The Way of
Phenomenology

The Way of Phenomenology

CRITICISM
AS A PHILOSOPHICAL DISCIPLINE

Richard M. Zaner

Pegasus
A Division of
The Bobbs-Merrill Company, Inc.
Indianapolis

This book is one of a series, Traditions in Philosophy, published by Pegasus in cooperation with Educational Resources Corporation, which has developed and created the series under the direction of Nicholas Capaldi, Professor of Philosophy, Queens College, New York.

The Bobbs-Merrill Company, Inc.
4300 West 62nd Street
Indianapolis, Indiana 46268

Third Printing 1976

Library of Congress Catalog Card Number: 77-114178
ISBN 0-672-63611-5 (pbk.)

For Dorion Cairns,
with deep respect

"For in the immediate world, everything is to be discerned, for him who can discern it, and centrally and simply, without either dissection into science, or digestion into art, but with the whole of consciousness, seeking to perceive it as it stands: so that the aspect of a street in sunlight can roar in the heart of itself as a symphony, perhaps as no symphony can: and all of consciousness is shifted from the imagined, the revisive, to the effort to perceive simply the cruel radiance of what is."

—James Agee, *Let Us Now Praise Famous Men*

Contents

The Most General Characters of Consciousness
  The Noetic Stream of Intentiveness
  Intentive Syntheses and Inner-Time Consciousness
  Evidence
  Actional and Operative Strata
  The Self
  Positionality and Objective Sense
  Review: Stratification and Foundedness

Preface

"The eagle never lost so much time
as when he submitted to learn of the
crow."

—James Agee,
Let Us Now Praise Famous Men

A sense of desperation inevitably overtakes one who begins, then tries to carry out a project whose very idea seems impossible. The temptation, felt more than known, is to try in one last gasp to buckle with matchless finesse the loose chains he hopes are silver, but somehow knows are only dross.

In this study, whatever its patent audacity in attempting to portray the incredibly fertile fields of phenomenological philosophy, I have, I fear, submitted more to the crow than to the eagle, and my efforts to fly with soaring grace may be but the awkward perchings at the feet of stolid crows. Still, perchance there will be some salvation even if that embarrassment be true: sometimes philosophers must move like moles in order to show, not a fanciful mountain of thought made from mere hills, but the very real mountain which lies beneath the surface, hidden even from the eagle's acute eyes.

My aim in this study is to have written more than a 'mere textbook'. It is to attempt an original study which seeks to make it possible for those as yet unacquainted with the ways of phenomenological philosophy to be brought to some understanding of it. It is one of my firm convictions that one learns philosophy only by philosophizing, and only slowly coming to appreciate, with increasingly critical perception, what he has been doing all along. This is, if anything, even more true of phenomenology—for I, with Husserl, conceive of criticism as *one of the disciplines of philosophy,* and, if I am right, its fundamental one. I hope to have shown, not that criticism is the fundamental dimension of philosophy (that being an entirely different study), but that phenomenological philosophy is most accurately conceived as criticism now firmly established on its own sound foundations. What criticism in philosophy signifies, we shall have to see as we proceed.

From these convictions, two consequences naturally follow. First, it is as complete a mistake to interpret phenomenology as merely one more 'ism' or metaphysical 'point of view' as it would be to interpret logic, ethics, or any other philosophical discipline in that way. *It is a field of inquiry integral to the nature of philosophy itself,* was dimly seen as such by many previous philosophers, and is currently practiced as such by many today. Second, one can 'learn' phenomenology only by actively engaging in it; and I do my best here to put matters in such a way as to involve you in the course of these soundings. I am aware, nonetheless, that considerable guidance is not only helpful but necessary in such a discipline, for the field is brambled with extraordinary difficulties, both terminological and systematic, having to do with the field itself and its own particular problems.

I have attempted to minimize the former by finding ways of expressing the many complex notions in intelligible English. If this sometimes raises the ire of my phenomenological colleagues, hopefully it will not alienate them. The conviction behind this is quite simply that this sort of linguistic effort is very much phenomenological in character, practiced continually by Edmund Husserl, Dorion Cairns, Alfred Schutz, Aron Gurwitsch, Maurice Merleau-Ponty, Martin Heidegger, and many others. What I have tried to do is find terms and expressions that make good sense in English, not with the grandiose aim of beginning a lexicon of terms, but merely to demonstrate that every genuine phenomenological insight can be expressed in English without compromise or undue stylistic awkwardnesses. I am not fully happy with my efforts thus far, but I do believe this is a good beginning for showing that even the most difficult of phenomenological notions can be articulated in perfectly understandable, if carefully used, terms. One need not literally transliterate Husserl's terminology into English. After all, he himself, having been trained as a mathematician first, was obliged to make use of an already available philosophical vocabulary, and finding much of it unsuitable, slowly began to carve out his own terms and expressions. Indeed, one of the outstanding features of his career is his constant growth, modification, and rethinking, not only systematically, but terminologically. It is not unnatural to attempt, then, a similar continuation.

I have also tried to surmount some of the systematic obstacles, not by obliterating them or by simplifying them beyond recognition, but by striving not to treat every important phenomenological issue—my choice will doubtless leave some feeling cheated, but there it is. And with respect to those I have treated, I have tried to leave much of the deeper analyses merely suggested. I felt it fully justifiable to show the *kind* of thing involved in critical study, and to indicate the *kind* of thing one finds thereby. Doing this, the reader ought to be able to go off on his own. Even so, I have found it quite necessary to wade through a good many of these details, especially in Chapter 4, where the theory of consciousness is engaged. There was no alternative except to move resolutely into some of the fantastic detail one quickly learns to expect in a criticism of consciousness. Even in that chapter, not everything is treated, however; to have done so would have required a book many times more lengthy than this.

In the belief, finally, that issues are the most important theme for such a book as this, I have dealt with the prominent men in the discipline only in the context of the thematic issues themselves. I have also tried to map out some of the ways leading to phenomenology—and I believe that they are many, even though I have gone through only three. I have also tried to map out something of the historical background of it, and some of the reasons that critical philosophy is one of the most urgent necessities of our times. Only an appreciation of the issues themselves can make this plain, however; and this was but another reason for focusing my study on 'the things themselves'.

My hope is that a careful thinking-through of this text, coupled with a study of the original sources themselves, which are increasingly available in English, will provide the reader with the basis from which he can venture out into critical philosophizing on his own.

*   *   *   *   *   *

Dorion Cairns, to whom this book is gratefully dedicated, along with Aron Gurwitsch, Alfred Schutz and Maurice Natanson have all had their influence on my understanding of phenomenological philosophy. I hold them all responsible for having shown me its urgency. None of them, of course, can take the blame for the way in which I have come to view the discipline, even though I believe that this way is not, in the end, inconsistent with what I learned from them.

I must also mention here the importance for this book of my many and wonderful conversations and consequent close friendship with Alec Ritchie, of the University of Newcastle, Australia, while he was a Visiting Professor at The University of Texas in the spring of 1968. These talks proved to have been the real stimulus, unknown to Alec, for my resolve to try to explain phenomenology in decent English. His comprehension of the language, and his amazing understanding of the discipline itself, proved to be a decisive factor for me.

For hearing portions of the first parts of the study during the first part of this past summer, I wish to thank my good friend Herbert Spiegelberg and the members of his Workshop in Phenomenology at Washington University, St. Louis. Their receptiveness to different ways of expressing old things, and their genuinely helpful comments, are gratefully acknowledged.

The award of a Summer Fellowship by the National Endowment for the Humanities made it possible for me to have the time to write this study, and is gratefully acknowledged.

Limitations of space unfortunately dictated the unhappy decision not to include an extensive bibliography which had been originally planned. Several of my students nevertheless should be acknowledged for their considerable efforts in that plan—George Agich, Donald Laughlin, Edward Lawry, and George Oberlander. It is hoped that the footnotes at the end of the book will provide at least some indications for further study.

And, for their patient endurance and sustenance of these efforts during a most trying summer, my wife and daughter must here receive my publicly proclaimed admission of a deeply private pact.

Austin, Texas
August, 1969   RMZ

Prologue

"We cannot know our world until
we find a compass that can chart
what world we know."
—Theodore Spencer, *An Act of Life*

Writing a book is an act of audacity. Not only does the author presume to know something and to be able to communicate it with honesty and accuracy, but he outrageously supposes that what he thinks he knows is worth committing to print and is of value to persons whom he does not know. Which puts, as simply as possible, the obvious but frequently buried question: Why write books at all? Or, more pointedly, why did I write this book? To neither of these questions do I, at least, have a satisfactory response, except the book itself. The proof of this, as with any other pudding, can only be in the eating. And since anyone who chances to pick up this book must be hungry, I owe it to him to say a few more words about what he may expect to find here.

Besides the fact of my own audacity—for I do indeed believe that what is said here will be worth it!—it seems only fitting that you, the reader, be reminded, at the outset, of yours. For you, too, must be a bit outrageous: you presume that you are capable of learning from books, of understanding, and thus of passing judgment on what you read, whatever that may be. But rightly understood, audacity is not only in order, it is necessary. The only appropriate response to an author's presumptions, especially if he writes philosophically, is philosophical criticism and self-criticism—the

more finely tuned the better; but in no case can the necessity of criticism be left unstated, unrecognized, and unap-
preciated.

This involves several things. Among others, it means that
nothing written here can be accepted as gospel. If you will
permit a rather bad simile, every book, and especially every
textbook, is always and essentially the gospel *according to*
. . . the author. Books do not write themselves, nor do they
fall ready-made from some handy Bookstore in the Sky. By
the same token, no reader can pretend to sit back and take
things in, as if the act of understanding required nothing
of him but that he sit there and be pounced upon by the
words and arguments of the book. Certain current myths
to the contrary notwithstanding, learning something, understanding it, does not just happen by rote; it is neither like
the measles nor like being led to slaughter, but requires an
attentive and critical mind and, perhaps most important,
almost unbridled enthusiasm. Only he who, in Thomas Wolfe's
wonderful phrase, "has hunger for it," can attain to knowledge.

In plain terms, *I* am writing this text, and the opinions,
judgments, and evaluations are mine, all mine—for better
or for worse. This is phenomenological philosophy *as I see
it,* presented in the best way I can at this time in my life.
It could not be otherwise: it bears my name, and hence I
must bear the responsibility and be held accountable for it.
If an author succeeds or fails in his task, he is, I suppose,
free to assume whatever credit or blame he thinks he de-
serves. These are his affairs, to live with as he will. But suc-
ceeding and failing are by no means easy to assess. In a
clear sense, all that can really be demanded beforehand is
a kind of pact between reader and author: that we recognize each other's joys and agonies, that we take each other
seriously, honestly, and critically at the outset, and then to
see what happens.

II

Permit me to put the matter somewhat differently, as it

is, I believe, more important than it may appear at first sight. Whether phenomenological or not, what is it that philosophers claim to be about? It seems to me that our current philosophical setting demands the serious posing of just this question—one too often left to so-called introductory courses, and even then too rarely faced squarely. Asking the question is crucial, and not simply in view of the unprecedented numbers of philosophers now alive and actively working and the sheer diversity of starting points, styles of thinking, methods, problems, and so on—all of which create a sort of crisis of confusion. There is also a wide divergence among philosophers today—and we seem more sensitive today that the same was true in the past, though not so severely—as to what it is they think they are doing in their work, which is not always the same as what they in fact accomplish! More seriously, philosophy itself has become, in our times, fundamentally *problematic.* For reasons which can and, later in this text, will be made explicit, no philosopher can rest easy in his own discipline, for just that has grown to be deeply at issue in our times. The setting of philosophy today is even more pressingly hedged than in former times by its radical opposite, nihilism.

The past one hundred years, but especially the past few decades, have witnessed a fundamental *relativization of perspectives.* This is particularly evident as regards history and the social world, although these are not the only phenomena which reveal this circumstance. As for history, what may be called historicality and historicity have become an intimate part of our daily lives. By the former, I mean to indicate what Wilhelm Dilthey called the rise of historical consciousness: that each of us is increasingly made to be aware of the historical character of our world and all its objects and events, ourselves included. Nothing we experience, it seems, and most of us realize it in one or another way (this being the significant factor here), can any longer be interpreted statically, without reference to history— whether it be ourselves, a psychiatric case, political events, natural happenings, science, art, or religion. But this referral to history has also become highly problematic, for it is not at all clear what exactly is meant by an affair's being 'historical,' much less what 'history' itself means or how knowledge of things past is even possible. We realize the naivity of the metaphor that would depict past events, objects, and people as a kind of massive repository of data and the view of the discipline of history as a kind of steam-shovel busily digging up those data and reconstructing the past 'as it really was'—a phrase which, we realize, does more to conceal than to reveal the genuine issues and phenomena. We have, in short, come to realize the relativity of historical standpoints, sometimes to the point of becoming historicist in our views, of reducing everything solely to their historical conditions. We live and breathe in the milieu of historicality.

But this phenomenon gives way to another: historicity. For we not only find ourselves continually faced with the enormous difficulties of establishing the meaning of, and the possibility of knowing, past events generally, but we have come to recognize that we are ourselves historical creatures through and through. As a consequence, we begin to suspect that there is no privileged perspective from which to view the past—or even ourselves, it seems. We also suspect that our unavoidable interpretations of past events, past philosophies, and so on, are themselves *disclosures of ourselves,* of what we take for granted, of what we value and believe in, in fact, of what we are. It has begun to dawn on us that for an historical being to interpret 'the' past is for it to interpret *its own* past, and this interpretation is, in truth, an expression of how that being sees itself, whether or not it says something about the past.

That the blooming of historicality and historicity in our midst bear hugely complicated and even questionable fruit, uncertain as to its value and destiny, is only part of the current philosophical scene. The same kind of relativization has happened at the level of the social world as well, in what one may call, in at least one of its meanings, the rise of social consciousness and, as its interesting and curious consequence, the rise of a kind of cognizance of sociality. In simplest terms, I mean to indicate that contemporary men, whether butchers, artists, philosophers, or scientists, are deeply informed by a bewildering view of the diversity of cultures and social contexts. And with this consciousness of socio-cultural diversity, with its apparently inevitable relativization of perspectives on norms, morals, modes of actions, and so on, there has arisen a whole new set of philosophical issues, not the least of which is the nature of philosophy itself: is it not itself but a mere expression of a particular social milieu?

Equally important, are the very ideas of 'the social' and 'culture,' which have become decisively problematic. What is it for something to be 'social'? What is the 'cultural'? How is knowledge of other, sometimes radically different, social worlds even possible? Am I not so much a creature of my own culture that knowing another, in any significant way, is impossible? We can no longer naively assume that there is a kind of underlying 'psychic unity,' as it used to be called, or 'human nature' common to all of us through all time. In short, the emergence in our times of the consciousness of social relativity has relativized our perspectives, persuading some that social relativism is the inevitable, although somewhat uncomfortable, conclusion.

With this new awareness of historicity, there arises a parallel one of sociality: the recognition that our own styles of acting and thinking, our framework of conceptualizing, with its own context of values, and approaches, is not shaped and focused only by our own socio-cultural (and historical) milieu, but also that framework (in terms of which we are able to pose any meaningful questions at all about other cultures), is as much an expression of what we ourselves are as it might be of these other cultures. As social beings, deeply informed and determined by our own nexus of social values, concepts, and the like, our interpretations of other cultures seems to disclose the nature of our own being as much as that of other cultures.

I am fully aware, as I believe you are, of the many sticky

issues these phenomena have necessarily tacked onto them. Hopefully, I will be able to make some sense of them in the course of this study, and thereby suggest to you something of the character and value of phenomenological philosophy. At this juncture, though, all I want to stress is the general situation and something of its consequences for us. The relativization of perspectives, sometimes quite radical, prompts our mutual recognition of the problematic character of philosophy itself. There is no reason whatsoever to think that philosophy is somehow exempt from this relativization, not even the fact that something called 'philosophy' has been around for several millennia. And that circumstance makes it necessary for us to recognize several matters about the writing and the reading of philosophical texts—and to consent to what follows from that. Above all, as we shall see in this book, this recognition and this consent are absolutely crucial if we hope to understand phenomenological philosophy.

More immediately, though, I am concerned about making it unmistakably clear what it means to say that I am writing, and you are reading, this book—beyond the truism is a truth we need to grasp. There will be a number of things said here of whose truth I am not so thoroughly convinced that I can parade them before you without qualms—more, I suspect, than I am now willing to admit. I am by no means sure I understand something I am supposed to understand, according to my own credentials, in order to be able to write this book. This is a fact, if you will, which it is essential to have out in the open, especially in view of the relativization already mentioned.

This fact, however, as I understand it, is not merely a dialectically inverted excuse, given in advance, to forestall my possible future embarrassment over what I shall say. Nor does it signify an unwillingness on my part to face the rumble, and the nimble minds of my readers who are possessed of the mythic fire for truth; nor is it, I hope, an exercise in false modesty.

To the contrary, my initial confession is essential to the

philosophic enterprise itself—for a writer, as for his readers, for a lecturer, as for his auditors—whatever else may be meant by the adjective 'phenomenological.' A word of explanation is necessary here. I propose to take the term 'philosophy' literally and historically: *'philiasophia,'* that is, the love of truth, or the quest for knowledge. Taking a number of shortcuts and keeping the discussion as brief as possible, the following is what I understand by that. Philosophizing is a quest which assumes the form of questioning, and begins, necessarily, from two central exigencies.

(1) The admission, the acknowledgement of intellectual poverty, of my own not-knowing, my self-recognition of ignorance that 'wonder' forces upon me. In Edmund Husserl's terms,

> . . . anyone who seriously intends to become a philosopher must "once in his life"[1] withdraw into himself and build anew all the sciences [i.e. knowledge] that, up to then, he has been accepting. Philosophy—wisdom *(sagesse)*—is the philosopher's quite personal affair. It must arise as *his* wisdom, as his self-acquired knowledge . . . a knowledge for which he can answer from the beginning . . . If I have decided to live with this as my aim—the decision that can alone start me on the course of a philosophical development—I have thereby chosen to begin in absolute poverty, with an absolute lack of knowledge.[2]

This admission of having to be, as Merleau-Ponty expresses it, a "perpetual beginner,"[3] is the recognition of the necessity for resolving the perplexity or the ignorance, through the careful asking of systematically delineated and organized questions.

(2) This follows from the first: an existential commitment by the individual (you and me), a willingness and resolve to make a concentrated effort to comprehend himself and his world with intellectual honesty, openness, and courage. Philosophy, in so far as it seeks knowledge, sets itself radically against what Plato calls, in the *Phaedo,* "misology" and "misanthropy," or what Gabriel Marcel calls "misosophy"[4] or the deliberate distrust, rejection, and denial of rational in-

quiry of any   kind or the   self-conscious   choice of nihilism.

In a way, then, philosophy's beginning in history is the beginning each of us must make *for himself:* the ultimate assumption, made blatantly and audaciously by the early Greeks, that (a) there is a *cosmos,* not chaos—since all things compose an ordered whole, it makes sense to seek to know the principles defining that 'order,' and (b) man, as the possessor of *'logos,'* can cognitively apprehend and 'say' what that cosmos and its order are. But to achieve this, it is essential that we do not begin with the presumption that we *already* are in possession of that knowledge. While assuming that the quest is not in principle impossible, we cannot naively assume that we already have it. Whether or not we do, must be critically determined.

I said that the initial acts of ignorance and commitment are manifested by questions. What is it 'to question'? And which questions come into play, and why? Keeping the discussion still as brief as I can, a question, taken in its root signification, is an articulated, step-by-step involvement of a 'one-who-does-not-know-something' who seeks to know, in the task at hand—namely, the task of 'seeking-to-know.' To question is to bring something into question, though what that something is may be only dimly seen, in view of the seeker's own admitted not-knowing which he seeks to resolve. Hence, to question is also for the questioner to draw back from that which he brings into question, to distance himself from it, in order to question it. As will be stated later, after further ground has been prepared, this distancing is a specific shifting of attention signifying a disengagement, without which questioning would not be possible.

The quest, accomplished through questioning, is not itself a giving of opinion, but is rather a *re-quest for a response which would resolve ('answer')* the quest. Thus, questioning is closely bound up with another activity, that of responding. If someone accepts the question as addressed to him (myself or another), the question *engages* him, it obliges him to respond or become a partner in my quest. There is thus a double sense of responsibility inherent in this joint endeavor of questioning and responding. As questioner, I bear the responsibility in my question, to listen to all responses, to be responsive to would-be 'answers,' and to make sure, through further critical questions, that I fully understand and assess the responses. As responder, I bear a coordinate responsibility: to respond responsibly, and to recognize and accept responsively, the responsibility of answering and of being open to explain, clarify, and if, need be, to defend my responses before the one who questions.

The acts of questioning and responding, I think, express the fundamental form of communication, i.e., of 'speaking together' and, thus, of giving what is properly one's own to the other, and are found most clearly in *dialogue*. My questioning, *by its very character,* opens me up to possible responses to which I am obliged at the very least *to listen critically;* my questioning is thus already a kind of sharing, and a request to share, my not-knowing *if,* and much hangs on that 'if,' I am truly questioning and not merely playing at it, in whatever form this may take. Similarly, if I have the audacity to respond, i.e., to accept that sharing or to agree to share that which is my own, that which is my purported 'answer,' this *of itself* opens me up to the dialogical pursuit of further requests, further responses, and so on, until (and if) the point is reached where the responses have resolved my questions— or, until (and if) we together reach the *truth that frees me (or us) from* ignorance and *for* knowledge. To question and respond is thus to commit yourself to dialogical co-re-questing and co-re-sponding in pursuit of the freeing resolution that will end the dialogue.

All of this implies two basic points. First, if philosophy is essentially this activity of questioning and responding, that is, dialogue, then it is a mode of what Marcel calls *"disponibilité"*[5] or literally, an openness and being-available which is dialogically involved in and committed to the pursuit of knowledge and truth. It is, therefore, a kind of *invitation to others* to engage themselves in a similar way. In short, Descartes' well-known injunction, in the "Preface to the Reader" of his *Meditations,* is fundamental to philosophical thinking. Expecting, as he says, no praise from "the vulgar and without the hope that my book will have many readers," he goes on to insist:

> On the contrary, I should never advise anyone to read it excepting those who desire to meditate seriously with me, and who can detach their minds from affairs of sense, and deliver themselves entirely from every sort of prejudice. . . .
>
> And inasmuch as I make no promise to others to satisfy them at once, and as I do not presume so much on my own powers as to believe myself capable of foreseeing all that can cause difficulty to anyone, I shall first of all set forth in these Meditations the very considerations by which I persuade myself that I have reached a certain and evident knowledge of the truth, in order to see if, by the same reasons which persuaded me, I can also persuade others. And, after that, I shall reply to the objections which have been made to me by persons of genius and learning to whom I have sent my Meditations for examination, before submitting them to press . . . This is why I beg those who read these Meditations to form no judgment upon them unless they have given themselves the trouble to read all the objections as well as the replies I have made to them.[6]

I shall have occasion to discuss this important passage later on. For the moment, it is essential only to emphasize again that Descartes hits upon a fundamental dimension of philosophizing: the injunction or invitation to us to commit ourselves with him to the mutual pursuit of truth, even if that truth be that there is no truth. Whether or not Descartes succeeds or fails, it should be stressed, is literally to be determined by these others. Regardless of what he believes himself to have discovered, whatever may be his confidence in them, his invitation commits him to the necessity of the others' critical appraisals. And this raises the second point I want to make explicit.

Earlier, I mentioned that your audacity as a reader means that you must be critical. The basic reason for this can now be seen. To say that the central dimension of philosophizing is questioning and responding, that it is dialogue or a systemic invitation to mutual meditation, is to say that it is always a critical and self-critical act. Every philosopher asks questions and gives responses; these responses, however, are essentially *epistemic* in character, knowledge-claims of one kind or another. Every response claims, minimally, to be a response to the question asked, however tentatively or categorically the answer is given. To that extent alone, every response is epistemic, or is a claim to know. This fact, in and of itself, makes a doubly critical involvement necessary—so long, that is, as there is a serious commitment to the quest. Briefly these are:

(1) The response, as such, supposes that the language used is in principle understandable. Thus it is always open to critical questions bearing on its clarity, consistency, and intelligibility, all of which may be called *internal criticism.*

(2) The response also claims to be about the affairs brought into question by the question. Hence it is always necessary to determine whether the claim is relevant and accurate. The response, as epistemic, supposes that these affairs *are,* and *are as asserted;* it also supposes that these affairs are accessible to others, especially to the questioner, and that the questioner can go to them and find them to be as claimed. Hence, critical questions are always possible and necessary concerning whether these affairs exist and whether they are as they are claimed to be. These kinds of critical questions may be called *external criticisms.*

Much more will have to be found out about criticism, but for the moment this will do. Thus, for instance, if one asserts in response to a question, that 'the soul is the principle of the body,' one supposes not only that one's language is clear and intelligible, but also that there is such an affair as 'the soul,' that it is as asserted ('principle of the body'), and that others can, if they desire and make the necessary effort, critically check to determine whether these supposals hold up. Of course there is more to it than this, and we shall later have to explore this in greater depth. The point for now is clear enough, however: to the precise extent to which philosophy involves questioning and responding, it is the dialogical invitation to others to engage themselves in this activity, and thereby to become responsive and responsible critics of themselves and of others.

III

My initial confession, then, is not at all a way of avoiding possible future embarrassments, but is inherent to the philosophic enterprise itself. Every philosophical assertion, and the questions underlying them, displays the fundamental grounds of the philosopher's own thinking—its internal demands, requirements, articulations, and presuppositions, and their rationale, if any—and necessarily opens up the way for dialogical criticism of its claims and its assumptions, indeed, of the very questions posed. *This is manifestly true of my linguistically expressed thoughts as found in these pages.* Hence, strange as it may sound, the requirements for reading this text is that a kind of dialogue must go on—as it must in the meaningful reading of any philosopher's work. Not only, then, is philosophy an act of audacity; it is also an act one can undertake, whether as author or as reader, only with great caution, if not with fear and trembling.

All of this is to say that philosophy is essentially a *reflective and reflexive* discipline. The philosopher reflects on all manner of affairs; but among them is his own philosophical activity and its results. This distinction between reflective and reflexive will later prove to be a foundational one. For the moment, though, I mean to indicate this difference, and the consequent fact that every philosophy is essentially under the requirement that it be able at every moment to account for its own possibility. R. G. Collingwood put it very well:

> Philosophy . . . has this peculiarity, that reflection upon it is part of itself. The theory of poetry may or may not be of service to a poet—opinions on that question have differed—but it is no part of poetry. The theory of science and the theory of history are not parts of science and of history; if scientists and historians study these things, they study them not in their capacity as scientists or historians, but in their capacity as philosophers. But the theory of philosophy is itself a problem for philosophy; and not only a possible problem, but an inevitable problem, one which sooner or later it is bound to

raise. . . . the philosopher is under an obligation to study the nature of philosophy itself.[7]

Being reflexive, philosophy is also an eminently personal act, something which only the individual self does from within the inner reaches of his own solitude. Hence, dialogue always has its necessary counterpart, meditation. Every philosophical act, then, is an original one, one which is *mine*, as my life is *mine*, and this circumstance is not one that can be ignored. To the extent that I try to leave out this essential point, to the extent that it is not livingly expressed in your thinking and in mine, everything becomes what Heidegger calls mere idle talk *(Gerede)*.[8] As we shall have to see, however, to call it a personal act is by no means to say of philosophy that it is valid for no one but the person who expresses it. Science is the product of acts of theorizing, inferring, observing, and so on; to forget that essential connection is to make nonsense of science. But to emphasize it is by no means to reduce science to mere private and relative bias. There are criteria to scientific thinking and doing; so, too, are there criteria to philosophical thinking, even more so, inasmuch as philosophy is a pre-eminently personal (reflexive) act. In fine, philosophers pretend to knowledge which others can also assent to (in some sense, to 'objectivity'), but that fact does not and should not hide the essentially reflexive character of the act itself. If anything, it makes philosophizing far more responsible as a discipline.

The problem concerning which questions are properly philosophical is not one that can be taken up here. Nevertheless, several chapters of this study have direct bearing on it, especially Chapters 2, 3, and 4.

One thing does stand out clearly now, in any case, and needs to be stated explicitly. The sense in which this book is mine is surely in no way trivial—it cannot be naively taken for granted as so obvious that it calls for no discussion. In simplest terms, I have selected the topics, I have done the examination, I have chosen what to include and what to exclude, and so on. More significant, however, is this: if philosophy is essentially a matter of philosophizing, and so, too, for phenomenological philosophy, then this study is itself necessarily *philosophical and phenomenological.* It is not *about* phenomenology, as if the latter, any more than philosophy, were something that could be chopped up into easily digestible chunks and then comfortably assimilated: learn the jargon, and then magically you have learned to philosophize or phenomenologize. This is my philosophico-phenomenological act, consecutively worked out in the English language, and can be understood only if you, the reader, actively engage me critically. This is a phenomenological study of phenomenology, some of the 'ways' into it, something about its historical background, and some of its prominent concerns; but it is patently the way in which I, at this time in my career, understand this discipline. If this be arrogant or too idiosyncratic for some, then, so far as I can see, both philosophy generally and phenomenology particularly are both arrogant and idiosyncratic. But, if you will, that is not only not bad, it could not be otherwise. The thing to do, as I see it, is neither to bemoan that nor give it up in despair; it is rather to keep a highly critical eye on everything I, or any other philosopher, writes. Ultimately, I believe, nothing can substitute for thinking through these matters on which I shall dwell for yourselves; and when it is a matter of my commenting on some other philosophers, nothing can ultimately substitute for your consulting the originals themselves. In both cases, it is unavoidable that you consult the 'things themselves,' whether the 'things' be philosophers' writings or the issues. In both cases, my basic claim is that, if you do 'check me out,' you will find them to be as I assert; I need not add 'hopefully,' since every philosopher in his very act of philosophizing admits his own liability to error, if not his own folly.

IV

The difficulties of introducing phenomenology are notorious, and quite sufficient to dissuade even the hardiest of souls. The reasons for this, however, are easy to appreciate, and will become even more obvious as we proceed. On the one hand, if one should decide to treat the works of those philosophers who may justifiably be classed as phenomenological, one is faced with two equally pressing difficulties. As Herbert Spiegelberg has shown, having undertaken this courageous task,[9] settling on a defensible criterion for defining 'justifiable inclusion' and selection of philosophers, is itself inordinately difficult. The 'movement,' as he characterizes it, is literally jam-packed with philosophers in one way or another aligned with it. But even if one could satisfy that demand, it remains to do the actual examination—and it turns out that, by practically any criterion of selection, the number of philosophers one must consider is rather large. Hence, if one does the job at all well one finds it minimally necessary to write at least several volumes (as did Spiegelberg), and to have mastered the works of numerous philosophers—Heidegger, Sartre, Merleau-Ponty, Scheler, and others, to say nothing of Husserl—each of whom is a genuinely original philosopher fully deserving of a lengthy study in his own right.

Even if one elected to treat only the work of Edmund Husserl, the inaugurator and central figure of the phenomological 'movement,' one is faced with a truly formidable amount of material. At the time of his death in 1938, he had published at least six major works and a number of important shorter studies, engaged in a great deal of correspondence, and more significantly, produced an incredible amount of writing during the five to six hours he devoted daily to philosophical writing in the more than fifty years of his active career. The latter comprised over 40,000 pages of manuscript in Husserl's own shorthand, as well as some 7,000 pages of longhand transcriptions worked out before 1938 by his assistants and collaborators—principally by Edith Stein, Eugen Fink, and Ludwig Landgrebe (who also edited and published one entire volume, approved by Husserl, after Husserl's death[10]). These were later collected into the Husserl Archives at the University of Louvain by Father H. L. van Breda (who saved Husserl's wife, library, and manuscripts from the Nazis), under whose direction these manuscripts have been painstakingly transcribed, collated with other manuscripts and lectures, annotated for publication in the *Husserliana* series published by Martinus Nijhoff. To date, twelve of these volumes have been published, and many more are to come.

Still, despite Husserl's decisive impact, phenomenological philosophy far exceeds his efforts, not only in terms of the number of other philosophers actively engaged in working within the discipline, but also in terms of the new thematic concerns and issues taken up by them. Hence, not even a study of Husserl's works would do justice to phenomenology. Nevertheless, a mastery of them is necessary to the understanding of the discipline and its specific problems, as well as of the other philosophers working within it.

Beyond the matter of the sheer bulk of material, then, there are considerable difficulties pertaining to the themes and problems treated by these philosophers. One must master an extraordinary amount of highly technical terminology— terms which are not always used consistently from thinker to thinker, nor even within the body of a single man's work. More to the point is the inherent difficulty of the issues themselves: notably, but not only, the themes of establishing the foundations of such affairs as the life-world *(Lebenswelt)*, intersubjectivity, man (person, self) and, in the work Husserl produced especially, the very complex strata of consciousness (its processes, temporality, meaning-bestowing functions, and so on). Literally everything can be, in some respects, open to phenomenological study. What this involves and how it is possible, will hopefully become clear as we proceed. In any event, it is obviously in no sense possible to speak of phenomenological philosophy as a 'school' or an 'ism'; not even the more neutral term 'movement' does justice to its character. It is not 'a philosophy,' but rather, as I hope to make plain, an inherent dimension or discipline of philosophy itself. To attempt to give a fair and yet manageable philosophical examination of it, then, is a difficulty of the first order. Which judgment only underscores the somewhat outrageous character of my effort. Rather than trying at this point to give some indications of phenomenological philosophy, however, I want instead to proceed by way of an indirection—hoping thereby to creep up on it and snare it unawares.

Husserl sometimes compared himself to an explorer who had come upon an entirely new and vast land. It is one which had in some ways, he knew, been suspected by other explorers; indeed, its existence, he felt, had been suspected throughout the course of modern philosophy, particularly since Descartes. Some past explorers had actually gone to its very borders, but did not, for one reason or another, make that last and decisive effort. Able himself, at first, to make only very rough sketches of some of the more outstanding features of the terrain—and at times getting lost in the dense undergrowth, coming up against apparent chasms which could not be spanned except by first building adequate walkways and bridges, and so on—Husserl realized that a very carefully executed map, with consistent and intelligible markings and guidelines, was absolutely necessary. At the same time, the fascination of the landscape itself—whose thorough examination became his prime task and goal—was there, unexplored and compelling, calling for attention. To insure that he would be able to get and keep his own bearings, but even more so that others would follow his course to confirm and extend his findings, Husserl divided his efforts between soundings, probings, searchings, and cartography, with periodic speeches designed to solicit and guide the work of the others. Each time he again took up the trail he found, as do all explorers, not only new sidepaths and connecting ridges, as well as new prominences, but also different perspectives—all of which forced additions, corrections, modifications, and even the recognition of mistakes made earlier from haste or momentary loss of vision. Thus, too, his sketches and maps were constantly being revised and changed, each time becoming more accurate and detailed. Indeed, the detail at some stages became practically prohibitive—in different terms, some of his works are such that almost every sentence could easily be a chapter title.

But, as is true of any stranger in an at first strange land, Husserl was mainly concerned with only certain of the features, gave only a cursory glance at others, while still others held his attention not at all, even though he was doubtless aware of their presence or would certainly not have been surprised to learn of them. Even what most attracted him,[11] did not fully reveal its secrets. Still, his discoveries and his invitations to others to travel to the place did attract the attention of many seekers who, having other interests, or, thanks to Husserl's pioneering efforts, better perspectives, were able both to explore other features and to refine even more the maps he had made. Among these, as is to be expected on any frontier, were the usual cluster of adventurers, pirates, and momentary sight-seers; but there were also a good many outstanding explorers as well. And Husserl himself continued to probe further and further, eventually earning the reputation in certain quarters of being a real maverick, a radical in his own land. Others did, however, take up the invitation and its challenge, and set out for the new land, with sometimes remarkable results, and confirmations.

With that began what Husserl always regarded as an urgent necessity—*the forming of a genuinely communal undertaking, a 'science' in the highest, or most fundamental, sense,* with each person confirming or disconfirming the results of others' work, probing further and returning to report and share the findings with one another, thus casting new light on ground already won and on that currently being explored, and thus building up a common, intersubjectively grounded fund of knowledge.[12] At the same time, a development both reasonable and inevitable also took place: the other explorers, each in his own way and according to the requirements of his own style and concerns, found new or even different features, felt it necessary to modify and reassess Husserl's maps and findings, reached different conclusions concerning the lay of the land and its limits and character. Some even contended that the 'path' Husserl took was set in terms that in the end prejudiced his findings, or that it was not the only 'path' one could or should take, or that it was itself an impossible one. A few, from comfortable seats at home, pontificated that there was not really any land at all beyond the comfortable borders already familiar to any level-headed man.

There thus developed a number of more or less divergent views and visions, and with them a number of 'phenomenologies' worked out with more or less detail by their respective authors. Some argued that they had found still unexplored paths in Husserl's own orbit. Others argued that they had found traces of earlier explorers, which even Husserl had stressed, as we shall see. Still others began to contend that they found much more than mere traces; that, indeed, the so-called new land had already been hit upon and actually explored.[13] And so the air began to be filled with rumors and whisperings, even loud voices, all contending for 'going beyond,' 'old party-liners,' 'influences,' 'convergences,' 'foreshadowings,' and 'parallels.' And so it goes. All of this is doubtless inevitable, as are the quarrels and squabbles, the extensions and revisions, which crop up around any seminal figure.

Without in the least baptizing or condemning any of these, and without even making the slightest move in the direction of writing a history, however exciting this would be, of this story, one thing does stand out clearly. It is this: phenomenological philosophy is to be likened neither to a tremendous edifice, each of whose bricks is cemented firmly in place, nor to a seed which, when properly planted, issues forth rare blooms, nor yet to a vast syllogism whose premises need only to be punched in, the rest to follow with proud deduction. It is rather, I think, at least preliminarily, captured with remarkable accuracy by the analogy of the explorer.

The sense of phenomenological method, furthermore, is very much like that of the explorer when he turns to the task of recording where he has been and how he got there.

Learning to think phenomenologically is very much like learning to read and actively use these records, the maps, guideposts, markings, and other paraphernalia of the explorer's and mapmaker's trade. The sense of phenomenological statements is very much like that of an explorer's statements, for the meaning of both is similarly twofold: in so far as they claim to be descriptions of the 'land,' *they are at once epistemic* (knowledge-claims concerning the land itself) *and communicative* (that is, invitations and guides intended to enable others to know what to look for). Thus, as will become clearer as we progress, the much talked about but less frequently understood business of 'description' in phenomenology is by no means a simple matter, any more than are an explorer's 'descriptions' a simple matter—both inherently involve much more than just 'telling it like it is.' What else there is, we shall have to see, for it is far better to 'see' things in action than simply to 'talk' about them. But, at the heart of the matter is the insistence that *every knowledge-claim is necessarily at the same time methodological, and vice versa.* There is no such thing as a 'method,' as distinct from what is discovered thereby; and what is discovered is inseparable from the 'way' one got there. Every 'descriptive' claim is not only an assertion about a certain state of affairs, thus requiring internal and external criticism, but also serves as a guide for others to bring that state of affairs to self-givenness, thus making criticism possible and rendering the entire undertaking necessarily intersubjective. More generally, epistemology, or more particularly, philosophical criticism, and methodology are strictly co-ordinate and inseparable disciplines, precisely because epistemic claims are also communicative guides, in philosophy no less than in explorations.

The analogy can be pressed even further. The explorer is not unlike the beatnik of the 1950's. He has little patience with hide-bound pontificating; he insists that the only basis for forming judgments about the place he has been, and thus for evaluating his descriptions as well, is the 'Like, I've-been-there' attitude. In other words, he justifiably will accept only those judgments and descriptions which have been framed on the basis of a direct seeing or witnessing of the landscape itself. It is the things themselves which must be the final arbiters. In Dorion Cairns' succinct terms, the fundamental methodological principle of phenomenology is that

> No opinion is to be accepted as philosophical knowledge unless it is seen to be adequately established by observation of what is seen as itself as given "in person." Any belief seen to be incompatible with what is seen to be itself given is to be rejected. Toward opinions that fall in neither class—whether they be one's own or another's—one is to adopt an "official" philosophical attitude of neutrality.[14]

Thus the phenomenological philosopher explicitly and rigorously adheres to the principle that epistemic claims formed on the basis of a direct encounter with the affairs about which the claim is made are more justifiable, in general, than are claims formed on the basis of either no encounter or merely an indirect encounter with those affairs. Evidence that will support a claim is stronger in the one case than in the others; similarly, confirmation and disconfirmation are stronger in the former than in the latter. Thus, for example, if it is judged that the Statue of Liberty is green, the evidence here is stronger if the one judging is actually experiencing the statue with respect to its color (that is, visually, since that is the best available way of experiencing color), than if one's claim is made on the basis of a recollection of the statue, a picture of it, or someone else's claim that it is green.

V

Thus, phenomenological philosophy bears some resemblance to traditional empiricism, for thinkers like Locke and Hume recognized something like that maxim of evidence. The fundamental difference here, however, is that traditional empiricism held a severely restricted form of it: philosophical knowledge is either (1) restricted to individual things (usually thought of as physical) existing in space and time, or (2) to perceptions established on the basis of sensations or impressions. Phenomenology, on the contrary, insists that such restrictions are critically unjustifiable, and are plain biases to be rejected.

What that form of empiricism obscured, and led one to believe as nonexistent or to ignore or officially deny, is that our experience is far richer than empiricism could admit. Not only are there different ways of experiencing the same thing—sense perceptually (in different modes), remembering, imagining, depicting, expecting, and still others—but some things are not at all accessible or reduceable to sensory perception—for example, one's own mind and mental processes (only Berkeley seems to have appreciated this), the minds of other persons and animate beings, numbers, logical forms, values, and still other affairs. Also, *these differences themselves* can be grasped and studied, and 'difference' is not itself open to what the empiricist understood by sensory perception. Furthermore, not only may things be given 'in person' (in the ways appropriate to each), but *self-givenness itself* may be grasped and studied and contrasted with modes different from it. From such bases a theory of evidence can be developed. Thus, while phenomenological philosophy, as critical philosophy, shares empiricism's insistence that philosophy be attentive to things themselves as experienced, it differs from empiricism in its contention that experience is seen to be, when critically viewed, much wider, more articulated, and far more complicated than empiricism traditionally acknowledged it to be.

In any case, this philosophy is far closer, in letter and spirit, to empiricism than it is to many traditional rationalisms. It differs profoundly from any philosophy that first sets up formal definitions and postulates, or material hypotheses, and then proceeds by a method of formal deduction, more or less on the model of mathematics or mathematico-empirical natural science.

> To take conceptual stuff already on hand and fashion a cloak of theory for objects *in absentia*, then called in for a partial fitting—that is at best only a way to botch together another in-

genious misfit to hang away with how many others in the lumber room of history.[15]

As with the explorer, the phenomenological philosopher is concerned with getting to the 'things themselves,' in the way appropriate to each, and without in the least presupposing that speaking of 'things themselves' is already a form of metaphysical realism (which it is not, as we shall see), and to determine what and how they are experienced to be, as accurately, adequately, and clearly as possible, on the grounds of the best obtainable evidence. He is also concerned with having his claims confirmed, disconfirmed, modified, or corrected, if need be, by others—*where confirmation or cancellation is derived from inspection of the affairs themselves in question.*

But to insist on the less obvious feature of epistemic claims—that they are methodological guides for others—is not to say that phenomenological observations are easy to come by, and certainly it is not to say that all one has to do is to understand the language used and their truth or falsity will be magically grasped. Without judging whether an actual explorer (in the familiar sense) or the phenomenological-critical philosopher has the greater difficulty, they clearly are very different in important respects. This is especially true as regards the 'things' about which they respectively talk, as well as the 'ways' they each arrive at their respective destinations. But what these 'things' and these 'ways' in phenomenology actually are, is a question which can be answered only as we proceed.

For now, to conclude this prologue, I only want to draw out the analogy a bit further. If someone is really anxious to find out what an explorer has discovered (and he is not required to be anxious, or even interested), then it will not do simply to *tell him about* all the grand scenery, the treacherous chasms, the scintillating views, the hardships and joys. If he really wants to know, then let him embark on the journey; or, if that seems a bit too formidable, let him go on a guided tour. But let it also be clearly understood that because the tour has a guide does not mean that the voyage will be any less demanding or that he will not have to put out considerable effort on his own. Indeed, really making the trip can only mean doing it oneself, guided by someone else—in this case, me. But my presence does not signify an exemption from critical attentiveness or phenomenological alertness on your part.

1

Ways to Phenomenology

"Do not be bewildered by the sur-
faces; in the depths all becomes law."
—Rainer Maria Rilke,
Letters to a Young Poet

From The World Of Daily Life: The Uncommonness of Common Sense.

I think the best way to begin is with an indirection. You are walking down the street; it is the holiday season and you are absorbed in thinking about the gifts you must buy. It is late afternoon and the sidewalks are swarming with people. But you do not notice them, even though from time to time you are jostled. You adroitly sidestep light poles, parking meters, and people. And then you are momentarily jolted out of your absorption when another person coming toward you seems about to bump into you. You step to the left, and so does he; then he goes to the right just as you, too, move that way. Back and forth you both go, at first surprised, then irritated, then slightly embarrassed. Finally you stop and let him decide, only to see that he, too, has, with a laugh, also stopped. Sensing the comedy of this dance, you both pass it off and go on your respective ways. A common event, quickly forgotten along with other similar familiar incidents in our daily lives, but the ripple of recognition inherent in it will shortly give us pause for thought.

Typically, in our everyday lives, we are concerned with things displayed about us. We can also say that our particular 'concerns' may be of many different modes, and that we may focus this concern or that concern on many different things, aspects, or qualities of things, and so on. Thus, at some time, I might be in a gallery contemplating the purchase of a painting of a landscape having a tree similar to the one which once grew tall and strong in my backyard. My attention may then shift, nostalgically, to that once-upon-a-time tree of my youth. The clerk asking me a question jolts my attention back to the painting, forcing me to pay attention now to its qualities, price, and so on. The jolt I experience will probably be accompanied with a cluster of other feelings which meld with one another—irritation, dismay, resignation, eagerness to have done with it, and so on—giving the total experience its own specific tone and atmosphere. The feelings variously rise, submerge, interlace, pass, fade away as the momentary shock is replaced by my now refocused attention on the business at hand.

Later on, say, talking to an acquaintance, I may recall my earlier affair with the clerk and go on to relate my nostalgia. The acquaintance nods sympathetically, says a word now and then, drinks his tea, looks at his watch and soon announces he must leave. I see him to the door, express the usual social amenities and receive his in return, and the man departs. Again, a quite typical and familiar sort of encounter; nothing at all remarkable or uncommon has occurred, any more than in the countless other incidents in our daily encounters with persons and things in the life-world.

Imagine, however, some variations in these three scenes. The man with whom you danced in the first, say, does not dance, but instead stops abruptly, salutes, and begins to recite Poe's "Mask of the Red Death." Something, you suddenly know, is amiss, and you tuck your eyes hotly into the corner of your cheek and swiftly move off. In the second, the clerk in the gallery jolts me back from my reverie by suddenly slapping me on the head, knuckling my ribs, and winking slyly at me with eyes laid like tombs in the ground of his leering face. Again, something is just not right, for anonymous clerks just do not do that sort of thing—and I remind him of this in quite unsubtle terms, while I turn and indignantly march out.

In the two original scenes (A and B), a kind of jolt or shock is experienced, but certainly not as drasticly as in the variations (A' and B'). In both A and B, the shock is mild, and is found in the quick refocusing of attention—busied with one thing, you are obliged to focus on something else. But in A' and B', there is not only an abrupt refocusing of attention but a sudden emergence of something else: the usual, typical ways in which 'people' are 'supposed' to act is broken down and you are suddenly *made aware* of this. That is, where A and B require you to take stock of your immediate surroundings and the affairs at hand, A' and B' shock you into an awareness of what you had been taking for granted without question all along—the way shoppers or clerks behave. In the latter scenes (A' and B'), you must stop and think; it is necessary to assess the situation precisely because it does not conform to the typical, taken-for-granted expectations of daily life.

Consider now a variation of the third scene (C). Suppose that when the acquaintance sits down and you begin to talk with him, instead of nodding, chatting, and so on, he begins to sound like a record running at ever-slower speeds. You bend over to find out what is wrong (people just do not sound like that!) and hear, ever so softly, a faint 'tick-tick-tick. . . .' What then? It is neither a matter of refocusing attention in any usual sense nor of having to reassess the hitherto taken-for-granted assumptions about the ways 'people' are supposed to act in one situation or another. Here you are forced into a more radical awareness. What was taken for granted is not simply that this man is a certain typical kind of person, but that that 'thing' is a human being in the first place, and this assumption is jarred loose from its deep moorings in a lifetime of encounters and dealings with what you have been accustomed to calling 'human beings'—and not just *calling,* but *acting toward and being reacted to* as such.

Whatever may define 'human being,' or whether or not it is proper to call automata 'human,' if we focus briefly on this variation (C') we can begin to see something of genuine importance. Suppose something like that actually happened to you, that you learn that that 'thing' sitting next to you is an automaton. Notice the shift of attention and attitude, and the accompanying emotions, values and actions. Where before you were not at all disposed to reach out and, marveling, tweak the nose, stroke the skin, pull the hair, prod the chest ('How in the world did they do it?'), you would now in all likelihood not be at all hesitant to do just those things—but to what is now experienced as not 'human' but as an 'it.' 'It' is somewhat strange and fascinating since it so closely resembles 'other humans'. However it may stand with mannequins and men, what such a case does, in effect, is to force into awareness, though it may be only momentary, a fundamental, taken-for-granted assumption that had hitherto been operative but not recognized as such. It is fundamental, for it is not simply a matter of a kind of momentary eyebrow-raising regarding the peculiar conduct of an anonymous other (A'), nor is it a sort of shock over the behavior of a clerk whose actions are most untypical (B'). It is not a matter of being forced to question the actions and roles of others, but *of there being others in the first place.*

What, after all, assures you that that thing which sits next to you in class, at the cafe, in the bus, is an other human being, with all that that implies by way of having his own life, values, actions, and so on? Is it not at least barely possible that what you so commonly but implicitly suppose, not simply as to how certain types of people should act (clerks, teachers, employees, legislators, parents, hippies, crooks, and so on), but as to there *being others at all* in the world, that this assumption or implicit belief or acceptance is one which does not stand up to critical inspection? However you may be disposed to answer such questions, what must be stressed is (1) that we all make use of precisely such assumptions all the time, and (2) that on certain occasions we can and sometimes are forced by circumstances to raise just such questions. Now, what these two points indicate is something most intriguing and crucial about the structure of our everyday world.

In the first place, however simple and straightforward our daily lives may seem, they are in truth terribly complex. Having merely scratched the surface of this complexity in three examples, we moved a bit further with the variations. Consider only A and A', noticing especially what we typically do *not* do: we do not 'dance,' much less become ruffled, as was the case when the other person was in front of us, when, say, we bump into a parking meter (you might get ruffled, but the meaning of it is quite different when it is the 'other man'); we do not doff our hats in greeting to doors, stop lights, trees; we do not blush in embarrassment at the sounds of trains, cars, or at other city noises (yet we do experience just such feelings when it is a matter of another person).

In short, we take it for granted that not all things in our world are strictly alike, that they are different for our experience, and that our usual attitudes and actions show this without our having to think about it at every moment. Our world, in other words, is a *stratified* one, and this stratification finds its expression in our usual ways of acting, thinking, and speaking. Moreover, sometimes we can and do 'stop and think'; motivated by circumstances and events, or sometimes just by our own desires, we pause and take stock of these and of our own taken-for-granted attitudes regarding them. In B' and especially C', the motivation to take stock is quite strong.

In the second place, consider that experience of surprise or shock which occurs. When you are forced to stop and think, even if only momentarily, this is a *kind of disengagement from* the texture and style of the concerns of the moment. You step back, as it were, from those hitherto prevailing concerns, and this stepping-back and 'taking-stock' involves an apprehension of those affairs that you have not hitherto noticed at all, or if so, only marginally. In short, the disengagement through shock is a *kind of reflective grasping,* both of things in the environs and of your own typical ways of dealing with them. It is, as we noted in the Prologue, to draw back from, or to 'distance' yourself as regards these concerns; thus, we find here one of the rudimentary forms of questioning.

This kind of disengagement and motivated reflection has been captured with rare sensitiveness in Theodore Spencer's poem, "The Enlistment," [1] some of which is well worth quoting here. In the poem, a man walks up to your door and asks what time it is; you reply, and he asks, "But whose time? Yours or mine?" What would you do, Spencer asks, when the usual ways of asking and responding break down?

> You could not speak as if he were your neighbor,
> Give him a Coca-Cola and talk of taxes;
> He'd look at you, and not take off his hat.
> And if you asked him in, he would say, "No,
> I'll stay right here; here in the open door."
> You'd find yourself both with him and alone;
> Looking outward at his curious eyes,
> And looking inward at what you'd forgot. . . .
> You'd probably wait, looking into his eyes,
> And all you'd say would be, "Yes, I know."
> Some usual thing, something you'd said before
> (You and I, we've all said it before,
> Unaware of what it meant till now, unaware
> That once we've said it, we have changed our world.)
> And having said it, suddenly you would look
> Beyond the door, beyond those strong eyes,
> And going beyond would come back through those eyes
> And find those eyes your own. "Yes. I know."
> You'd suddenly say, and would not ask him in.
>
> You would go out: and he would not be there.
> Seeking yourself you would go out to find him.

The disengagement and reflective apprehension of what you have until now been unaware of effects a crucial shift. Suddenly you are shocked into an awareness of *yourself*: "And going beyond," you "come back through those eyes / And find those eyes your own." That is, the jolt of the uncommon, emerging in the midst of the common, awakens that in you of which until now you were not aware, and by so doing effects a subtle shift in you and a change in the world itself. You now see it, for the first time, really. This leads to a third point.

With this shift there emerges the recognition of what before seemed so obvious and commonplace that it called no attention to itself. Now you find the obvious quite suddenly transformed. Having recognized it, "we have changed our world." Like someone who suddenly discovers that he is lost in a city, the things which surround us in our daily lives, things usually familiar and cozy, now stand out as strange and alien; what was common is now seen as most uncommon, the usual as uncannily different. We begin to perceive that "things as they usually are" in the everyday setting of our lives, have dimensions and depths, as do we ourselves (these being inseparable), only dimly suspected before. As in Wallace Stevens' *Blue Guitar*,[2] we learn "A tune beyond us as we are." That blue guitar, which changes "things as they usually are," I learn "c'est moi. The blue guitar / And I are one."

The more we bring into focus our taken-for-granted ways of dealing with things as we commonly take them to be, the more does this sense of their, of our, strange novelty stand out. You begin to feel like one who, although having walked down a particular street countless times, suddenly sees a tree, a house, a porch, as if never really seen before—though, of course, it has been seen, and just for that reason does it stand out now as 'the same yet different . . . somehow'!

We may now begin to appreciate the fact that our usual attitudes, which seem so natural and easy, are at bottom characterized not only (as already stated) as a set of concerns for the things commonly displayed about us, but also as a kind of implicit suspension of the possibility that these things that hold our attention might be otherwise than they appear in our usual daily concerns and experiences.[3] Certain of our experiences do, nevertheless, force us to step back from our engagement, our deep-seated acceptance of things as they usually are. Played upon by the blue guitar, we are jolted back, we disengage, step back from, and apprehend these things and ourselves in a changed way. In such momentary encounters, to be sure, our reflective experience, our wonder, is usually dropped and we go about our affairs, the shock fading into the backdrop of things and experiences typified as 'peculiar and strange'—a typical dimension as much a part of our common lives as what is familiar.

This disengagement and reflective apprehension may itself be focused upon; it may itself be sustained, and we may thus try to move more deeply into this hitherto unexplored terrain. But how to do so, when the prime thrust of the usual, the obvious, seems to be to suspend just such a move? As Husserl has pointed out,

> I find continually present over against me the one spatial-temporal reality [*Wirklichkeit*] to which I myself belong, as do all other men found in it and related to it in the same ways. This "reality," as the word itself already indicates, I find to *exist there,* and *I take it just as it gives itself to me as existing.* All doubting and rejection of the data of the natural world alters nothing in the *general thesis of the natural attitude.* "The" world is as actuality [*Wirklichkeit*] always there; it is at most here and there "other" than I supposed, this or that is so to speak struck *out of it* as being "illusion," "hallucination" and so forth—out of it, it, in the sense of the general thesis, the always existing world.[4]

Most often, in other words, moments of doubt and uncertainty bring into focus only a segment of the world, only certain of our taken-for-granted beliefs and assumptions about it, but *not it itself as such,* nor our rooted belief in it as 'there.' How indeed are we to move more deeply into what Husserl calls the "general thesis of the natural attitude," when just that "thesis," that fundamental acceptance at the base of all our concerns and activities, seems to resist that move, seems to reassert itself even in the midst of our doubtings and puzzlings? Referring to this natural attitude as "my being in reality," Maurice Natanson addresses just this difficulty:

> It is not a question of sharpening some special sense, of looking in some extraordinary corner of the mind, or of locating the philosopher's stone. What is called for, above all, is that each one of us examine his style of being in the world at the level of ordinary, common-sense life, so that the philosophical character of that level of experience be clarified . . . What, then is it that the character of common-sense life is going to reveal which will make being in reality understandable? The direct answer is curious: the mark of common-sense life, the very essence of its style of being, is its failure to make itself an object for its own inspection . . . That common-sense life has a style, has an essential structure, is an insight that necessarily transcends the understanding of common-sense men . . . Yet it is exactly that absolute awareness of the style of our being in common-sense life which must be made an object for inspection if the datum of being in reality is to be gotten. And this is the most difficult of all tasks, largely because what it is that is required of us is exactly the problem. There is a built-in mechanism of protection in the stream of daily life which guards against this awareness; philosophy is an effort to crack this barrier.[5]

Yet, if what I have suggested in this section thus far rings true at all, then Natanson's judgment concerning common-sense life, earlier affirmed by Alfred Schutz,[6] requires some modification. For, while it is certainly the case that our usual style of doing and thinking within the life-world is mainly characterized by (1) being attentive to, or being concerned and busied with, the things in the environs (and neither *as* experienced by us, nor our experiencing them *as such*), and (2) a suspension of the possibility of their being otherwise than they are experienced and believed to be, still there are certain kinds of experiences which are not only characteristic of our life-worldly being but also break with just these two central features. I have suggested that such a disengagement occurs, however minimally or momentarily, with such simple cases as that in A and A', and that the break is even more pronounced in cases such as B' and especially C'.

To be sure, these are only momentary, and the stepping-back and taking-stock is correspondingly brief. But what must be stressed here is, as Natanson insists, that we are not engaged in a kind of metaphysical easter-egg hunt. A kind of release from the deep moorings of the general thesis of the natural attitude *occurs*. The problem, then, is *not* to try and find a way of pulling oneself up by one's own bootstraps (how free oneself from common-sense when common-sense is precisely geared against that freeing?). It is not, more generally, as if phenomenological philosophy had to be brought in from the outside in order to "crack this barrier." Quite to the contrary, that sense of uncommonness which makes this "barrier" stand out is already within the texture of the common itself.

What is required, and is within our freedom to do, in order to focus explicitly on that fundamental 'thesis' which grounds us in the lifeworld, is *to sustain that kind of shock and disengagement systematically and then methodically to explore in depth what then is disclosed to us.* This can be done, for precisely that astonished vision which becomes explicit in these types of momentary experiences can itself be focused upon. Doing that, with care and attentiveness, is to move toward, if not into, phenomenological philosophy. For what concerns such a philosophy is neither the affirmation nor the denial of that from which we disengage ourselves, but rather the methodical exploring and probing, in the setting of and through reflective wonder, of this 'new land': that 'world' in so far as it is experienced by us, and ourselves in so far as we experience it.

As Husserl emphasizes, while the constant affirming of 'reality' is the texture of our daily lives, the denial of it is itself but *another thesis* or supposition, one which affirms the non-being of that reality. That is, unlike Descartes' attempt at universal doubt, the phenomenological philosopher is interested neither in affirming nor in denying anything, but in exploring, or, as I shall want to say later, in *making explicit* what has hitherto been *implicit*. This effort leaves untouched the 'general thesis'; just as in the experiences we briefly touched upon, the thing itself—the anonymous stranger, the clerk, the acquaintance—remained all along 'there' before us, so here, the 'world' and all it includes—values, physical things, other people, myself, institutions, etc.—remains 'there' all along. If I read this disengagement correctly, only our attitude toward the world undergoes a shift; *our attention shifts from that of engagement in to that of focal concern for the sense and strata of the very engagement itself.* This 'way,' then, is obviously open to anyone who wants to follow it. When the explorer returns, he invites others to go and see for themselves what he claims to have discovered, and he leaves at their disposal the 'way' he followed. But it is not the only way. So we now must turn to several other paths.

The Way of Criticism of Naturalism and Subjectivity.

A good deal was said above about 'experience' and the necessity to study it carefully. Indeed, many phenomenologists, and especially Husserl, will insist that this 'study' must be 'scientific.' Such a view does not, on the face of it, seem very different from one prevailing view. Whether there is any difference or not, it is true that an emphasis on 'science' as the prominent, if not the only, way of acquiring knowledge of existing things generally (including human experience), is quite widespread; it even filters down into the actional and value structures of daily life. Certainly a commitment to the thesis is fundamental to traditional empiricism, naturalism, positivism, and much of analytic philosophy and pragmatism. It is also a central tenet in the most influential theoretical view today among the sciences of man—namely, behaviorism. The questions implicit in section I—what is 'experience'? how can it best be studied?—have already, it seems, received their definitive response. Like all responses, this, too, is an epistemic claim and therefore necessarily requires critical questioning.

Following out the implications of certain central issues and tenets of traditional empiricism—especially Hume's distinction between 'matters of fact' and 'relations of ideas' [7]

—a large number of philosophers and theoreticians, though differing on some issues, have held the common view that genuine science and the science of experience are the same. This thesis has usually been held along with a number of others. For example: (1) science is concerned with the realm of 'matters of fact,' and is thus strictly *empirical.* (2) 'Empirical' means 'what is experienced,' and this in turn (3) is usually assumed to be synonymous with 'what can be observed, directly or indirectly, by means of the senses.' The latter (4) is taken at the outset to be more or less what Hume had understood by it—one form or another of 'sense-data-' or 'stimulus-response-theory.' Since (5) the only *non-empirical* knowledge is found in logic and mathematics ('relations of ideas'), (6) any claim to the effect that there are 'essences' or 'affairs knowable *a priori,*' other than what is learned from 'relations of ideas,' is merely expressive, or is nonsense. These theses are usually held along with a nominalism: nothing in logic or mathematics yields knowledge of the world, and only individuals, open to sense perception, really exist. Knowledge consists of propositions, and propositions are of two kinds: analytic and synthetic. Thus, if one claims strict necessity, and thus *a priori* status, for a proposition, it can only be analytic (its truth-value being strictly determined by the meanings of the terms used, it says nothing about the world). If one claims to be speaking of something other than the meanings of the terms used in the proposition, the claim is by definition synthetic and hence only probable, never necessary—and thus falls within the province of empirical science. Thus, all knowledge of 'matters of fact' *derived from and based upon* sense experience is always and essentially a matter of empirical science.

In such a view, to experience something is always passively to take-in sensory data (literal *aesthesis*) that, of course, are *in themselves* unconnected, unordered, unrelated to one another—a phantasmagoria of bits and stuffs causally imprinted on and thus real modifications of the perceiving organism's sensitive surfaces. I shall return to this conception in greater detail in the next section of this chapter. For now, it is important only to note that in its terms, all 'order' and 'regularity' arise *only* from and as a consequence of *nonsensory* processes—whether they be Hume's 'associative principles' (or 'custom and habit'), Kant's system of 'categories' and 'schematism,' or classical psychology's 'judgment' and 'memory.' Thus, this view simply takes it for granted that, as Schutz points out, "the only alternative to controllable and, therefore, objective sensory observation is that of subjective and, therefore, uncontrollable and unverifiable introspection." [8] In brief, what is 'sense perceivable' is assumed to be 'overt' and thus 'objective' data (behavior) alone, and the 'subjective' is uncritically assumed to be 'private' and therefore 'inaccessible' to scientific inquiry. Since only the latter yields knowledge of the world, we cannot *know* what is not overt; the subjective is epistemically forbidden, locked in the prison of the private. In order to get at what transpires behind the cell doors, if anything, it is therefore necessary to either rely on 'reports,' or subject the 'subjective' to 'translation' into scientific language, or reduce it to data that are 'overtly observable,' or else simply regard the whole distinction between 'public' (objective) and 'private' (subjective) as either nonsense (all that exists is physical) or as merely linguistic convention. In every case, and one can think of even more than these, the 'subjective' is held in epistemic suspicion; *if* there is the 'subjective,' then getting to it *always requires special techniques* devised solely on the grounds of the prior assumption which *glosses* from 'empirical' through 'sensory perception' and 'sense-data' to 'private and inaccessible' to inquiry.

The basis of this conception is what Husserl calls the "naturalization of consciousness," [9] which is, he believes, not only radically mistaken but at the heart of the historical process resulting in the crisis of western man. In substance, Husserl claims, the central thesis which underlies this naturalization is that, as he says,

Whatever is, is either itself physical, belonging to the totality of physical nature, or it is in fact psychical, but then merely as a variable dependent on the physical, at best a secondary "parallel accompaniment." Whatever is belongs to psycho-physical nature, which is to say that it is univocally determined by rigid laws.[10]

Since what is primary is physical nature, the "rigid laws" which are supposed to explain all empirical events and objects, including mind and mental events, are those pertaining to physical nature. Hence, even if the 'psychical' is theoretically admitted, it is *of necessity* to be treated either as (1) translatable into or reduceable to what is physical (i.e., 'overt behavior'), (2) held in abeyance until such procedures become possible, or (3) rejected as (minimally) nonscientific and therefore inaccessible and unknowable ('private').

Precisely to the extent that the view in question rests on some form of sense-data theory, it is unavoidably involved in either of two commitments, both of which are absurd in Husserl's sense—that is, each is evidently inconsistent with itself.[11]

(1) On the one hand, if the theory of sense observation invokes a theory of physical causality to account for the occurrence of 'stimuli' impinging on the organism's sensitive surfaces, then *naturalism*, or some variation of it, in its specifically modern sense, follows. That is,

> Naturalism is a phenomenon consequent upon the discovery of nature, which is to say of nature considered as a unity of spatio-temporal being subject to exact laws of nature.[12]

What is, is ultimately physical or dependent upon the physical—a unity of spatio-temporal and causally interconnected material particles in motion—and is therefore *knowable only as physical.* Thus does naturalism *begin with the assumption* that only empirical science can yield knowledge of the world.

Furthermore, 'empirical science' is for this view assumed at the outset to *mean* an ordered knowledge of measurable quanta; hence, for it, mathematical physics and chemistry are taken as the *model of all science*—and this, again, quite without question. Solely to the extent that a field of study uses the techniques, methods, and principles of this model is it judged to be 'scientific.' Reductivism is essential to this view, precisely because, corresponding to the ontological thesis that all is physical or reduceable to it, is the epistemological-methodological thesis that all 'sciences' *must* be evaluated by reference to mathematical physics in order to be legitimate. Accordingly, all questions concerned with the justification of knowledge are to be answered by other, equally empirical inquiries—all of which ultimately are to rest on some mode of sensory observation. The latter means the passive imprintation by sense data; hence, psychology and physiological optics serve as the epistemic ground for adjudicating the claims to being 'science.' At the same time, these disciplines are 'sciences' solely to the extent that they model themselves on mathematical physics, and thus follows the essentially circular, and ultimately single-storied, conception of knowledge and reality. It also follows that philosophy, in so far as it yields knowledge, is legitimate and justified only if it is a kind of janitor in the house of science; its proper roots are in science, and its task is strictly the analysis, clarification, and interrelating of empirical scientific results.

(2) On the other hand, if the theory of sense observation invoked to support the conception is like the sense-impressionism of Hume, then a thorough-going skepticism is inescapable. In such a view, since all knowledge of 'matters of fact' is restricted to impressions, and their consequent 'ideas,' one can literally say nothing about the *essentially recondite sources or causes of impressions,* any more than one can inquire into the ultimate nature of the mind either as to its receptivity or as to its ways of making connections among ideas.[13] Precisely because of this double-pronged skepticism, it is obvious that neither sensory observation nor any form of 'internal perception' of the mind can be relied upon as supportive of scientific claims to knowledge. Indeed, *the entire scientific edifice must collapse,* precisely because the claim it makes to be a knowledge of objective states of affairs *cannot* be justified. All one can 'know' are *his own* 'impressions and ideas.' Getting beyond this subjectivism is possible only thanks to our customary and habitual beliefs, but custom and habit cannot function as epistemic justifiers since they are themselves rooted in and

derived from impressions and ideas. This conception, like the first, necessarily entails a vicious circle.

It would seem that the only viable way to support the conception in question is one form or another of naturalism, or behaviorism. But is this really viable? Notice, first, that such a view *must* regard all phenomena, universally, as physical; or, if some do not immediately seem to be this, then one must 'translate,' 'reduce,' or 'transform' these data into other ones which *are* physical, or, 'overt' and therefore 'objectively observable.' If some phenomena resist this move, they must be ignored, and this ignoring is considered both necessary and legitimate.

Such translation of 'subjective' into 'objective' data—the thesis that, for instance, psychological affairs, like 'needs,' are ultimately but the behavior of nerve-tissues, which are biophysical or biochemical imbalances, essentially presupposes the acknowledgment that there are phenomena *that are not the same* as 'natural' or physical data. The insistence on translation requires the counter-naturalist thesis that *not* all things are 'natural' in the naturalist's own sense. If they were, 'reduction' would not be at all necessary, even heuristically. Therefore, whether these phenomena be taken as 'illusions' or 'private' appearances, they cannot *for that reason* be ignored. Even if only illusory, they must be susceptible of study in themselves, and hence must be accessible, as *genuinely* illusory and distinguishable from the nonillusory, and the criterion in reference to which 'illusion' alone has its meaning must be able to be justified within the framework of the theory itself—which is essentially impossible in this single-storied conception, since 'criteria' *cannot be at the same level* as that for which they serve as criteria.

Second, it is always philosophically relevant to ask what happens to the phenomena that, it is claimed, not only can but must be 'translated.' To argue for the latter's necessity is to presume that it is *possible,* and that nothing essential is thereby lost. Notice, however, the requirements for any such translation or reduction: there must be two sets of data— that to be translated and that into which they are to be translated—and furthermore some sort of 'guide' ('dictionary') for doing the translation to assure that the translating is done properly. And, of course, there must be a way of defining 'properly' within the terms of the proposal itself. But does any of this make sense within the framework of the conception?

The one set of data, the 'subjective,' is assumed at the outset to be 'private.' Private to whom? Why, to the one whose data they are, whose behavior is observed, and *they are by definition accessible to no one else,* including the observing scientist who seeks to do the translation. They may be 'reported' or seemingly 'recorded' by instruments, but the data themselves remain essentially available only to the one having them. In short, these data, subjective and private to the utmost *in terms of the theory itself,* are inaccessible for the translation. Even 'reporting' and 'recording,' after all, are not only *at a remove from the actual data* themselves but involve, on the part of the observer, several or more *inferences* whose premisses, however, cannot themselves be made legitimate since they concern precisely these 'private' data. Finally, the necessary 'guide' for the translation is not, as it must be if the translation is even possible, one which contains *both* sets of data and appropriate 'rules' for defining 'proper' translation. First, if the 'guide' *did* contain both, then the one set of data, the 'private,' would *not* be as assumed, for it would be quite available to anyone possessing the guide. Second, the only alternative for the task at hand are the objective data themselves—a step many theorists are inclined toward, but which is a patent *petitio principii,* since *by definition* one set cannot have anything in common with the other. Third, the 'rules' by which the translation is to be done (usually, 'logic') are not at hand, since, in a consistently held naturalism or behaviorism, even these must be at the same level, or have their source and justification in the 'objective data'—and thus cannot function as 'rules.' Therefore, not only is something 'lost' in the translation, but, in truth, *the whole of the subjective is never had in the first place.* On these grounds naturalism and behaviorism are theoretically in· the same bind as the most radical skepticism.[14]

The thesis concerning 'private' data, then, is completely unjustified and evidently self-contradictory. But what of the other part of the thesis, that concerning the restriction of knowledge to objectively observable ('overt') behavior, whether coupled with an ignoring or an outright denial of 'subjective' data? What is it 'to observe'? Well, it is to be stimulated passively by some causally efficacious source (light reflecting off a surface and drumming into the eyeball). What is it to be 'stimulated'? Well, it is to have certain neurophysiological consequences 'inside' the organism, which neural commotion eventually winds up 'inside' the cerebral cortex. Of course, the latter data are *not* themselves 'objectively observable' *in principle,* as we have already seen, even if 'reported' or 'recorded.' But if it is true that human beings respond, not to externally existing objects open to inspection by a multiplicity of observers, but strictly to 'stimuli' which are by definition 'internal,' and thus also private, to the organism of the supposedly observed organism, *then no data of any kind are observable, much less objectively verifiable, by more than the one unique organism which alone has the data.* There is simply no way for *me* to observe and then theorize about what *you* experience by way of sense-data—unless, of course, I *covertly,* and inconsistently, *assume* that some data are not private and inaccessible but shared with others, even though this is never stated in the theory. Furthermore, what must be explicitly recognized is that the *observing theoretician* (scientist or philosopher) *himself cannot be excluded* from this theory of his. What applies to human behavior *must* apply to *his* behavior. If all *he* has as data are also sense-data, which are by definition private to him, *then there are no objective data anywhere to be found.* The so-called 'objective' data, ironically, turn out to be just the opposite—*on the grounds of the theory itself.* The theory makes impossible what it makes necessary.

Finally, it is evident that such theories as these remain essentially blind to a decisive point. They are themselves, in the strictest epistemic sense, *products* of specific human activities—for instance, 'explaining,' 'observing,' 'inferring,' 'theorizing,' to mention only a few of the more obvious ones. But if this is true (as it is), and if 'activities' of this kind are 'mental' (as they are) and thus 'subjective,' *then these theories are utterly incapable of accounting for themselves* in their own terms. As Schutz remarks, even the most refined behaviorism can merely explain the behavior of the *observed* (and not even that, as we saw), never of the *observing behaviorist himself.* Such a behaviorism simply takes for granted, as does naturalism, that there is a common social world in which there are not only human persons acting and interacting, but observing scientists and theorizing philosophers as well. It presupposes, in short, "that an intersubjective understanding between scientist B and scientist A occurs neither by scientist B's observations of scientist A's overt behavior, nor by introspection performed by B, nor by [imaginative] identification of B with A." [15] Scientists talk with one another while observing behavior, no less than do philosophers; and both proceed to write books—and neither the one nor the other can be accounted for, in the terms of the theories themselves.

Such theories fail to recognize that every empirical science is necessarily *naive* in its starting point and foundational presuppositions. To say this is not, as Husserl points out, to indulge in pejorative name-calling, for 'naivity' means only that every empirical science necessarily proceeds on the basis of presuppositions that are taken for granted. As Husserl emphasizes,

> It is true that natural science is, in its own way, very critical. Isolated experience, even when it is accumulated, is still worth little to it. It is in the methodical disposition and connection of experiences, in the interplay of experience and thought, which has its rigid logical laws, that valid experience is distinguished from invalid, that each experience is accorded its level of validity, and that objectively valid knowledge as such . . . is worked out. Still, no matter how satisfactory this kind of critique of experience may be, as long as we remain within natural science and think according to its point of view, *a completely different critique of experience is still possible and indispensable* [my italics], a critique that places in question all experience as such and the sort of thinking proper to empirical science.[16]

However *self-corrective* science, and a philosophy basing itself on it, may be it is by no means *self-critical:* the justification of its foundational assumptions—epistemological, axiological, methodological—is not a possible task for empirical science. What is called for is a rigorous critique of experience, including that which goes into empirical science itself; and *this critique lies at another epistemic and systemic level.* The very existence of science, the fact of experience, requires a multileveled philosophical position. The failure to recognize this is tantamount to becoming enmeshed in a vicious circle. As Kant had already shown, however much some of our knowledge may arise from sense experience, it cannot at the same time be justified by that sense experience.

Thus the criticism of naturalism and behaviorism has delineated a series of urgent questions and the necessity of meeting these with another level of inquiry. The criticism shows that despite all claims to the contrary, the naturalization of consciousness in truth vitiates the very possibility of posing, much less resolving, these issues, thereby marking out the positive nature of *another* task. First, what is called for is the systematic grounding of all knowledge and experience; the positive impulse is for foundational inquiry in the sense of the systematic unraveling and criticism of the presuppositions of knowledge and experience. Second, and more particularly, the criticism shows that it is evidently inconsistent (absurd) to treat 'subjectivity' or 'psychical' phenomena as if they were 'nature' or reduceable to 'nature.' It thus shows the necessity of doing something other than 'naturalizing' consciousness: first and foremost, to discover what the 'subjective' itself is, in its own terms and for its own sake, initially and before any effort is made to determine its actual and possible relations and interrelations with the physical, the somatic, the social, and so on. What are the essential features of consciousness itself? What is it 'to experience' objects in the world? What are these 'objects,' considered strictly *as* 'objects experienced by consciousness' (whether *as* sense-perceived, *as* remembered, *as* judged, *as* believed, *as* doubted, or whatever)?

Indeed, the sense of the criticism is that the conception of science implicitly operative in naturalism in all of its forms is far too narrow, too restricted, too uncritical, to do justice to the phenomena. The fundamental intuition, so to speak, of naturalism is quite correct—that is, its impulse to science —but its vision is askew. The systematic study of experience, of consciousness and its objects, must be scientific, a science focusing on essences:

> If knowledge theory will nevertheless investigate the problems of the relationship between consciousness and being, it can have before its eyes only being *as the correlate of consciousness* [my italics.], as something "intended" after the manner of consciousness: as perceived, remembered, expected, represented pictorially, imagined, identified, distinguished, believed, opined, evaluated, etc. It is clear, then, that the investigation must be directed toward *a scientific essential knowledge* [my italics.] of consciousness, toward that which consciousness itself "is" according to its essence in all its distinguishable forms. At the same time, however, the investigation must be directed toward what consciousness "means" ["intends"], as well as toward the different ways in which—in accord with the essence of the aforementioned forms—it intends the objective, now clearly, now obscurely, now by presenting or by presentifying, now symbolically or pictorially, now simply, now mediated in thought, now in this or that mode of attention, and so on in countless other forms, and how ultimately it "demonstrates" the objective as that which is "validly," "really."
> . . . The sense of the question concerning legitimacy, which is to be put to all cognitive acts, must admit of being understood, the essence of grounded legitimation and that of ideal groundableness or validity must admit of being fully clarified, in this manner—and with respect to all levels of cognition, including the highest, that of scientific cognition.[17]

That 'scientific cognition,' however, is no longer what naturalism thought it to be—namely, empirical—but is rather the foundational and rigorous effort to disclose, explicate, and analyze the essential features of consciousness and its objects—always considered strictly as correlates. The criticism, then, delineates another 'way' to phenomenology, conceived not as one more 'ism' alongside others, but *as a set of central issues and themes, and the effort to realize a truly foundational philosophy.*

In section I, it was suggested that one 'way' in which a central set of themes, and the task of carefully contending with them, can arise is through the jolts and shocks which occur in daily life. Here I have suggested another 'way,' namely, through critical dissatisfaction with prevailing theoretical notions, which sets up the *very same* set of themes and tasks. In section III it remains to lay out still another 'way' into phenomenology.

The Historical Nexus.

There is nothing substantially new in the ideas clustered around naturalism and behaviorism. Both the theory of sense perception and the emphasis on science have their historical roots. As Husserl showed in his last work, *The Crisis of European Science and Transcendental Phenomenology,* [18] not only these but a good deal else besides were already present in the writings of Galileo and Descartes. With Galileo, nature is conceived of as a thoroughly rational universe accessible by means of a strictly rational science—which for him means *mathematical* science. Geometry, and especially geometrical measurement of quanta, became conceived of as the ideal, the model of all knowledge of nature 'as it really is.' Hence, the workaday rule-of-thumb ideas and procedures pertaining to natural things (distances, shapes, velocities, volumes, and so on) become interpreted as *approximations* to the 'real' mathematical forms which are determinable with precision.

Geometry, as a science of precise measurement, is thought to provide a method of definitively overcoming the relativity of perceptual experience and the limitations of the practical art of measurement. In this way, it was believed, one can attain the ideal of absolute, invariant truths transcending the idiosyncracies and variabilities of perceptual life. At the same time, the latter receives an interpretation that gives rise to a fundamental style of treating perception, and generates an entire constellation of issues unique to that style. Since the book of Nature is written in mathematical terms, and perceptual things are merely approximations to these mathematical forms, perceptual life generally is taken as a kind of second-class citizen in the domain of Reality. What is perceptually experienced is an illusion, an *appearance* of what really exists, and the latter is the system of particles in motion determinable by mathematical techniques.

Taking mathematics, and geometry in particular, as already-established acquisitions at the disposal of anyone who can master the appropriate tools and methods, and as the model of genuine knowledge, everything else becomes either quantified or interpreted as depending upon quantifiable affairs—i.e., *extension* becomes the prime property of Nature, along with motion, which is to say, measurable displacement. Galileo's first step, then, is already an *abstraction* whereby only the corporeal, extensional, measurable aspect of things and the world is considered.[19]

From this emerges one of the central themes of modern philosophy. For if nature 'really' is a system of corporeal particles in motion determinable by mathematics, and if perception does not disclose that system, then accounting for the discrepancy becomes an urgent problem. The logic of the mathematization of nature makes necessary a specific inquiry to explain *why it is that we do not experience what we would were we able to apprehend perceptually what nature 'really' is in itself.* Beyond that, it becomes necessary to account for why it is that our perceptual experience yields not only a realm of appearances, but that *specific and remarkably consistent illusion we in fact concretely experience.*

Our perceptual apparatus, for whatever reason, does not disclose the genuine being of nature—assuming, as do most modern and many contemporary philosophers, that physical science alone tells us what nature really is. How can that failure be explained? And how can we account for the specific and regular 'appearance' which our perceptual experience does disclose? These basic questions form the core of the 'problem of knowledge' in its specifically modern sense. It is an *urgent* set of issues, moreover: for on its solution rests the fate of the newly developing sciences of nature. Only if the claims to knowledge of the 'external world' can be justified, will these sciences be made secure.

The fundamental style of treating perception then flows quite naturally: the theory of sense perception, and thus the theory of knowledge of the external world, are strict consequences of the assumption that nature as it really is, is explained to us by mathematical-physical science alone. The 'theory of ideas' *(Vorstellungstheorie)* gives the fundamental way in which those problems are posed and solutions attempted. Already present, in at least germinal form, in Galileo and more fully developed by Descartes, this theory, and its attendant dualism, came completely into its own especially in British empiricism, and was brought to even further fruition by Kant. Following out some of its principal features, it soon becomes evident that it gives rise to certain pressing questions which are irresolvable within its own framework. Appreciating that historical development, but especially the problematics of the theory of ideas, constitutes a third 'way' into phenomenology.

The theory has a unique style which is typical of most philosophical positions from Descartes through the nineteenth century philosophers (and many after them). Recognizing that there are obvious and important differences among them, we can state it in the following terms. Mind is an autonomous sphere unto itself; it is a closed interiority.[20] That entity is a kind of container, a sort of place where things happen called 'sensations,' 'impressions,' or 'ideas.' The mind is a thing *(res)* with certain determinable *contents,* furnishings, with which it works. Events also go on within the mind: it has certain functions, operations or faculties—memory, judgment, willing, feeling, cognizing, and the like—by means of which its contents are combined, ordered, compared, separated, and in general dealt with.

This closed domain stands opposed to 'external' things in general, including that external body which embodies it but is considered as nonessential to it. There are, then, two 'worlds' standing off against one another, as ontologically independent but coordinate *substances.* As such, neither requires the other in order to be itself, nor is any reference to the one requisite for knowledge of the other. They are mutually exclusive and self-sufficient parts of a totality: Reality. The one, 'nature,' is the world disclosed and analyzed by mathematical-physical science—accessible only by means of elaborate techniques. The other, 'mind,' is that which, when analyzed, should yield the solutions to the basic questions, for it is the mind that is responsible for the 'appearance'; and it is mind's limitations in its perceptual equipment that account for its failure thereby to apprehend 'reality.' As it happens, though, mind has a most peculiar characteristic: *prior to all analysis* it seems to have contact with (perceptions of) the world of objects 'outside' it. In more ordinary terms, one usually believes that the objects with which one deals every day are really as they are experienced to be. How is that possible, if mind is, *after analysis* and according to the theory of ideas, seen to be a closed domain, having to do only with its own ideas? How can mind and nature at all have to do with one another?

The solution to that question is already contained in the starting-point which yields the very question. Expressed in a different way, the theory asserts that what we, in our naive ('vulgar') attitude, believe, turns out not to be the case. The difficulty is to try and determine (1) what we *really do* experience, and (2) why we believe it to be the same as what *really* exists. And it is precisely here that the theory of ideas comes in. What must transpire in order for the mind, which is 'inside,' to experience nature, which is 'outside'? *Either* the mind must go careening out of itself, through its sense organs, over to the object (say, a tree), and then bounce back again 'inside,' proclaiming as it slides back, 'Lo! There is a tree yon; watch out!'; *or,* the tree must 'come to' the mind. Quite in keeping with a long tradition reaching back to the Greek Atomists, Epicurus and Lucretius, the theory of ideas opts for the latter. The specific problem is how, in particular, the thing which is 'there' could 'travel' over 'here' where the mind is, and yet be experienced as 'over there.' Modern science provided just the mechanism for this, without resorting to Lucretius' 'little pictures' sent off by objects and lodged in the eye. In ways determinable by physical science, the object 'acts' on the senses, 'causing' an 'idea'[21] to be imprinted on the sense organ. A causal chain is set up that eventually results in sensory stimulation.

In short, mind deals with objects only through ideas in the mind. These ideas are peculiar in two ways. First, they are taken to be *representations;* that is, they *re*-present or 'copy' the object that caused its appearance in mind in the first place. Second, ideas by nature *'come from'*—either from the world, from God, from the imagination, or from the mind itself. To understand them, is to seek their origins. Hence, epistemology is necessarily conceived as *causal-genetic.* And, in a precise analogy to what 'the incomparable Mr. Newton' had done as regards Nature, knowledge is thought to be 'built up' out of 'simple ideas' ('atoms'), with 'complex ideas' (like configurations of atom particles) constituting knowledge. To justify knowledge is thus to 'analyze' complex ideas into their simple components.

We normally believe that we know full-bodied things like apples and children, which physical science, and the theory of ideas, tells us are *really* extended particles in motion. Why do we believe the former when the latter is what really occurs? The simple ideas (or impressions) are actually thought to occur, but because of habit and custom, and the operation of that other mental analogue of physical nature, 'association' (which works like gravitation), we are led to think that what are *really* simple ideas are complex ones; we think that an apple is really simple, a 'one' thing, when in reality it is complex, a 'manyness.' How do we know the latter? Only by carefully analyzing our ideas into their parts does this become apparent; hence, our normal experience is merely appearance, and only philosophical theory can make this appearance stand out.

The theory of mind that emerges is thus an effort to provide the solution to the two prime questions, and thereby to also ground the possibility of knowledge of the 'external' world. Nevertheless, precisely because mind is encapsulated, closed on itself, it cannot *in principle* come into contact with the real world. The bridge of ideas is, of necessity, only problematic, for the mind, a strict immanence, can know only its own contents and activities. Everything else is only probable, just because knowledge of anything not an immanent component of the mind requires special techniques if mind is to get out of itself; but since these techniques, which are also in the mind as methods or ideas, are also immanent, knowledge of anything not mental is always mediate and hence only probable.[22]

What we normally call things, then, are only clusters of ideas in and connected by the mind, either necessarily (Kant) or merely contingently (empiricism). In either case, things are strictly products of the mind's own operations or habits. Thus, what began as a systematic effort to demonstrate the justifiability of knowledge of the external world known by science (whose validity was never questioned), ends up as an encapsulated subjective idealism. The 'things themselves,' which it had been the hope could be firmly reached by cognition (mathematics mainly), become either unknowable 'noumena' or else the dark secrets of which Hume spoke.

Besides what has already been pointed to, there are three fundamental assumptions to the theory. (1) *The concept of 'things-in-themselves' is legitimate:* it is necessary to conceive that things as they appear to us perceptually are not things as they really are. The distinction, made fully explicit by Kant, is conceived as one between what is or can be experienced and what is not and cannot be experienced.

(2) It is also assumed *that there are things-in-themselves,* and not only that it is proper to think them. The argument is simply that if there are 'ideas' and these are taken for granted as 'coming from' somewhere, and are '*re*-presentations of' something, then there must be a something that both 'causes' them and of which the ideas are copies. The rub here is just that no sense can be made out of this momentous '*of*' and '*from*' within the theory itself, as Berkeley clearly saw (even though he lapsed back into it himself). What is that 'something'? As Locke honestly said: "I know not what."

(3) A final and decisive assumption is *that the cognitive subject is a self-subsistent and self-existent entity, and that there are other such entities* (external things) *ontologically on a par* with the cognitive subject.

The cognitional relation between these ontologically co-ordinate, mutually independent entities is such that, if there is a cognizing, the *immediately presented* object of the cognizing is something that is internal to, an immanent component of, the cognitive subject itself (ideas). Hence, the prime epistemic question: given that there is no knower immediately acquainted with anything except what is immanent to his own mind, how it is possible for him to know anything else? Kant's extension of this to the case of self-knowledge merely intensifies the problem.

The typical move is to the mind's immediately presented object. But this object is assumed at the outset to be a 'copy,' and thus the problem merely gets restated: how does it happen that certain representations represent realities (are true) and others do not (are false)? For the everyday person, on the contrary, the question is simply whether there really is this or that object. Hence, the theory has the additional problem of accounting for why it is that normal experience does not conform to the requirements of the theory. Why are we deceived and why do we not know that we are deceived?

To account for this anomaly, the theory not only must assume what we have seen about the nature of ideas, but also that it is the 'object' which is active (causally), and the 'subject' which, as Kant made clear for the first time, is passive—that is, a capacity for being affected, or imprinted, by the causal action of the thing itself. The passive organism *receives* stimulations, whether aware of it or not. Hence, sensing in its purest form *(aesthesis)* is the sheer reception of 'data.' Once the data are received, then the mind's own processes come into play: what in normal life I believe to be 'over there' can now, it is thought, be shown to be a function of *nonsensory* processes going on in the mind—habit, judgment, memory, etc.—as a result of which what is *actually* received 'here' is *believed* to be 'there.'

The trouble with the entire theory, quite apart from what was stated earlier, is that it gives rise to problems, riddles, and certain vital questions that cannot even be posed within the framework and the theory. Parallel to Husserl's criticism of naturalism, Marcel, Sartre, and Merleau-Ponty argue that the traditional theory of ideas is an outrageous objectivism, guilty of what Merleau-Ponty calls "worldly prejudice."[23] Consider the notion of 'impressions,' or 'sensations.' On the one hand it is said to be an *actual objective* occurrence, which can even be measured and thus detected by an observer. On the other hand, since 'sensation' is experienced by the perceiver, it is essentially subjective and private in the terms of the theory. In a futile effort to rescue the theory from this subjectivism, the 'sensation' is magically reconverted into an *object:* it is said to be what I actually perceive! Hence, it becomes both subjective and objective, both perceiving and perceived.

As Sartre says,

> No synthetic grouping can confer an objective quality on what is in principle of the nature of what is lived. . . . Sensation, a hybrid notion between the subjective and the objective, conceived from the standpoint of the object and applied subsequently to the subject, a bastard existence concerning which we cannot say whether it exists in fact or in theory—sensation is a pure daydream of the psychologist.[24]

And Merleau-Ponty insists, in the same vein, that "pure sensation would amount to no sensation, and thus to not feeling at all. . . . We make perception out of things perceived. And since perceived things are obviously accessible only through perception, we end by understanding neither."[25] William James had already pinpointed this "psychologist's fallacy"— that *"great* snare" which consists in the *"confusion of his own standpoint with that of the mental fact* about which he is making his report." Studying another's mental state or experience (with its object), the psychologist, viewing the same object, "gets easily led to suppose that the thought, which is *of* it, knows it in the same way in which he knows it. . . ."[26]

With this objectivism, another riddle occurs. If our only contact with the world is with sensations, then everything which is not that, or not reduceable to it, must be given over to the subject—and hence be without objective significance. Thus, the theory invariably takes the sphere of *values* and that of *meaning* as purely subjective, and therefore as unknowable except by the subject—and this is not genuine knowledge since it is not objective. The *relativization of value and meaning or significance* seems a necessary consequence of the theory.

But, of course, the theorist is himself a perceiver and a knowing-valuing subject. He also writes books, presumably to and for other, similar subjects. If his theory is to make sense, it must hold for him, too. Thus, since value judgments, and judgments concerning what things 'mean' to the subject, are strictly personal affairs, the theorist can judge neither those of the other nor even his own, since neither of these is epistemic. Both are simply expressions of the subject's own private states, and no one can know anything about any of this—*not even that they are private and emotive expressions!* Since all a theorist himself can know of anything other than himself, including other human beings, are sensations located within himself, it is nonsense to speak of anything 'other' at all, much less write books about them. The insuperable riddle of *solipsism* necessarily follows, for the very question concerning the existence of other human beings cannot even be meaningfully posed within the strict framework of the theory of ideas.

While most of the philosophers adhering to the theory were typically anxious to show that their philosophical results were commensurate with the beliefs and notions of 'the vulgar,' the truth of the matter is that the nature, structures, dimensions of common sense were not even made thematic, much less accounted for systematically. Thus, the appeal to common sense could only be uncritical. As we will see later, Hume probably came the closest to seeing the issue here; but his appeal to 'custom and habit' did not focus on the problems, and indeed, turned out to be but a kind of happy magic saving him from radical skepticism. Hence, along with all the other problems, the entire field of what Husserl calls the 'life-world' remains as a prime theme for inquiry. Along with it, the themes of intersubjectivity, embodiment, self, the experience of time, and still others remain as well, either as riddles within the theory of ideas, or as incapable of being asked within its framework. The understanding of these kinds of issues constitutes a third, historical 'way' into phenomenology, or critical philosophy. The more one finds critical shortcomings, in other words, the more one begins to demand the development of a truly critical and critically justified philosophy. Just that is what Husserl sees as the historic mission and basic sense of phenomenology.

The Inherent Direction of These 'Ways.'

Holding as close as I dare to the analogue of the explorer, if one sets out to guide others to a different land, he must surely help them to take each step one at a time, until they are able to 'see' the land for themselves. Phenomenology is nothing if it is not philosophical first of all. Hence, everything said about philosophy must also be realized here; and, it should be obvious, one 'way' into phenomenology must be a preparation in the discipline and history of philosophy. The fundamental demand, as we shall see, of phenomenology is that philosophical criticism itself become a solidly founded discipline of its own. Hence, I have continually stressed the dialogical-critical task of philosophy, and have tried to engage these tasks concretely.

But what of that other great thrust of philosophy, the effort to obtain a synthetic, constructive vision of 'what is' as such? My response is brief, but not at all unappreciative. No such attempt can be carried off unless (1) it can be shown to be a *possible* task and to proceed on grounds that are justified—which necessarily entails a foundational critique of consciousness and of reason and its abilities. Also, (2) such an effort must be thoroughly *self-critical*, capable of accounting for its own possibility at every step, and each of its steps is critically justified as the effort proceeds. In short, be the synthetic results of such theorizing what they may, they systematically presuppose philosophical criticism and self-criticism. Hence, the focus on the latter *in no way* prejudices the former, but rather must remain neutral to it, disengaged from it, in order to fulfill the required critical task. Such criticism cannot be taken for granted; not only that, it requires development on its own.

And this point is a first 'way' to come to an appreciation of phenomenological philosophy, a way already made earlier in different terms. When Hume made his famous distinction between 'matters of fact' and 'relations of ideas,' for instance, it seemed to him, and many after him, to be the final word on the nature of knowledge. But this very conception itself *presupposes* not only that there is another *kind* of knowledge (neither of 'facts' nor of 'relations') but that this other kind cannot be accounted for in terms of the distinction between 'matters of fact' and 'relations of ideas' which supposedly exhausts the kinds of knowledge. This knowledge, *a priori* and synthetic in Kant's sense, is precisely *Hume's philosophical assertions themselves*. The condition for the possibility of making such critical assertions is not and cannot be the same as the condition for the possibility of making claims about 'what is.' As we shall see, Hume himself came close to seeing just this difference, which Kant for the first time appreciated.

Seeing this difference is made possible by the adoption of the critical attitude of phenomenology. This attitude requires a 'stepping-back' from any philosophical (or other) theory and an inspecting of it *without presupposing either acceptance or rejection*. Such criticism may and sometimes does result in one or the other; but both acceptance and rejection themselves presuppose that critical disengagement and inquiry have been done.

In Section I it was suggested that something very much like this disengagement is found in everyday life, not only in the examples chosen, but much more generally. After all, it is very common to be asked to 'look at things as I see them' —that is, disengage yourself from your own standpoint for the moment—or to consider several alternatives of action without initially consenting or denying either. A quite similar step is found more formalized in empirical science: the meaning of objectivity requires a critical stepping-back from the scien-

tist's own specific and personal biographical situation in order
to permit the repeatability and verifiability requisite to scientific work. For the strict purposes of inquiry, scientists can
and indeed *must* remain neutral to the results of an inquiry,
in order to insure that they will not 'pre-judge' or 'prejudice'
them. Whether *in fact* this is done is not pertinent to the issue; the 'objectivity' stands as an *ideal* to be attained through
progressive effort, not something achieved or even necessarily
achievable in fact. And social science, where the injunction
is to ignore one's own (the scientist's) biographical situation
and stock of knowledge, and to understand the meanings
which actions have for the social agents whose actions they
are, presents an even more obvious instance of disengagement and neutrality requisite for the purposes at hand.

What is important is to focus on this act itself, wherever
it may be found and to whatever degree. Consider the activity of criticism itself, ignoring the specific issues treated—
e.g., in sections I and II above. Several relevant points already stand out. (1) To be able to criticize presupposes the
possibility of disengagement and neutrality as regards all
position-taking (acceptance, rejection, or something in between) toward some claim (a thesis, theory, or total position).
(2) Unless that be possible, no pursuit or claim of knowledge is possible. (3) It is the basic meaning of that 'invitation' which is essential to philosophy. (4) Criticism is at
least of two kinds, internal and external, and the 'invitation'
is basically to engage in this critical effort.

Recall the passage from Descartes' "Preface."[27] Two significant points are made: (1) although he is meditating, is
a kind of solitary self in quest for truth, his meditations are
explicitly an invitation to others "who desire to meditate seriously with me"; and (2) such *comeditation* is a form of dialogue
and is possible only if these others can "deliver themselves
entirely from every sort of prejudice. . . ." To insure that
these injunctions are kept, he sent his work to others before
publication, and then published both the work and the responses, along with his own responses to the latter. He then
warns all subsequent readers "to form no judgment" on his

Meditations until and unless they have also studied the entire document.

What Descartes did is essential, if sometimes only implicit, to every philosophical claim or set of claims. His act of sending out his work is an overt exhibition of the inherent nature of criticism in philosophy. To see this still more clearly, consider any philosophical claim *just as a claim,* regardless of its specific content—for example, Descartes' claim, "I think, therefore I am." Supposing, for the sake of simplicity, that the language is intelligible and clear, that internal criticism has been done: what is the character of the *claim as claim?* It is a *supposal* that *there is* something (the 'I'), and that *it is thus-and-so* ('thinking, and therefore is'). Disregarding the obviously richer content and complexity of Descartes' claim, we can distinguish two different affairs here.

On the one hand, there is the *supposal itself* (the claim as claim); on the other there is *the state of affairs about which* the supposal is made. Furthermore, the supposal itself shows distinctions beyond its linguistic dimension: it supposes (alleges) that there is some X, and that X is 'thus-and-so.' Nor is this all, for the supposal that X is, and is thus-and-so, is also a supposal that its being and being thus-and-so are affairs which are *other than* the supposal itself. Hence, the claim as a supposal inherently alleges that X and its being thus-and-so are *accessible independently of the claim,* that, in principle, anyone, including the claimer himself, could go to X itself, and if he does, he will find X to be and to be as supposed by the claim. That is, the supposal includes the *co-subjective (comeditative) accessibility* of the things judged (claimed, supposed).

A final characteristic may be mentioned, without of course exhausting the features of supposals. Every claim inherently and necessarily points towards something which would *ground* it, which is the 'reason' or 'evidence' for the claim's being asserted with one or another *modality*—as 'positively certain,' or 'true in all likelihood,' or 'doubtfully so,' or 'positively false,' and so on.

Thus, Descartes' claim supposes that there is an entity ('I') which is a thus-and-so ('thinking self'), and that 'therefore' (in one appeal to 'grounds') it is such-and-such ('existent self'). It supposes that others can also find this entity, and that if they do 'go to it,' they will find that there is such an entity and that it is as Descartes supposes. The claim is also asserted as apodictically certain (its major appeal to grounds, the 'evidence' of 'clear and distinct ideas'). Hence it alleges that each of us will be constrained by the 'thing itself' to assert it similarly, in view of the grounds on which it is made.

It is crucial, however, to note one thing: *none of us is forced or constrained to do any of this.* The nature of the claim as claim is that it *invites* us to do what is necessary—'go to the things supposed and supposed as thus-and-so'—in order to see for ourselves, to 'check it out.' We *may,* but are *not forced,* to do it. *But if* we take up the invitation, we are then obliged to engage in a specific task: 'comeditation,' or *criticism.* This 'going and checking,' whether done by Descartes again and again, or by others of us, is what comeditation or criticism requires; hence, it entails the dimensions of criticism mentioned above. Each claim stands in need of constant criticism, which it may or may not actually receive, but without which the claim is epistemically incomplete. This means that every claim stands in need of *being accounted for,* or at least of *being accountable for,* and doing this 'accounting' involves 'going and checking' the features of the claims mentioned, and others as well.

To criticize a claim, then, presupposes the possibility of disengagement and neutrality, the cosubjective accessibility of the things supposed as supposed, and the possibility of reiterable grounds or evidence. From these considerations, two general points stand out. (1) The very idea of knowledge is inseparable from the idea of grounds or evidence. (2) Our own act of viewing the 'claim as claim' is precisely the same kind of act of disengagement and neutrality already emphasized. This act is in fact done, and we have already done it many times here. To be sure, we all do it with greater or lesser success, finesse, or ability. But *what* we do is, first, *to focus attention* on one affair, or aspect, and therefore *to disregard* others. We ignored the specific content of Descartes' claim and focused on it simply as a claim. Second, in this focusing we strive *to maintain our disregarding* or disengagement, to keep out of consideration those affairs or aspects which we initially decided, for reasons which must themselves be critically reviewed, to disregard for the purposes at hand. Third, this *striving is an effort to remain free from prejudgments,* from prejudicing the results of our focusing on or attending to whatever it may be. We strive to focus and to disregard: that is, we have in view an *ideal.* We aim toward a goal, that of complete freedom from prejudgments (prejudices). Thus, as Husserl insists, "Must not the demand for a philosophy aiming at the ultimate conceivable freedom from prejudice . . . instead of being excessive, be part of the fundamental sense of genuine philosophy?" [28]

Let us return to the first general point, that 'knowledge' is inseparable from 'foundations.' Picking up our considerations of the claim as claim, suppose that I say, "The water in the pool is cold." What is it, to 'account for' or to 'ground,' such a claim? Being a relatively simple case (for our purposes, at least), the answer is at hand: if I want to account for it (to show its reason, to give its evidence, to justify it), I walk over to the pool and stick my feet in—or, depending upon what I meant, and determined through internal criticism, by 'cold,' and if I want more precision, I put in a thermometer or even a finer instrument. In short, I 'do' something, and this *doing is a turning to the state of affairs about which the supposal is made,* in whatever way, depending upon what is in question. To 'ground' it is to 'show its reason' or 'evidence,' to 'justify it.' *It, the state of affairs itself,* must be 'seen' or 'experienced' to be *as supposed.* [29]

If what is supposed to be the case is found to be so, the supposed state-of-affairs *coincides with or agrees with* the state of affairs itself. If what my toes feel, or what some instrument reads, coincides with the supposal made ('the pool is cold'), then the supposal is 'true'; if they conflict in some way, then they do not coincide, or only partially coincide or agree, and the supposal is 'false' or 'unlikely' or some other such modality. What is crucial here is the *kind of thing done* in order to 'check out' the supposal—that 'doing' called 'grounding' or 'finding evidence.' Depending upon what is called for (what the specific supposal is), and upon what sorts of affairs are in question (as supposed), the 'thing done' to obtain the supposed 'grounds' or 'evidence' will vary. But the 'doing' is always a 'going to the affairs or complex of affairs' judged about (supposed or claimed) to see if they are as supposed.

What is called criticism and what is called grounding or evidence turn out to be two sides of the same coin: to criticize is to seek the grounds or evidence for what is criticized. And this process is something done, is an experience of a specific kind, requiring checking the supposal both internally and externally. Every claim to knowledge requires criticism and grounding. It must be 'held accountable,' and the philosopher 'self-responsible.' In order to do this, I must *hold the claim in abeyance* until and if the grounding or evidence can be displayed, if at all, or to whatever degree. This 'holding in abeyance,' finally, is the act of disengagement and neutrality we have pointed out in this chapter.

What these considerations suggest is that the act of criticism and grounding include the act of focusing-and-disregarding made possible by that of disengagement and neutrality. *These acts constitute the 'ways' to phenomenology, just as the themes (only partially) disclosed thereby constitute part of the sense of phenomenology's task.* If one turns to Husserl's many writings on 'phenomenological method,' the infamous concepts of 'epoche' and 'reduction' are not at all the monstrosities they are sometimes portrayed to be. What Husserl is always concerned to point out is precisely that complex of acts. Thus, when he first formalizes the 'method,' he considers Descartes' 'methodological doubt.' But a careful reading shows that it is not at all this doubt which he means;[30] rather, it is the *"attempt to doubt"*:

It is . . . clear that the *attempt* to doubt any object of awareness in respect of it *being actually there necessarily conditions a certain suspension of the thesis* [which one attempts to doubt]; and it is precisely this that interests us.[31]

Just as Husserl is interested in the *attempt* to doubt and its 'suspension' of the thesis, so, too, the effort to 'step-back' from a claim and criticize it involves a 'disengagement' *from* and a remaining 'neutral' *to* it. One neither accepts nor rejects the thesis or claim—until and if it can be critically grounded. The notorious 'epoche' means neither more nor less than that. Of course, one *must constantly maintain* his focusing and disregarding while he is engaged in his critical effort —and this maintaining is fundamentally what the 'reduction' means. There is, then, nothing mysterious or recondite about either methodological concept. Phenomenological method is not a proposal for a kind of metaphysical treasure hunt, nor is it an esoteric doctrine pontificated from on high to a privileged few gifted souls. *It is no more nor less than philosophical criticism and grounding carried out to their fullest extent—to the foundations.*

2

The Sense of Phenomenology

"It is . . . to let all these things, each
in its place, and all in their rela-
tionships and in their full substances,
be, at once, driven upon your consciousness, one center. . . ."

James Agee,
Let Us Now Praise Famous Men

Philosophical interest may focus on a variety of matters.
Throughout, the fundamental dimension of philosophy's
concern is that of criticism. Criticism is not a whim of the
philosopher, but has its ground in that pervasive philosophical, indeed human, activity called claiming. In fact, it is not
excessive to suggest a more general thesis: not only epistemic
claims, but every claim—whether axiological, ethical, metaphysical, religious—necessarily invites philosophical criticism.

Phenomenological philosophy is first of all philosophical
criticism. Precisely because of this, is it eminently relevant
to every dimension of human life. But even so, what uniquely
characterizes this specific philosophical task? A first clue is
already on hand. Phenomenology is characterized (1) by the

universality with which criticism is systematically practiced, and (2) by the affairs on which it is brought to bear. What these latter are will not concern us in the present chapter, but a preliminary indication can be given.

When I disengage from a claim in order to criticize it, what happens to the claim, or 'thesis,' thus disengaged? What is it to disengage myself from the claim? Clearly, if I consider Descartes' claim, "I think, therefore I am," *nothing at all* happens to the claim. It remains precisely what it was, only now I do not myself either engage in believing, denying, or affirming it. Nor, for that matter, do I attempt to determine, initially, what follows from it, what significance it may have for his philosophy, and so on. These are obviously important matters, but are determinable only if I first of all understand it *as a claim:* it is a *supposal* that such and such is the case. Similarly, I know that Descartes affirmed the claim, believed he had evidence for it, and attempted to derive consequences from it. These, too, I take note of: the claim *as* affirmed, *as* believed, and so on, is also part of what I, the critic, must examine for its meaning, presuppositions, and evidence.

This is surely familiar. As any critical historian knows, he must *abstain* from pronouncing judgments on the affairs studied until he has, so to speak, allowed them to speak for themselves. The critic, whether historian or not, must *let things be* exactly what and as they are in order to be able to do his task. The task of philosophical criticism is that of determining what the 'things themselves' (for instance, claims) are, to describe them *as* they are, and to engage in that most difficult of tasks, critical assessment and evaluation.

But suppose now that I set myself the task of critically understanding *my own* beliefs: what must then be my project? *Precisely the same thing,* only now matters quickly become entangled if I am not most careful. I know, as you do, that I can and do examine my own claims (values, beliefs, etc.)— sometimes because circumstances oblige me to do it, other times because I want or need to do so. I know, too, that each of my own beliefs has a certain meaning for me: some have the sense of being rather personal, others of being shared. Among the latter are some having the sense of being shared by only a few (my family, my region, my culture), while others have the sense of being more general, even universal —for example, that there are other human beings than myself in the world and that they are more or less 'like' me. Whether or not I am correct in any of these beliefs, I know that they are there, and that they have these meanings for me and us.

But how do I know this? I know it because, when I do 'step back' and critically consider them, without either affirming or denying, *I take them as beliefs I do indeed find in myself,* and as such they are seen to be supposals I hold (we hold), which have such meanings. Every belief obviously has other dimensions. Thus, I find (and I believe that you will find—itself a belief we all share and could criticize!) that I believe the tree outside my window is not only a physical object but a living thing, one which I planted; it is also an object I believe to be 'over there' in my yard, one which could be and has been seen by others. Moreover, it is an object believed to be impermanent (it could be destroyed, it will one day die, and so on), beautiful, precious, potential firewood, and the like. Any one belief can be seen to have a *complexity of strata,* to be more or less private or public, personal or universal, in scope, to be more or less clearly known or understood, and to have a specific placement in relation to other beliefs.

All of these, and other characteristics are disclosed and could be analyzed in depth in one or all of these strata, without at any time affirming or denying any of them. Of course, I note, these beliefs *are* affirmed or denied by me, the one whose beliefs they are; some, I also know, are affirmed and/or denied by others. Insofar as I step back and consider them, I simply note that this is the case, but as critic I do not now 'live in' that acceptance or rejection. What is important here is the *shift of attention*—in Agee's terms, that shift of consciousness "to the effort to perceive simply the cruel radiance of what is" [1]—by virtue of which I now focus on the belief *as such* *(as* something I accept, deny, believe in, and so on), and study it in respect of its complexity, scope, stratification, evidence, placement, presuppositions, and the like.

That shift of attention, along with its disclosure of the correlation between myself-as-believer and the belief-as-believed-by-me, *can be generalized,* brought to bear on those beliefs, claims or theses having the sense of being inherent to human life as such, to science, to art, or to consciousness as that whereby I am at all aware of anything whatever (geometrical figures, theories, physical things, other human beings, myself, phantasms, social institutions, or anything else). Each of these can be examined, while in the systematically adopted attitude of disengagement, as regards its inherent sense, strata, scope, and the like. The aim of this difficult task is to bring out or *to make explicit* those structures that remain merely *implicit* and taken for granted, in order to make possible a thorough critical understanding of them and permit their assessment. *This task is phenomenological description,* and is what phenomenology seeks in its initial thrust—an aim the 'method' is designed to realize.

That mistakes of all kinds are possible is obvious. Hence, as will be seen in more detail later, philosophers engaging in phenomenological description necessarily invite and require the comeditation of other philosophers—to confirm, disconfirm, or modify every finding. Only those claims which can be verified on the basis of the best available evidence pertaining to the specific affairs in question can be said to be admissable into the corpus of phenomenologically acquired knowledge. Phenomenology is, in this regard, no different from any other area of philosophic concern, and all are under the same formal requirements pertaining to knowledge of any sort. Intersubjective verifiability, fruitfulness in elucidating the affairs being examined, systemic connections to other branches of knowledge and inquiry, and other criteria, apply equally to any claim to knowledge—although what is to be done to realize them will obviously vary depending upon what is in question.

The upshot of this preliminary reflection is quite apparent. Contrary to a common way of regarding it—as one more philosophical 'view' or 'position' on things alongside other, equally plausible stances (idealism, realism, positivism, etc.)—*phenomenology is rather one of the systemic disciplines of philosophic concern.* In this sense, it is analogous to logic, ethics, aesthetics, or epistemology. Therefore, the crucial question in this respect is not at all whether phenomenology is a 'point of view' preferable to, say, analytic philosophy or pragmatism, but, to the contrary, whether it is, as I believe, the more fundamental *task* of philosophy itself—as opposed to ethics, logic, and so on.

Precisely to the extent that phenomenology is one of the disciplines of philosophy, it by no means coincides with the work of one man, Edmund Husserl. However original his contribution to philosophy was, the kind of discipline toward which he worked in his career is one which has had many historical precedents. Therefore, this chapter must set out at least some of these precedents. But the phenomenological task of criticism is not merely one 'branch' of philosophy alongside other, equally fundamental 'branches.' Accordingly, it will also be the burden of this chapter to try and show that (1) phenomenology coincides with philosophical criticism, properly speaking, and (2) this discipline is the most *fundamental* task for philosophy.

The Tendencies in Previous Philosophy.

A great many philosophers, in modern times especially, have set out central ideas which, when focused on, can be seen as leading to the kind of discipline Husserl called phenomenology. Three of these will be dealt with, and only *some* of the focal themes of their work will be examined.

Descartes: The Invitation to Evidence.

It is well known how Descartes, deeply disturbed over the barrenness of the intellectual situation of his time—in which firm grounds neither for knowledge nor for personal conduct[2] were provided—resolved "like one who walks alone and in the twilight . . . to go so slowly, and to use so much circumspection in all things, that if my advance was but very small, at least I guarded myself well from falling." (*Discourse*, p. 91) His advance was to be, he hoped, toward the true foundations of all knowledge—a major theme in his, and in most subsequent philosophy. If such foundational knowledge is synonymous with "what is completely known and incapable of being doubted" *(Rules*, p. 3), then it is imperative that

> *our inquiries should be directed, not to what others have thought, nor to what we ourselves conjecture, but to what we can clearly and perspicuously behold* and *with certainty deduce; for knowledge is not won in any other way. (Rules*, III, p. 5)

Such knowledge is science in its most profound sense. It is philosophical knowledge—that kind of "true and evident cognition" which is alone capable of investigating and discovering the "first causes" or the "principles" of all things *(Principles,* "Author's Letter," p. 204).

This grounding is of the utmost importance for Descartes, who saw the entirety of genuine knowledge on the analogy of a building (*Discourse*, p. 89): if its foundations are not secure, the edifice will collapse, regardless of the energies spent to shore it up. Only if the old edifice is demolished and the construction begun afresh on firmly established cognitions will genuine knowledge be possible. Merely probable knowledge, mere conjecture, however insightful, will not do for the task. But how is it to be accomplished? What assurances are there that the efforts at doing it are effective and the results achieved thereby true? Such questions set in relief Descartes' fundamental concern with *method* (how to achieve true cognitions) and with *evidence* (how to be assured that such cognitions are genuine and thus to guarantee that one will not fall into error). As he insists, "it were far better never to think of investigating truth at all, than to do so without a method" *(Rules,* p. 9). By the same token, it is essential that one be able to determine the true from the false in order to know that his method leads to what he set out to find. Hence, it is imperative for Descartes to determine *how to begin* in his quest, what path to follow, and which 'signs' correctly mark the way. The themes of *beginning* in philosophy, of *method* and of *evidence* are central to Descartes' efforts to give knowledge genuine foundations. These concerns show his prescience of an established discipline of criticism.

Guided by the unquestioned belief that mathematics is the prototype for all knowledge, his aim became that of developing a *mathesis universalis* (*Rules*, p. 13), with philosophy providing the foundational principles. The latter are to be secured through intuitions and deductions. This brings us to the core of Descartes' concerns. "By intuition," he writes,

> I understand, not the fluctuating testimony of the senses, nor the misleading judgment that proceeds from the blundering constructions of imagination, but the conception which an unclouded and attentive mind gives us so readily and distinctly that we are wholly freed from doubt about that which we understand . . . and springs from the light of reason alone. . . . (*Rules*, p. 7).

Intuition is strictly a matter of cognition, possessed or acquired only by a mind unclouded by other concerns and interests and focally attentive to the matter at hand. Furthermore, intuition has to do with "clear and distinct ideas" and these are intimately tied to being free from doubt.[3] Intuitions, far from being the nebulous, arbitrary hunches of which one usually thinks, are strictly *products of a rigorously rational process*—methodical doubt—and are cognitions of clear and distinct ideas. These alone provide the foundations Descartes seeks.

The problem of the *beginning* is therefore resolved: since 'certain' and 'foundational' mean 'indubitable,' one must begin by *attempting to doubt* all one's theories, beliefs, values, and ideas, in order to determine whether, and if, there are any at all which can withstand doubt. Thus, too, the problem of *method* is also resolved, again by the very nature of the project. Finally, the 'marks,' the *evidence*, which will tell one if and when he will have reached the 'foundations' are also at hand: what must be sought are *clear and distinct ideas*.

What are these 'ideas'? Descartes says,

> I term that clear which is present and apparent to an attentive

mind, in the same way as we assert that we see objects clearly when, being present to the regarding eye, they operate upon it with sufficient strength. But the distinct is that which is so precise and different from all other objects that it contains within itself nothing but what is clear. *(Principles;* XLV, p. 237)
Although referring to sense perception, which yields no intuitions, the point is readily understandable. Analogically, Descartes says,[4] I have a clear view ('idea' by analogy) of a visually perceived block of marble when, under optimum conditions for sight, which operates upon the eye with sufficient strength, I am able to see it in respect of its various properties and determinations—as opposed, say, to seeing it at night, in the fog, when my eyes are not functioning well, or I am just not very clearheaded at the time. Similarly, I see it distinctly when I see it *as it itself* and not something else (the table beneath, the wall behind, and so on). Obviously, seeing with (relative) clarity and distinctness requires attentiveness and an unclouded mind. The analogy to genuinely clear and distinct *ideas* is apparent: the idea, say, of triangularity is cognitively *clear* when it is understood with its particular content (meaning), and is *distinct* when it is cognized *as it itself* and *not* squareness or some other geometrical idea. The idea will be both clear and distinct when, attentive to what is now the task at hand, and having a clear head, I judge step by step—'triangularity is that property of closed, plane geometrical figures having three sides, each of which . . .'—apprehending all along the meaning of such concepts as 'line,' 'straight,' 'angle,' and the like, and cognizing *the whole idea.*

But these ideas must be cognized as *indubitable;* this is the result of the rational process of doubt, the intellectual effort to determine whether, if at all, *the opposite (contradictory) of an idea can consistently be conceived.* If the opposite is conceivable, the idea in question is not indubitable, since that very conceivability is the meaning of cognitive doubt. If it is inconceivable, the idea is precisely indubitable. Both conceivability and inconceivability, however, are strictly matters of rational cognition, not psychological feelings or imaginative constructions. Hence, indubitability is synonymous with the inconceivability of the opposite of the idea in question. To clearly and distinctly cognize the indubitability of the idea is to have an intuition of it.

The method of doubt, therefore, is inseparable from what is disclosed by the method, and in this Descartes has obviously seen a prime requirement of criticism. If evidence consists of intuitions, and these are clear and distinct ideas (the fruit of methodical doubt), then evidence is gained through this doubt alone. Evidence is a matter of *actually undergoing* doubt, or the *attempt* at doubt; it is a matter of experiencing (rationally) the 'itself-presentedness' of the idea in question as inconceivably otherwise. Descartes thus resolves to doubt, *to withhold his belief and judgment* as regards an idea, if it is at least conceivable that it is otherwise than believed to be. The famous precepts of method thus begin by his resolving

> to accept nothing as true which I did not clearly recognize to be so; that is to say, carefully to avoid precipitation and prejudice in judgments, and to accept in them nothing more than what was presented to my mind so clearly and distinctly that I could have no occasion to doubt it. *(Discourse,* p. 92)

The rest of the Cartesian quest is well known: Descartes' path takes him to the only thing which can withstand even the most rigorous and far-reaching doubt—himself. *The foundations of knowledge are first and foremost in the knower himself.* But to maintain this consequential thesis is by no means to rule out the possibility of error, discovered either by oneself or by others. "It must always be recollected, however," Descartes insists, "that possibly I deceive myself, and that what I take to be gold and diamonds is perhaps no more than copper and glass" *(Discourse,* pp. 83–83). Hence the act of sending his *Meditations* to others, and his emphatic invitation to others are by no means mere gestures. They are essential to his very conception of what is necessary for the establishing of the foundations of knowledge. It is thus necessary to distinguish carefully between Descartes' great *confidence* in his discoveries (as are most philosophers, after all), and the *epistemic claims* he makes about these affairs he confidently believes himself to have discovered.

What concerns us here, however, is not to interpret or defend or reject these claims. Rather, we should take careful note of the kind of project he saw as fundamental, the principles which governed his attempt to fulfill that project, and the ways in which he sought to execute it. These we have stressed: that the very nature of knowledge requires foundations; that the latter are inseparably connected to a method which is itself at once the self-evident starting-point for the project and is productive of the evidence for the foundations; and that the entire effort necessarily leads to subjectivity.

At every point, moreover, it is conceived by Descartes as essential that others be able to do what he did, and that if they do, they will find the same as he. What Descartes grasped as a prime task of philosophy—although, of course, he goes on to say much more—is that of *criticism*. With his central and significant ideas of 'beginning,' method, evidence, and the turn to subjectivity (mind), Descartes was clearly stressing the necessity for a *discipline* of philosophy quite independent of any metaphysical stance, even his own. That he himself went on to give such a stance is neither here nor there so far as this specific discipline is concerned. It is true, nevertheless, that he by no means fully appreciated the kind of requirements inherent in the task of criticism. This task is further advanced by Hume and Kant.

Hume: Of Skepticism and Magic.

In light of our discussion, the turning to Hume must seem peculiar, for he is assuredly the skeptical archenemy of the rationalist's ideal of giving apodictic foundations to knowledge. Moreover, it is mainly Hume's version of the 'theory of ideas' that has received the most severe criticism from phenomenological philosophers. It is Hume's theory of mind that has been critically opposed to Husserl's,[5] and it is Hume's theory of abstraction that Husserl took great pains to refute.[6] Finally, it is Hume's skepticism that Husserl believes, with Kant, must be definitively refuted in order to secure the possibility of science, both empirical and philosophical.[7]

Still, Husserl had great respect for Hume, and not simply in a negative sense. Indeed, Husserl remarked more than once that it was Hume who came as close as any previous philosopher to phenomenology. Noting that Hume's "sensualism" prevented him from becoming the "founder of a truly 'positive' theory of reason," Husserl emphasized that

> All the problems that move him so passionately in the *Treatise* and drive him from confusion to confusion, problems that because of his attitude he can in no wise formulate suitably and purely—all these problems belong entirely to the area dominated by phenomenology.[8]

Appreciating Hume's tendency toward phenomenology, then, is a matter of understanding the kinds of issues which concerned him, and how he proposed to resolve them, rather than his specific doctrines. What are these? And how do they lead to phenomenology?

The obscurities and infelicities of his *Treatise*[9] are notorious; so, too, are its minutiae, paradoxes, complicated arguments, and profusion of issues. All the same, the work is a remarkable *tour de force*, not only in its detailed undercutting of causal metaphysics but also in its frequently brilliant posing of central problems. For all his confusions, Hume is unmistakably clear as to his aim in writing it. Noting the sorry state of knowledge in his day (p. xviii), as Descartes had in his, Hume embarks upon "the only expedient, from which we can hope for success in our philosophical researches"—which is to quit the tedious and contentious noise and clamor, the busy bustle of debates over at best marginal issues, and

> instead of taking now and then a castle or village on the frontier, to march up directly to the capital or center of these sciences [logic, morals, criticism, and politics], to human nature itself. (p. xx)

Despite his aversion to laying claim to truth, Hume is completely convinced that all sciences are dependent on the science of man. This science, the "capital city" of all knowledge, must first be won before any other village or province can be conquered. Again, he is unequivocal:

In pretending therefore to explain the principles of human nature, we in effect propose a *compleat system of sciences* [my italics.], built on a foundation almost entirely new, and the only one upon which they can stand with any security. (p. xx)

Although he is here completely at one with Descartes, Hume's understanding of this "solid foundation" does distinguish him substantially from Descartes. For, he believes, this foundation can only be "experience and observation." Beyond this we simply cannot go. What appears to us is strictly what we can rely on; there is nothing 'behind' appearances, no 'substance' (pp. 139, 187–211, 638). What Hume proposes, then, in his march on the capital, is the search for the foundations of knowledge, one which he regards as lying self-evidently in man himself—thereby revealing another fundamental agreement with Descartes, both as to aim and as to the place where the foundations will be found. But the science of man is to be based strictly on experience and observation. The problem, then, is to discover what this proposal amounts to: (1) What does the appeal to "experience" entail, and what is understood by "observation"?, and (2) How can and does experience serve as the foundation for the science of man as the foundation, in turn, of all sciences?

(1) The question concerning experience is quite complicated. In fact, Hume's appeal goes in two very different directions, which he tends to conflate uncritically. On the one hand, there is the usual way of interpreting it: referring to sensory perception, in Hume's sense, his appeal is understood to mean that all knowledge derives from and is based on impressions and ideas. A knowledge of 'ultimate causes' is radically impossible. As such, Hume's philosophy is taken as an empiricism with all its usual trappings—an interpretation having Hume's apparently full endorsement (e.g., pp. xxi–xxii, 82, 87, 139, 157).

Such an interpretation, however, invariably creates curious and irreconcilable anomalies, not so much in the villages on the frontiers, but in the capital city. First, if Hume's appeal to experience is interpreted solely as asserting that knowledge is sensory in origin, and therefore never *in principle* yields certainties, then his frequent claims to "undoubted truth," certainties "beyond question," and other "unquestioned principles" are either mere rhetoric or are nonsense—his *caveat* against the infelicities of language notwithstanding. No appeal to *principles* would even be possible. Hence, that very thesis is self-defeating: the "in principle" is neither a mere 'relation of ideas' nor is it a 'matter of fact.' Second, on such an exclusivist interpretation of 'experience,' Hume's philosophical assertions themselves, as we saw, become radically unaccountable and unintelligible. However difficult it is, as Hume says, "to talk of the operations of the mind with perfect propriety and exactness" (p. 105), these difficulties cannot be confused with the *modality* character of the epistemic *claims* made about the mind itself, its operations and principles, on pains of vitiating the very sense of his proposal to build "a compleat system" of knowledge. Either that, or else one must, by some arbitrary criterion, decide to carve out whole chunks of his argument and discard them.

These considerations suggest that a narrow interpretation of experience is unjustified, and unfair to Hume's actual practice of his 'science.' There are indications from Hume himself for a broader understanding, although it is also the case that he is surely not consistent in developing them. He proposes to "observe" experience, wanting to apply "experimental philosophy to moral subjects," that is, to what pertains to man. Noting that there are differences between experiments in natural as opposed to moral philosophy, he writes:

> We must therefore glean up our experiments in [moral] science from a cautious observation of human life, and take them as they appear in the common course of the world, by man's behaviour in company, in affairs, and in the pleasures. Where experiments of this kind are judiciously collected and compared, we may hope to establish on them a science, which will not be inferior in certainty, and will be much superior in utility to any other of human comprehension. (p. xxiii)

What is meant by this "collecting and comparing" of "experiments"? To discover the powers and qualities of the mind, Hume's express aim in Book I, he must conduct "careful and exact experiments" which permit the "observation of those particular effects, which result from [the mind's] different circumstances and situations" (p. xxi). He is, I think, unusually faithful to that aim and method—a method which seems to have three basic ingredients. (a) It is clear from his actual analysis, that "to observe" the mind and its operations is *to reflect* on them, even though Hume does not expressly focus on reflection as a philosophical method. Instead, he variously uses such expressions as "consider," "find," "reason," "argue," "observe," as well as "reflect." The principal difficulty with his analysis here is that he rarely distinguishes between the "operations" of the mind *as observed* by him, and the "operations" which *he himself engages in as a philosopher* concerned to discover the former. He continually confuses what is *reflected upon* (observed or considered), with the *reflecting itself.* It is nevertheless clear that when he speaks of "experiments," what he both proposes and in fact carries out are *reflections* on the mind as set in a variety of circumstances and situations.

(b) His experimental method consists of a kind of *inventory* or geography of the mind and its ingredients. To be sure, his effort to take stock of the mind is frequently mixed in with critical discussions of other views, both philosophical and 'vulgar.' But at every point his aim is unmistakably clear: he "pretends" (supposes, claims) to "explain the principles of human nature" (p. xx), and this pretension is done by tracing "up the human understanding to its first principles . . ." (p. 266). That he winds up in "the most deplorable condition imaginable, inviron'd with the deepest darkness . . ." (p. 269), is irrelevant here. What is relevant is the kind of task done in what he calls his "experiments": namely, reflectively to consider the mind in as many and various circumstances as possible in order to determine its true character and limits. This reflection is a matter of making an accurate inventory of the mind's ingredients and operations, and the various interconnections among them. This inventory purports to be nothing less than the theory of mind that will ground the theory of man generally. Thus, although Hume would by no means acknowledge, much less be happy with this, he is in fact embarked on an inquiry to delineate the *essential* features and principles of mind, and thus is implicitly on the road to criticism.

(c) His method involves an *appeal to others* to reflect or observe with him and see for themselves whether or not he is correct in his claims. Hume is enormously confident (most of the time) that his findings will be confirmed by everyone (e.g., p. 23), but he expressly enters a *caveat* (already noted) against the interpretation of this confidence as implying a dogmatism or "conceited idea of my own judgment" (p. 274). Indeed, it seems no extravagance to suggest that his railing against the rationalists, and against the faintest hint that he himself might have indulged himself in an absolutist word or two, is in truth more negative than positive in import. It is more an earnest desire to avoid dogmatism or conceit than it is a disclaimer of the possibility of discovering principles.

The appeal to "experience" must therefore be understood in much broader terms than is usual. Not only is it a *thesis* concerning the origin and ground of knowledge (experience in the more restricted sense), but it is also a methodological injunction to "experiment and observe" in an effort to determine the "nature of mind" itself. It is therefore crucial to distinguish the two senses of experience—and especially to grasp the sense of "experiment" (hence, experience) the philosopher must perform. What the philosopher finds must always be submitted to criticism, and this invitation to others to follow him in his studies (p. 273), is an essential ingredient in the appeal to experience. In his method and its requirements, Hume has given several of the prime themes of phenomenology, and has adopted very much the same conception of criticism which we found nascent in Descartes.

(2) The second question (asked above)—how can and does experience serve as the foundation for the science of man?—can be treated more briefly. The critical distinction, without which Hume's entire effort is a shambles, is between *experience as reflected upon* and *experience as reflection*. If we maintain

the distinction, as Hume rarely does, then it is clear that the search for "solid foundations" is for the principles of human nature.

Hume's *Treatise* literally abounds in such principles. In his own terms, "experience is a principle, which instructs me in the several conjunctions of objects for the past. Habit is another principle, which determines me to expect the same for the future" (p. 265). That both habit and experience are founded on the "imagination" is also a principle, however "inconstant" the imagination is. Beyond these are the principles of the division of perceptions (pp. 1–2), of the association of ideas (pp. 10–11, 92–93), of belief (pp. 96–97, 624), of the connection of cause and effect and the inferences one may legitimately draw therefrom (p. 139), and of custom (pp. 102–03, 135–35), and so on.

Hume never tires of reminding his readers that neither natural nor moral philosophy can penetrate to the "ultimate principles," and any suggestion that one of them can is regarded as a presumptuous extravagance unworthy of consideration (pp. xx–xxii, 263–73). Despite his splenetic feeling (p. 270) that "we have, therefore, no choice left but betwixt a false reason and none at all" (p. 268), Hume does in fact make numerous claims to have disclosed, truly, the nature, operations, and principles of human understanding. Whether he regards these claims with skepticism or not, they are there as such and demand critical assessment—as he repeatedly acknowledges, while also admitting the possibility of his having erred (pp. 105, 623).

His skepticism, like Descartes' dualism, is in its philosophical status an epistemic claim supposedly issuing from his study of man, and thus is open to criticism. It is, in other words, as he clearly sees, a *philosophical stance,* a *conclusion* supposedly reached *after* "a cautious observation of human life" (that is, *after criticism*). With this emerges one of the most intriguing features of his philosophical labors—one he does not, unhappily, pursue or even see as such. If he had, he would have found himself in the midst of phenomenology.

Since the point is so important, it must be made as explicit as possible.

Hume writes:

When we trace up the human understanding to its first principles, we find it to lead us into such sentiments, as seem to turn into ridicule all our past pains and industry, and to discourage us from future enquiries . . . We would not willingly stop before we are acquainted with that energy in the cause, by which it operates on its effect; that tie, which connects them together; and that efficacious quality, on which the tie depends. This is the aim in all our studies and reflections: And how must we be disappointed, when we learn, that this connexion, tie, or energy *lies merely in ourselves, and is nothing but that determination of the mind, which is acquir'd by custom*[My italics.], and causes us to make a transition from an object to its usual attendant, and from the impression of one to the lively idea of the other? (p. 266)

Without quarreling with him, note Hume's response to this: philosophically, a "total skepticism" must follow. On the one hand, the subject is "nothing but a heap or collection of different perceptions" (p. 207; also p. 635) that do not themselves form any self-identical whole. On the other hand, objects and their connections are products of subjective operations (which implies a self), that is, beliefs arising from custom and habit. Hence, radical skepticism is inevitable.

The only thing which saves him from it is the peculiar circumstance that *it matters not the least to us in our daily lives.* "Carelessness and in-attention alone can afford us any remedy" (p. 218). The "natural propensity" inherent to us in our daily lives, is to go blithely about our affairs as if things really were as we believe them to be. But when we analyze them philosophically, we can plainly see that things are not as we believe, but are merely consequences of our belief. We must either resolve to reason not at all or else to reason— and then find ourselves in a total skepticism.[10] Thus, Hume concludes, even though we *as philosophers* ought to preserve our skepticism, the *fact of human life* is that "if we believe, that fire warms, or water refreshes, 'tis only because it costs us too much pains to think otherwise" (p. 270).

But how can this be? What *is* this happy but wholly magical characteristic of daily life that so easily resolves the excruciating dilemma of radical skepticism? What is it which "lies merely in ourselves" to account for the lucky legerdemain, the carelessness and inattention, of common life?

Hume's response is at once evasive and yet strangely compelling: "belief." Although we know, philosophically, and with *genuine certainty* for him, that ideas are not *really* connected (any more than impressions are), *we come to believe* in connections and really existent objects as a consequence of the effects of contiguity, resemblance, and regular and repeated conjunctions among ideas (pp. 93, 96–97, 102). As he puts it,

> We find from common experience, in our actions as well as reasonings, that a constant perseverence in any course of life produces a strong inclination and tendency to continue for the future. . . . This habit or determination to transfer the past to the future is full and perfect; and consequently the first impulse of the imagination in this species of reasoning is endow'd with the same qualities. (pp. 133–34)

With Hume, we desire more; we wish to "push" our enquiries, till we arrive at the "original and ultimate principle" (p. 266). What is this "secret operation" (p. 104), that can produce such a strong belief in a connected, continuing objective world and subjective self, and which can alone save us from total skepticism? And, if it is so potent for common sense life, why is it not equally significant for the philosopher? Why is belief pejoratively called "mere belief" and "nothing but" custom and habit?

What Hume utterly fails to see is the very *sense* of his own analysis at its nodal point. He brings us to the brink of a discovery of immense significance for his own express aim and leaves us dangling. What is so crucial about his study is that while he does see clearly that "what lies in ourselves" is that which accounts for connection and regularity, he yet fails to push his inquiry into that region of "belief" and "custom"—*and just that region is precisely what must be examined, on Hume's own terms, as essential to "human nature."* Just that strong inclination is responsible for the belief in the world and in ourselves. And Hume confessedly takes this for granted (p. 218).

Husserl is clearly correct, then, to discern behind Hume's skepticism and its radical formulation of the problem of accounting for objectivity as well as the mind, an entirely new kind of "world-riddle" *(Welträtsel):* "the riddle of a world whose being is a *being produced from subjectivity* . . . that and nothing else is Hume's problem." [11] The greatness of Hume, for Husserl, lies in the fact that he was "the first to *treat seriously the Cartesian focusing purely on what lies inside.*" [12] By raising this problem, not only does Hume effectively challenge the objectivism of causal metaphysics and the naive realism of everyday life, he also, unwittingly, advances the discipline of phenomenology a giant step forward.

It is therefore necessary to see Hume, along with Descartes, as one of the most important and influential precursors of that critical discipline: in his aims, his methods, and his implicit disclosure of the foundational place of everyday life and of subjectivity.

Kant: The Phenomenal Labor of Consciousness.

If a discussion of Hume seemed initially strange, including only a relatively brief mention of Kant must appear outrageous. After all, Kant is surely the great proponent of transcendental philosophy, with its rigorous effort to establish the conditions for the very possibility of the objective world in terms of consciousness—and phenomenology certainly shares that aim. Restricting himself in his first *Critique* to phenomena, he emphasizes the fundamental place of inner time, the synthetic character of the understanding, the necessity of the transcendental ego, the importance for knowledge of sensory perception, and other notions which seem part of the phenomenologist's stock in trade. Husserl's antimetaphysical leanings seem unquestionably similar, finally, to Kant's attitude toward dogmatic metaphysical speculation. "Indeed," Gurwitsch says, "in the history of modern thought between Kant and Husserl one does not find a theoretician of subjectivity who is of comparable depth." [13] Nevertheless, Gurwitsch goes on to point out that Husserl clearly had a preference for Hume. Although he does acknowledge that Kant had a presentiment of phenomenology, Kant, Husserl believes, was misled into constructions on his own.[14]

This preference for Hume was largely because he clearly and seriously grasped the fundamental problem of accounting for objectivity in terms of subjectivity, but without any leanings towards metaphysics. It is also due, it would seem, to the way in which Hume set up and carried out his "experimental" inventory, or "mental geography."[15] Husserl was nevertheless also highly critical of Hume's results.

The tendency of Kant towards phenomenology is thus quite difficult to assess. This is true even though there are many apparently obvious parallels between Kant and Husserl. A brief account of Husserl's relations to Kant will help at once to clarify that difficulty and to pinpoint Kant's contributions to the phenomenological problematic.[16] Quentin Lauer is surely correct when he says that "the first of the great philosophers to influence Husserl was Kant (though much of the influence was indirect, being filtered through the neo-Kantians)."[17] Indeed, in *Ideas, I* (1913), Husserl explicitly says that it was Kant who first truly perceived the fundamental sense of phenomenology, "although he was not yet able to appropriate it and recognize it as the center from which to work up on his own line a rigorous science of Essential Being."[18]

The misgivings Husserl had about Kant's "formalism" became more pronounced as the field of phenomenological inquiry became clearer. By the time of his *Formal and Transcendental Logic* (1929), Husserl reached the critical conclusion that Kant had "asked *no transcendental question* about [logic], but rather ascribed to it an extraordinary apriority, which exalts it above such questions."[19] In reaction to Hume and empiricism, Kant correctly stressed the apriority of logic; however, largely because of the way he understood Hume's criticism of causality, Kant was anxious to show the possibility of synthetic *a priori* judgments. But in thus focusing on the synthetic, he simply took it for granted that *analytic a priori* judgments were beyond doubt, exactly as Hume had done. That these are *a priori,* Husserl does not contest. What Kant failed to grasp, however, is that they are *not for that reason* immune to questions concerning the ways in which they are grasped and made evident through acts of consciousness.

No matter how tautalogous a judgment may be ('A is A'), it still is *grasped as such* by an act of consciousness that has articulated phases in which 'A,' the 'is' and finally 'A' are grasped in the ways peculiar to being the 'subject,' the 'copula,' and the 'predicate' of a judgment. Beyond this, *the judgment as a whole* is also grasped *as such;* and its tautological character itself could be grasped and explicated, compared, theorized about, and so on. But Kant does not see any of these affairs. Suzanne Bachelard puts the issue here clearly:

> Only when one has grasped that the logical formations are, in their way, *objects* can one ask the transcendental questions of their subject . . . When one considers the concept, the judgment, etc., as objects that exist over and against the contingent multiplicity of our subjective acts, one can wonder how these objects have precisely the sense of objects, even though they originate in our subjective activity. This "even though" *leads* us to reflection. Then logic must necessarily be examined along two lines, the objective line and the subjective line. . . . Paradoxically, only when one fails to see the logical formations detach themselves from subjectivity with the sense of objects does one fail to raise the truly subjective problems regarding them. . . .[20]

In essence, Kant simply presupposed the existence of logic and thus does not raise transcendental questions concerning it. For him, it is clear that logic is in no sense a "subjective science." The suggestion that logic can and must be examined in "the subjective line" is tantamount to suggesting that logic is but empirical psychology.[21] This suggestion would never be accepted by Kant. As Husserl argued later in *Krisis,* the difficulty is (1) that Kant never gave a radical critique of psychology either, and thus (2) failed to see that not every inquiry into subjectivity is psychological in the empirical sense. Indeed, this bias is found at the center of Kant's own critical position: the notion of 'inner perception' through which knowledge of the mind (qua phenomenon) is obtained has "a strictly psychological sense" for Kant.[22]

At the root of the difficulties Husserl finds (with Kant) are two consequential assumptions, both of which set Kant off as fundamentally dependent upon Hume. First, the concept of 'things in themselves' is legitimate; second, *there are* 'things as they are in themselves' as opposed to things as they appear to us.

These assumptions, we saw, are at the heart of modern philosophy since Galileo. Kant, however, aggravates the situation in his theory of cognition by maintaining that one cannot even apprehend *himself* or his mental processes *themselves* (as noumena), but only obtain these as phenomena. Hence, one is in principle restricted to appearances, both as regards the world and one's own consciousness. For all the *a priori* machinery of forms, categories, and schematism, Kant is unable to rid himself either of Hume's skepticism or of dogmatism, without positing the necessity of things in themselves, if only as a "merely *limiting concept,* the function of which is to curb the pretensions of sensibility."[23] When I perceive something, all I have presented are the data which appear; but I can *think about* this, and when I do, I *conceptually* see that the 'appearance' must be an 'appearance of . . .' *something* (which I do not perceive but only *think*).

Hume, finding no anchor in experience to correspond to this 'thought,' concluded that it was mere custom and habit ('belief') which gives rise to it, and consequently fell into radical skepticism. Kant, seeking to avoid that, and dogmatism as well, concluded that while the senses may lead one to *think* that one experiences things themselves, we *know* that this thought is not in principle able to be given a base in perception (intuition). Hence, while the *thought* of things in themselves is not contradictory, it cannot be counted as *knowledge* since we have no possible sensory content with which to 'fill in' the concept. But, if the assumption of things in themselves proves to be unwarranted, Kant must fall into skepticism or dogmatism, precisely *because he accepts uncritically the Humean schema* of perception and, with some modification, of knowledge as well.

Beyond the well known difficulties of the notion of things in themselves, what is most problematic is its extension to the mind itself. "In fact," Husserl contends,

> Kant fell into a peculiar sort of mythical locution, whose verbal sense, it is true, refers us to something subjective, but to a mode of the subjective that it is essentially impossible for us to make intuited, either in factual examples or by genuine analogy.[24]

Kant is forced by his project to speak of consciousness, ego, and the subjective generally; and, the sense of his 'critique' *requires that it be the mind itself* on which he reflects. Yet, he cannot do just that, on two grounds. (1) 'Inner perception,' through which alone can one obtain knowledge of consciousness, is a *psychological* mode of awareness for Kant and is therefore incapable of yielding *a priori* judgments. (2) One obtains only the phenomenon of mind, and never the mind itself; hence it is impossible for us to speak of mind in more than a 'mythical locution.'

Husserl thus grew increasingly restive with Kant, even though he continued to maintain that Kant had a genuine presentiment of phenomenology. This foreshadowing is found especially in the first *Critique,* and it is to this we turn, ignoring the difficulties in order to focus on Kant's advancement of the discipline.

Just as Hume had lampooned metaphysical reasonings as productive merely of noise, however resonant, so, Kant caustically remarks, has metaphysics become "a battle-ground quite peculiarly suited for those who desire to exercize themselves in mock combats . . ." (p. 21), without, however, gaining so much as an inch of territory. Kant further argued that while metaphysicians have argued that the discipline of speculation is a 'science,' not only have they typically been guilty of "a merely random groping" among mere concepts, but they have dogmatically assumed what must be demonstrated—how and to what extent, if any, metaphysics *as a science* is at all possible. Inherent to this are two issues: (1)

what it means to designate an inquiry as scientific, and (2) whether metaphysics can be properly so designated.

Again echoing Hume, Kant expresses dismay over the paradoxical fate of metaphysics as it has hitherto been practiced: having the greatest pretensions to science and certainty, it has been dramatically lacking in any clear successes. But where Hume had not submitted the very sense of science to criticism, nor inquired into the possibility of those disciplines which do yield genuine knowledge (mathematics and logic), Kant insists that we must do both. Moreover, where Hume had despaired upon learning that the grounds of knowledge lie "merely in ourselves" and had concluded that "philosophy has nothing to oppose" his skepticism, Kant takes precisely that discovery as his point of departure—his famous "second Copernican revolution." And here is found that highly significant methodological move, the *transcendental turn.*

Noting that the natural sciences "learned that reason has insight only into that which it produces after a plan of its own . . . constraining nature to give answers to questions of reason's own determining" (p. 20), Kant suggests "a similar experiment":

> Hitherto it has been assumed that all our knowledge must conform to objects. But all attempts to extend our knowledge of objects by establishing something in regard to them *a priori,* by means of concepts, have, on this assumption, ended in failure. We must therefore make trial whether we may not have more success in the tasks of metaphysics, if we suppose that objects must conform to our knowledge. (p. 22)

Kant characterizes this as "our new method of thought, namely, that we can know *a priori* of things only what we ourselves put into them" (p. 23). Kant speaks of this method as "looking for the elements of pure reason in *what admits of confirmation or refutation by experiment*" (p. 23, footnote a). Like Hume, Kant submits that the method of "experimentation" so successfully used in the natural sciences be tried out in philosophy. He goes on to emphasize that this method, although modeled on natural science, differs in a fundamental way: "testing" cannot mean *referral* of future experiences *to the object* as that which would confirm or disconfirm hypotheses. Rather, since this "new method" proposes to "experiment" by supposing that objects must conform to our concepts, "testing" can mean only the determination of whether, by what right and under what conditions, these concepts are legitimately applied to objects.

This crucial problem can be decided only if it is demonstrated conclusively that there could not possibly be any object of experience *except* on condition that these concepts are presupposed. If it can be shown that experience and all its objects would be unintelligible without this presupposition, then the "experiment" will have been confirmed, and its results demonstrated to be *a priori.* Hence, it is necessary to turn to mind itself in order to "test" the proposal. This "turn" to consciousness with its specific methodological motif gives the basic sense to the notion of "transcendental."

Such a "confirmation" Hume had already obtained—there are no connections or regularities among objects of experience except for our 'belief.' But Hume failed to understand the sense of his own discovery, as we saw. Kant's revolution has the force of showing that Hume's skepticism was in effect misplaced: its ground is the inability to know the objective world *itself,* and, of course, the *self.* But, Kant contends, his new method shows that our *a priori* concepts and principles *cannot* apply to things in themselves anyway, but *only* to things *as we experience them.* It is only the latter which demonstrably conform to our concepts (p. 24). Hume had already made the transcendental turn, but did not know it (and to that extent he did not make the turn since it requires a critical self-cognizance!). Kant makes it explicitly, and in so doing began the examination of what Hume had called 'belief.'

This 'turn' is first and foremost a *methodological* move. His critique of pure speculative reason is a systematic probing, not of *whether* there is *a priori* knowledge, but of *how such knowledge is at all possible.* His critique, then, "is a treatise on the method, not a system of the science itself. But at the same time, it marks out the whole plan of the science . . ."

(p. 25). Hence, Kant, like Descartes and Hume, sees that the *method* for gaining access to consciousness is *inseparable from what one then discloses.*

Before any straightforward metaphysical speculation is legitimate, it is necessary for the philosopher to give a 'critique' of the ability of reason to engage in it. The consequence of the transcendental turn is that the inquiry into the conditions of the possibility of experience and knowledge of phenomena (appearances) purports to yield an entire 'geography' of consciousness (both as 'understanding' and as 'pure reason'). As Kant emphasizes when he speaks of the 'analytic of concepts,' he understands by this "the hitherto rarely attempted *dissection of the faculty of the understanding itself . . .*" (p. 103). To the extent that Kant *actually practices* this "dissection" he has set out upon a fundamentally phenomenological explication.[25] It is quite important to grasp its sense, even though Kant does not himself focus specifically on it in the *Critique.*

The "dissection," it seems clear, is the same method as that which he calls "abstractive isolation," and is used by him with great consistency.[26] Consider, for example, his use of it in the first pages of the transcendental aesthetic. He begins by noticing that there are different components in experience: thinking and sensing. He then "takes away" everything stemming from the former in order to determine what "remains." Further abstractively isolating, Kant finds the components of sensing itself: matter and form. Isolating the latter, he further delineates the forms of space and time, and each of these is then analyzed.

Quite parallel with Hume's conception of 'experimentation in the moral sciences,' Kant's actual practice of this method shows that it has four central features. (1) It is obvious that Kant believes that others who take the time to do so, can do what he has done and will find what he has found; the method is essentially a *cosubjective* one. (2) The method is a way of picking out *evident distinctions and differences* in consciousness—differences in components as well as in function. At the same time, (3) it involves a *focusing on and analysis of* the elements and functions thus delineated to determine their respective natures and places in the whole of consciousness, and a consequent disregarding of other elements. But also (4) it includes the *systematic comparison* of the elements in order to determine, first, what is due to what (what the understanding contributes, as opposed to perception), and second, what relations obtain between and among the isolated elements.

Precisely these procedures are essential to *criticism,* even though Kant does not apparently focus on them *as such.* For, it is clear, the "transcendental question" in its most basic formulation in the "deduction" cannot be resolved without first having the various elements (in this case, the categories) *already at hand. Obtaining these is a matter of "dissection,"* but Kant adopts it quite *uncritically,* for all its frequent use. Hence, one of the serious themes for phenomenology will be to ground that very method—that is, to determine its essential features and to uncover its basis (for Husserl, both are found in the nature of consciousness itself).

Kant's dissection is conceived by him as the proper task of transcendental philosophy. With it, he seeks to ferret out the "pure concepts to their first seeds" in the understanding itself and thereby to display their very possibility (p. 103). To that end, Kant develops his tables of categories and judgments, and then seeks to "deduce" them and to show how the organization of sensory intuitions by means of these categories is possible (the function of the "schematism"). By claiming to fulfill that dissection, Kant has in effect produced a theory of consciousness and its essential components (those required for the possibility of experience and knowledge).

What emerges is that consciousness is fundamentally *active* (as opposed to the passivity of sensibility). Without going into the details of his theory, it is easy to appreciate that the consequence of the methodological move is that Kant claims to have discovered the *essence* of consciousness, both as "understanding" and as "reason." This turning to the essentials of consciousness (but not 'in itself,' of course) is strictly necessitated by the transcendental turn itself. Turning to consciousness as that to which objects of experience must conform in order to be what they are, is a focusing on what is essential, both to objects and to consciousness.[27]

Kant's transcendental critique, then, is, in at least one of its directions, an effort to uncover and assess the 'pretensions' of sensibility and consciousness and to explicate ('dissect') their inherent 'claims.' It is also a criticism of the presuppositions of any possible metaphysics, and thus claims to disclose its limits and justifiability. The transcendental critique of pure reason necessarily leads to consciousness as the focus of the inquiry, which attempts to isolate the essentials of human experience and knowledge and to display their interrelationships. In all these respects, Kant's notion of 'critique' coincides with what we have called phenomenological 'criticism.' Hence, Husserl's judgment that Kant was the first to perceive the sense of phenomenology is clearly correct, despite the fact that Kant was misled concerning logic, inner perception, and the assumption of things in themselves. The development of phenomenological discipline will depend, however, on focusing these presentiments as explicitly as possible.

Recapitulation: Tendency Becomes Demand.

We have seen that phenomenology is to be understood as the discipline of philosophical criticism. This discipline can be characterized preliminarily as concerned with the explicit focusing on claims ('beliefs' in the broadest sense of the term), wherever they may be found—in science, art, religion, politics, everyday life, metaphysics, philosophy (including criticism itself). Descartes' acute sense of method and the requirements of evidence are major advances in the development of criticism. In the sense that 'claiming' is always 'believing' with one or another modality, Hume's philosophical labors yield unexpected rewards: his delineation of 'belief' as the core of human consciousness sets out a prime theme for critical inquiry. Kant's turn to consciousness, extending Hume's 'mental geography' to the transcendental, is a fundamental advancement of the thematic. Only an inquiry into consciousness can provide the kind of grounds implicit in the Humean notion.

Furthermore, Kant's transcendental turn shows that Hume's prime reasons for skepticism are in truth major *issues:* if everything does indeed "lie merely in ourselves," then consciousness is the necessary focus for every strictly critical effort. Thus, philosophical criticism develops in two basic directions, or better, at two levels. First, since every human engagement necessarily involves 'beliefs,' these must be subjected to critical explication and analysis. Phenomenology at this level is a *criticism of science, art, religion, and every other human engagement.* Second, since every 'believing' has its source in subjectivity (or consciousness), phenomenology must also be, at its deepest level, a *criticism of consciousness (and subjectivity) in all its strata.* Since every criticism requires that the affairs criticized be as fully explicit and clear as possible, *criticism requires and depends on an initial descriptive elucidation of these affairs.* Hence it is that phenomenological criticism produces descriptive theories of consciousness, the social world, perception, science, art, and so on.

The explicit focusing on 'beliefs' is a methodological move having the different aspects we have mentioned several times. The discussions of Descartes' attempt to doubt, Hume's experiment to produce a mental geography, and Kant's abstractive isolation or dissection, showed the crucial two-sided characteristics of critical methodology: that 'method' at once *leads to* the fields of critical inquiry and *discloses their essential features.* Descartes' reflections on method, no less than Kant's, moreover, have a central meaning for criticism: it must not only make use of 'methods' to fulfill its task, but more, it stands in urgent need of a *fully developed critical theory of criticism itself.* Phenomenology, thus, must be at one and the same time a criticism of all human engagements as well as of consciousness, and a criticism of itself.

A theory of criticism is necessary to criticism; phenomenology must also include a critical theory of phenomenology. To the extent that every empirical science, as well as art, politics, and so one, makes presuppositions that require philosophical criticism, Husserl, extending Kant's germinal insight into metaphysics, speaks of them as *dogmatic,* but in an obviously nonpejorative sense. It is thus clear that these sciences

> stand in need of "criticism," and indeed of a criticism which they are not able on principle to supply themselves, and that, on the other hand, the science which has the unique function of *criticizing all the others and itself at the same time* [My italics.] is none other than phenomenology.[28]

Descartes' goal of a *mathesis universalis,* Hume's vision of the totality of science based on the science of man and human experience, and Kant's effort to lay out the necessary grounds for experience and knowledge all point to the necessity for a *fully explicit and rigorously grounded discipline of philosophical criticism.* This discipline (or 'science,' as all of them, and Husserl, prefer to say) must be *first* in the sense of foundational; it must yield intersubjectively verifiable cognitions; it must be a science of 'beginnings'; it must focus on consciousness; it must be capable of yielding continuous and accumulated findings by a multiplicity of philosophers existing at different times and places (the 'science' must be genuinely *communal*). It must, in Husserl's phrase, be a *rigorous science,* dialogically critical through and through.

> As applied, phenomenology supplies the definitive criticism of every fundamentally distinct science, and in particular therewith the final determination of the sense in which their objects can be said to "be." It also clarifies their methodology in the light of first principles. It is therefore not surprising that phenomenology is as it were the secret longing of the whole philosophy of modern times. The fundamental thought of Descartes in its wonderful profundity is already pressing towards it; Hume again . . . almost enters its domain, but his eyes are dazzled. The first to perceive it truly is Kant. . . .[29]

What I have tried to show thus far are those features of each of these philosopher's ideas which unmistakably reveal this "secret longing." But the circumstances of philosophy, indeed of man, in our times are such that the realization of these tendencies cannot be postponed or left to chance. Not only does the *very meaning of philosophy require* the grounded discipline of criticism, but contemporary man and society have entered a phase of *crisis* unparalleled in human history—a crisis which concretely calls for a radically new understanding and clarity regarding man himself. It is to this that we must now turn to understand the requirements and urgency of critical philosophy.

The "Crisis" of Philosophy.

Among the many features of nineteenth century thought are two which are most impressive. First, there is a turning to the *de facto* world, either as a sphere for social and political *action* or as the only place where reason can be legitimately relied upon to yield *knowledge*—i.e., empirical science. Often they mutually reinforced one another, especially where empirical science was directly productive of technological goods and services at the disposal of the state or some power group. Second, that turn to the mundane was thought to be a rejection of metaphysical speculation; this, paradoxically, was shot through with metaphysical assumptions, and led to an extreme relativism and skepticism, given new life from the rise of historical consciousness and the new awareness of the diversity of cultures.

What both implicitly did was to naturalize consciousness, and included a wholesale, uncritical affirmation of the senses—sometimes expressed as a glorification of 'the practical,' either as political-economic-social *praxis* or as the epistemological ground for all *theoria*. These, in turn, implied a rarely expressed but altogether obvious denigration of the competence of reason to know reality or settle human disputes. Reason, indeed, has typically become viewed as fundamentally at the service of the nonrational: either biological formations or psychological passions (egotism), or determined by social or political ideas serving one's own social interests (ideology); or else as restricted in its legitimate functioning to the ordering and classifying of sensory data. In general, rational thought, except as it has been practiced in the framework of empirical science, is commonly seen as basically determined by nonrational forces—historical, social, etc.

Thus we have in our times witnessed the formal baptism of the *'point of view' mode of thought:* that any response to a question, and especially to epistemic questions, must first be seen as the expression of a certain 'point of view'—sociological, psychological, economic, political, etc.; Catholic, Protestant, Jewish, Buddhist; American, Russian, Chinese, English, etc.; democratic, republican, communist, socialist, 'right' or 'left,' etc.; and so on through a practically endless list. In philosophy as well this attitude has become almost a set pattern: one is usually interpreted as speaking (and is expected to speak) from an idealist, pragmatist, realist, Kantian, existentialist, analytic, or some other 'point of view.' And, if you do not speak *from and for* a certain stance, you risk not making any sense at all. Thus there has grown up in philosophy the notion that a philosopher's first job really ought to be to clarify immediately what 'position' he wishes to defend, what his 'point of view' is, and so on. Then, having settled his limitations and viewpoint, the discussion can proceed in the usual manner, with its stock-in-trade of thrusts and parries, charges and counter-charges, and with the usual results. Despite the passion of the plea (which, of course, one must have, even if it is cleverly 'cool'), he will have expressed but one more 'point of view' to be filed away in the plump pages of one more proud journal, which will itself be promptly placed in the already bulging files of the past. It might be periodically rescued, perchance, by some enterprising doctoral candidate, seeking something 'original' to write about, but this itself is destined for dusty burial in the same overstocked cabinets. In the meantime, little if any genuinely communal effort has been achieved, and the sense of philosophy becomes increasingly lost.

Such a fate is doubtless fitting for much of what passes for philosophy. But whether it be fitting or not is plainly a question that can be decided only by *criticism*—and this takes us a step further. So long as human reason is under suspicion, and consciousness either naturalized or ideologized, the bag is up for grabs to the loudest or most persuasive: as with the Sophists, argument, much less critical descriptive explication, becomes synonymous with 'winning,' and the rational standards of discourse fall into disrepute or are lost completely. Judging between conflicting views, positions, claims, is, however, a matter of rational cognition exercising rigorous standards. If the latter are degraded, the former become nonsensical, and choosing between one or another position a matter of mere momentary feeling and happenstance—not rational choice at all, but simple impulse. If the consequent relativism has any backbone at all, it necessarily ends in nihilism: the radical denial of the very possibility, not to say the significance, of the quest for knowledge. What commonly happens is that the skeptic or relativist becomes an expert smuggler, or a victim of 'double-think': standards somehow sneak in anyway, and at least the pretense of rational argument and discourse goes on.

To be human, in short, is among other things to think: the only question is not whether, but how well or badly. Much of our thinking is devoted to 'making up my mind,' or 'taking a stand' as regards something; hence, our thinking is commonly a matter of choosing what to do or believe in. To think, in these terms, is to take a position with respect to that 'something,' and this is unavoidably to appeal to standards, reasons, goals, without reference to which the position-taking is unintelligible, much less possible. To decide to do X is to decide to do it *rather than* Y, and hence is to appeal to reasons for X rather than for Y. Thereby, our thinking is inextricably opened to *critical questions,* of the kind discussed in this study. Since choosing not to choose is still a choice, moreover, it is also subject to the same conditions. Hence our thinking is essentially bound up with critical inquiry, and no amount of naturalizing or ideologizing of reason can circumvent that necessity for rational criticism except by deceit or utter ignorance. Being suspicious of reason, like skepticism or relativism, is paradoxically a position-taking, an appealing to 'reasons' and 'standards' that supposedly bind one to the position. By that very fact is necessitated a *form of inquiry not itself subject to the position in question, but which is not only presupposed by skepticism and relativism, but necessarily remains neutral to both—that is, criticism.*

It was already noted that the empirical sciences, especially those dealing directly with nature, were generally held to be exempt from the suspicion of reason. Why this was, and in many ways still remains so, cannot be investigated here. But the fact itself is significant. The sciences, their methods, foundations, and concepts, are all products of consciousness. They all issue from specific acts of theorizing whose very possibility makes the denigration of consciousness nonsense. If reason is restricted in its legitimate employment only to the sphere of empirical science, that very restriction is self-contradictory and makes that science impossible.

Another point to be emphasized is that the very fact that empirical science was regarded as exempt is highly suggestive. The existence of empirical science, with its multiple and complexly interrelated clusters of epistemic claims, methods, and constructions, in and of itself demands the philosophical discipline of criticism. Husserl insists, in this regard, that "only science can definitively overcome the need that has its source in science." [30] But the science in question cannot be empirical science, since this is what generates the need for foundational criticism. Nor can the kind of science needed be simply one more 'point of view' alongside others—for judging among such 'points of view,' or as it became formally baptized, *Weltanschauungen*, requires the same kind of criticism. As Husserl puts it, what is demanded is

a scientific critique and in addition a radical science, rising from below, based on sure foundations, and progressing according to the most rigorous methods . . . *Weltanschauung* can engage in controversy; only science can decide. . . .[31]

The exigency of our times is precisely for the kind of science already foreshadowed by Descartes, Hume, and Kant—one which is presupposed by every empirical science, by every human engagement, and by every 'point of view' in philosophy. This radical new science is phenomenology—the philosophical discipline of radical criticism. But what does the designation of criticism as 'radical' mean? Or, more exactly, what is demanded of thinking in its 'radical' critical employment?

The radical is that which 'goes to the roots' or grounds. Thus, the radical criticism of science, for instance, takes us to the *roots* of science—to *that without which science would not be that which it is.* In this sense radical criticism goes to the *essence* of science (or whatever is in question); it places its grounds in question and forces the *inquirer to encounter and abide with them as problematic.* In the strongest sense, radical criticism discloses the problematicalness of *the ground as ground.* The 'problem' (from the Greek, *problema*) is an obstacle, a jutting-out-place, preventing passage. [32] For something to be an obstacle it must, first, *refer to someone* for whom it is an obstacle, and second, it must *refer to that person's* (or group of persons') *context of concern or action* (which may be science, everyday life, or some other context). So long as the latter is maintained, and the obstacle prevents its realization, the person experiences the obstacle as a problem that calls for, but may not receive, resolution. He can no longer *remain* within it and thus a solution is *urgently* needed.

The problem as such, in its basic sense, is an *aporia* or impasse, and forces two realizations. First, the hitherto prevailing system of ideas, beliefs, values, and the like which led to the emergence of the problem in the first place, is seen to be inadequate and is thereby *called into question.* Second, a search for something new or different is needed in order to enable one to get out of the impasse. The more intense the impasse, the more radically is this prevailing context called into question.

The truly radical question, then, is that which forces a *foundational impasse.* It forces me, the one for whom the impasse exists and who seeks a way out of it, *to place myself in question* precisely because it makes problematical the ground as ground—including that which grounds me as a seeker. There is a critical need for that criticism which will take me to the roots, and without which the *aporia* must continue unabated.

But what is it, 'to go to the roots'? Granted that our present-day crisis demands going to the roots of science, indeed of reason and human life, what kind of project is called for in the notion of seeking 'foundations'? We already noted that every epistemic claim is complex or stratified; and several of its necessary strata were pointed out at that time.[33] Briefly, every such claim is (1) articulated in a judgment that is (2) expressed in a certain language; (3) it also supposes that there is the state of affairs *about which* the judgment is made, and (4) that the state of affairs is as supposed by the judgment. Beyond these, we also noted (5) that the claim supposes that this state of affairs is other than the claim and is independently accessible; and (6) that the claim alleges that there are 'grounds' for the claim's specific modality (certain, probable, doubtful, false, and so on).

Criticism is possible and necessary as regards every epistemic claim; indeed, the very disclosure of these strata is a prime task of criticism. In order critically to assess any claim whatever, it is, first of all, imperative *to make explicit* precisely such implicit dimensions; only then can the assessment (verification or disverification) proceed. In different terms, only if you already know what is at issue as regards any particular claim or set of claims, can you go on to determine truth or falsity. This process of 'making the implicit explicit' —that is, *descriptive explication*[34]—is essentially involved in criticism, and it is *a process of systematically explicating the presupposed or taken for granted strata of claims.*

The procedure can be generalized as regards any claim whatsoever, be it ethical, aesthetic, practical, or religious. Moreover, as we saw already nascent in Kant's work, the fullest development of criticism requires that it become transcendental—it must 'dissect' consciousness as that by means of which alone anything at all is experienced or known. Or, as Hume had argued, one can critically assess our claims to knowledge only by tracing up our ideas to their source 'in ourselves.' When this descriptive explication is thus generalized and formulated explicitly, it is clear that it is the fundamental meaning of 'seeking foundations': *foundational thinking is presuppositional thinking,* and this is what philosophical criticism requires.

The procedure can be further understood by generalizing several pairs of concepts, making clearer the 'demand' on thinking. Eugen Fink has shown that one can distinguish between 'operative' and 'thematic' concepts in the work of Husserl, or of any philosopher.[35] Whereas the latter are explicitly established and focused concepts developed for the analysis of particular problems, the former are unclarified and unanalyzed notions used by the philosopher in an unthematic way. For instance, 'custom' and 'habit' are operative concepts in Hume, whereas 'cause' and 'idea' are thematic. In Kant, the notion of 'dissection' is operative while that of 'deduction' is thematic.

Of considerable usefulness in the analysis of a philosopher's work, these concepts can also be fruitfully extended to philosophical issues as well. Thus, instead of risking terminological confusion with a term such as 'presupposition' in the explication of epistemic claims, and especially of consciousness, it will be far clearer to describe their strata as *operative* (or implicit). As opposed to these operative strata, there is what Husserl calls its *thematic* object. If I judge, for instance, 'The house is red,' what I am focally attentive to (what is *thematic*) is the house itself, in respect of its color, and I am only implicitly (operatively) aware of the various strata uncovered thus far.[36]

By the same token, the operative and thematic can be usefully extended to foundational thinking generally. As both William James[37] and Husserl[38] have shown, every act of consciousness has the same essential structure: each has its own thematic object or field[39] and its operative strata, and the task of radical criticism is fundamentally, as we will later see in detail, to explicate these. To seek foundations, then, is to uncover as fully as possible (ideally, to do so completely) the thematic and operative strata of consciousness, and of every human engagement generally. Since not every stratum is at the same level, moreover, there is the further task of displaying their systemic interconnections.

A second pair of concepts is equally useful for clarifying the nature of our procedure. Criticism is a matter of reflection. In our usual lives, we are for the most part attentive to the various objects (in a broad sense) of our actions and awarenesses, whether these be acts of joy, perceiving, willing, judging, or any other. You are perfectly able, of course, to shift your attention from one thing to another. Thus, I might at one moment be interested in a particular glass as something to use in order to get a drink of water, but then shift my attention to its color; I may then become attentive to the particular hue of the color of the glass, and so on. In such cases, it would be patently wrong to say that my attentional shift either falsely *reified* or created the color or its hue. The shift does not make either into a separate entity, nor does it manufacture them. Rather, they were there all along—only I did not happen to notice them. And when I do, they are then presented to me *as such:* the color is the color of the glass, the hue is a quality of the color of the glass.

To reflect upon something, similarly, is a shifting of attention. From being concerned with the glass, its color, or the color's hue, I can shift my attention to my visual perceiving of the color, or to the judgment I made about the one or the other. I might say, 'I like that shade of red on the glass,' and then stop and reflect on that judgment itself, noting perhaps that it has the logical form of class inclusion, or that I did not really mean what I said. In the same way, I can reflectively apprehend my own acts of consciousness, whether perceptual, judgmental, memorial, or other—and in respect of their different features. *What* I am able to apprehend is one thing; *that* I am able to do so, and to become more proficient at it, is quite another. The former will concern us later; the latter is the point stressed here.

It is thus possible to distinguish between *acts of reflection* and what Husserl calls *straightforward attending to objects.*[40] In both, there is another distinction which will give us the second pair of concepts, correlated to the shift of attention. To shift attention from one affair to another does not reify anything—i.e., *it is not an objectification,* as if the mere refocusing of attention somehow literally constructed a new object. On the other hand, when I do shift attention as noted, this does make the affair an 'object' for my new act. In order to distinguish clearly these radically different matters, therefore, and especially to indicate that attentional shifts in our actual experiences do not result in metaphysical constructions (objectifications), I shall designate them *objectivations.*

Accordingly, to objectivate is to advert or attend to, or to take note of, something to which I was not previously attentive (though, of course, I may have noticed it in the past). *Similarly for reflection:* when the various operative strata of epistemic claims were distinguished, for instance, they were in no way *objectified* but merely *objectivated.* It only made explicit (thematic) what was already there but merely implicit (operative).[41]

What is demanded of thinking, especially in the context of crisis, is that it be *radically critical.* To be critical is to seek the foundations, which task necessarily means to go to the roots of our operative lives and systematically objectivate these for the purpose of critical explication, analysis, and assessment. The task for the philosopher is a critical one, in both senses: the need is urgent, and it demands the rooting out of presuppositions (operative strata) in order that we become able to know what to hold by. Since, however, this task itself is one which yields epistemic claims (as did Descartes', Hume's, and Kant's), the work of criticism must by its very nature be continually criticized. *There is no criticism which is not essentially self-criticism;* and, when it is a matter of foundational criticism, the self-criticism must likewise be foundational. It is in this sense alone that Husserl wrote of the necessity for a "presuppositionless philosophy" —the philosopher must at all times seek to ground his own claims and operative concepts.[42] That this is never completely possible for any single philosopher is obvious enough; however, this is but one more sound reason for the urgency of developing the discipline of philosophical criticism into a genuinely *communal* effort and building up an increasing amount of accumulated findings. The task of this discipline is an infinite one, since its region of inquiry is literally the totality of human life.

Finally, it is clear that the question of method is inseparably bound up with what is to be studied by means of it. Or, to use an earlier expression, every claim in the discipline of criticism is at once epistemic and methodological, serving not only to disclose the operative and thematic dimensions of human engagements (most fundamentally, of consciousness) but also as communicative guides for others to go and see for themselves—that is, mutually to engage in the same task. The crisis of man and philosophy in our day makes such dialogical criticism all the more urgent.

The "Logos" of "Psyche": Criticism and Consciousness.

Each of us experiences himself as, and thus has the sense for himself of being an *object* in the world among other objects. At the same time, each experiences himself as a *subject for whom* there are objects in the first place. Thus, I know that, like other objects, I not only occupy a particular space (thanks to my body) but that because I do, no other object can simultaneously occupy it. I know that I am not only physically placed, but that like other objects I (as embodied) can be broken, picked up, looked at from various standpoints, touched, smelled, and so on. But I also know that I am not simply an object: I have the sense for myself of being the subject of experiences through which alone are objects at all given to me. Things exist for me only as correlates of my experiences of them.

But my experiences are of many different kinds, as are the objects I come to believe in as existent; and these objects, I realize, exist in different ways. Thus, I believe that the paper on which I now write exists, and should anyone happen to ask me how I know this, I would doubtless in my normal life think him slightly daft for even asking such a question. After all, I see it, touch it, could chew on it, and so on; and so, too, could he. On the other hand, I also believe that there is an enormous range of other equally physical things, the bulk of which I do not now experience, and most of which I have not and might never experience. Yet I believe that they exist. In different terms (as Berkeley saw quite clearly), to say that they exist means that either others do or could experience them, or experienced them in the past and do or could recall that; or that I myself do or could experience or recall having experienced them. In one way or another, in our usual daily lives, these objects exist for me (us) either as now or then experienced, or experienceable, or at the very least able to be experienced in some manner at some time by someone. Even those objects not now, or even never experienced, exist for us as correlates of *some* mode (if only a fictive mode) of consciousness.

But physical things are not the only things that are part of our life-world. There are also values, ideas, relations, numbers, music, meanings, institutions, mores, folkways, laws, beliefs, goals, reasons, motives, cultural and artistic formations and actions, and so on and on. These, too, 'are' for us only as in some fashion correlated to some mode of experience. Even so, such things as these, no less than the many different sorts of physical things, are experienced by me (us) as more or less independent of me (us). Even though I come to know the norms governing marriage in my culture, for example, only through my own experiences within and of my social world (experiences such as those intrinsic to the process of 'socialization'), still these norms do not have the sense for me of being created by my experiences nor of being dependent solely on me for their existence as norms of conduct in my culture. Although correlated with my experiences, objects are, *experienced as* having existed before I came on the scene, as existing even when I am not aware of them, and usually as going to continue to exist after I die.

This is, obviously, a very cursory glance at a really complex matter. Just as obviously, my point is not to lay out all the complexity. It is rather more simply to indicate a little of what it means to say that I am, for myself (and you for yourself), at once an object and a subject *in the world* of physical, cultural, and historical objects; and that these things and the 'world' they form, although they have the sense of being something on their own, are so correlated with my experiences that *even that sense* is something disclosed only in and through my own experiences.

I am simultaneously a worldly object and a worldly subject. But even to be able to recognize that shows that there is *another dimension* to my being: I am not only object and subject, but *am necessarily conscious of myself as such*, that is, *as worldly in this dual sense*. My being as subject is thus complex in a remarkable way: I am a *self-conscious* being, I am reflexively[43] cognizant of myself and of everything asserted thus far about being an object and a subject in the world.

Several clusters of issues thus emerge. Phenomenology is that philosophical discipline concerned with the critical explication of foundations. This task leads to consciousness. But the turn to consciousness confronts us not with an entity or substance, but with a highly complex and stratified concatenation of acts and processes of awareness by which the world and its objects (including myself as subject for whom there are objects) are disclosed and experienced in various ways. The being whose acts of consciousness accomplish this feat, has for himself the sense of being both object and subject, and of being reflexively cognizant of this complex. How does it happen that these objects (of whatever type) come to have the sense of being at once *for* the subject and yet not dependent on him for their being? (Whether they 'really' are dependent or not is not the question, obviously.) How can we understand and critically account for the *objectivity of objects, which objectivity is disclosed only through the acts and processes of consciousness of the subject?* How is it, furthermore, that the subject has for himself the sense of being both an object and a subject in the world? Finally, what are we to make of the reflexivity of the subject?

Clearly, phenomenology has a central set of issues to untangle, issues on whose critical clarification depends a host of other important problems: not only, as we saw, the sense and foundation of empirical science, but for the same reasons, those of art, religion, politics, the social world, history, and philosophy itself. In general, these phenomenological questions concern consciousness, or, as we may also say, mental or psychic life as such. In this sense, one can characterize the discipline as one which focuses on the 'psyche' —not, of course, in the sense of an empirical psychology. The concern for the psychical is a *foundational* one. More specifically, phenomenology seeks to explicate and analyze those operative and thematic features of mental life without which it would not be what it is. The focus on foundations is on the *essentials of consciousness.* In this sense, phenomenology may be called a *logos of the psyche: it is the rigorous and radical criticism of consciousness in respect of its being that whereby objects are at all encountered and of its being the locus of subjectivity.*

To recognize, seek to understand, and remedy, the crisis of modern man and philosophy, then, is necessarily to project that critical undertaking of developing and firmly establishing the discipline of phenomenology in the most thorough and systematic manner—that is, to develop critical philosophy as a rigorous science.[44]

The discipline of criticism is fundamentally a criticism of consciousness. Its requirements are exacting, as Descartes lamented after but one meditation.

> But this task is a laborious one, and insensibly a certain lassitude leads me into the course of my ordinary life. And just as a captive . . . I fall back into my former opinions, and I dread awakening from this slumber. . . .[45]

This is not a merely stylistic flourish, as Hume, Kant, and Husserl testify. For if we take disengagement and neutrality seriously, this means that we must go against the natural tendency of our normal lives, indeed even of consciousness, and rigorously refrain from 'living in' that tendency while at the same time attempting to study it—neither accepting nor rejecting, but focusing on it just as it is presented to reflection. What we encounter is a remarkable complexity in whose reaches it is easy to become lost and confused, from which we lapse insensibly back into the lassitude of ordinary life.

It is always imperative for the critical philosopher to keep two matters distinct: his own ongoing activity of reflection (and everything belonging to it), and the matters which he reflectively observes (and what belongs to them). Confusing these is both easy to do and is one of the gravest critical errors, as we have seen.

The task of phenomenology, then, is the reflective-descriptive explication, analysis, and assessment of the life of consciousness, and of man generally. Since his aim is to develop his discipline as rigorously as possible, and since that signifies that he must obtain the best possible evidence for the things to be studied, then clearly the phenomenologist must turn to *his own mental life.* The mental lives of others (human and animate) are, to be sure, experienced by him; but although we certainly believe that to be true, as beginning phenomenologists we cannot take it for granted. In any event, even if that is true, my own consciousness is presented to me far more clearly, fully, and directly than is that of the other person. Thus, if we want to focus on consciousness (as did Descartes, Hume, Kant, and others), and if we want the best available samples of it in order to make our descriptive judgments with the best evidence,[46] then there is no alternative except to reflect on my own consciousness, and each of you on his own.

Lest the bogey-man of solipsism disturb anyone, a word of explanation and solace is in order. First the solace: I presume that anyone who has the audacity to make claims about the mind is referring in his claims to something called 'mind,' and on the basis of *some* sort of acquaintance with that affair. If that were not the case, we would hardly give credence to his claim. When Hume claims this or that about 'mind,' he is not making a claim either about apples or merely about Mr. Hume's mind, but rather about any affair properly designated 'mind.' But, second, Hume has some basis on which one can make such claims, and that basis can only be his own reflective inspection of his own mind—

which is just what he says, as did Descartes. Only, third, he insists, therefore, that others can make the tedious effort to do the same thing—that they must reflect on their own respective minds, and if they do, they will find what he claims. The matter is precisely the same for anyone else. One of Descartes' most brilliant methodological insights is his systemic invitation to others to 'reflect along' with him. It is also very obvious. Only today we are troubled by this as suspiciously 'subjective'—largely because of our tendency to conceive 'objectivity' in such narrow terms that only sense perceivable affairs are thought to be objectively accessible and susceptible of cosubjective confirmation. That view is, we have seen, patently mistaken and even self-contradictory. It curiously ignores large areas of our actual experience of non-sense-perceivable affairs, which nevertheless are manifestly open to this procedure of objective checking: mathematics, logic, as well as the entire arena of philosophical discourse, and other areas as well.

So much for the solace. If anyone speaks about mind, he must do so on the basis of some presentedness of it, and this can only be in direct reflection on his own, which leads to subjectivity but not to 'subjectivism.' This brings up the explanation. Imagine a beginning laboratory class in biology, where the day's lesson involves dissection. The instructor has placed frogs at each desk. He asks each student to pick the left leg and note the tendon. The student has the job of looking at his own frog, not of rushing to the instructor and looking at his frog. Similarly, each of you has his own 'frog,' his own mind, and your job is to examine it, not mine. What you are asked to do is to study that mind in respect of its most general or universal features, and not what is merely idiosyncratic, however interesting that may be.

This is just what you must do in order to comprehend what any theorist of mind has to say. To check him out, you must inspect the best available sample of mind, your own, and see if you find what he claims. Obviously, doing this requires considerable practice and native talent; but so do cooking, composing, or chemistry. Hence, whether aware of it or not, every such theorist necessarily projects a 'rigorous science' of consciousness, with the open possibility of cosubjective 'checking' at its core. This means, strictly, that the only 'explanation' is in the actual doing of it, that each of us actually engages in systematic reflection of his own consciousness, to 'see' whether what follows in the next chapters is indeed the way it will be claimed. Dialogical criticism is no mere mouthing of words: it is the actual, laborious engagement of issues by each of us, in the silence of his own solitude.

Having a veritable universe before us, and only a few pages at our disposal, we cannot do more than scratch a few surfaces. If I can in that way at least get across the kind of thing involved in phenomenological criticism, I will have achieved my purposes.

3

The Theory of Consciousness

"These things that live on departure
understand when you praise them:
fleeting, they look for rescue through
something in us, the most fleeting of
all. Want us to change them entirely,
within our invisible hearts, into—
oh, endlessly—into ourselves! Whoso-
ever we are."
Rainer Maria Rilke, *Duino Elegies*

Some Historical Considerations: Franz Brentano.

The phenomenological criticism of consciousness in its
broad outlines and details, had already been worked out by
Husserl, both in the studies published during his lifetime and
in his then unpublished writings. Because of his phenomenal
productivity, and the enormous range of issues pertaining to
the theory of consciousness, all that will be attempted here is
a schematic treatment of only some of the more prominent
features.

Husserl saw himself as deeply immersed in, and as bringing to fruition, the fundamental tradition of western philosophy. He also claimed not only to have firmly established its
basic but hitherto only operatively-grasped demands—namely,
for criticism—but also to have advanced that tradition in a
wholly original manner. All this is focused on his detailed

investigations of consciousness. Some of the main historical lines for this development have been sketched. There are other thinkers who, in Husserl's judgment, were also influential: William James (in his *Principles of Psychology,*[1] already mentioned), and more particularly Husserl's philosophical mentor, Franz Brentano.[2] Although even a brief discussion of Brentano's important work is not possible here, some indication of his thinking is necessary in order to prepare the way for understanding the particular thematics leading to Husserl's theory.

Against the main trends of nineteenth century psychology, which were mainly physiological and experimental (on the model of the natural sciences), Brentano argued that the proper subject matter for psychology can only be psychic life itself, studied in and for itself. The methods of natural science are simply not relevant for this, mainly because of the kind of matters to be studied (for him, methods must conform to the affairs to be studied). And, comparing the matters studied in each of these sciences, one finds evident qualitative differences. Brentano is thus led to distinguish between two large classes of phenomena, psychical and physical, and to argue that different, although related, inquiries are necessary for the examination of each.

By 'psychic' phenomena he means 'psychic activities,' with the accent on *activity*. Such activities as hearing a sound, smelling a rose, seeing a color; but also believing, judging, inferring, doubting; desiring, fearing, loving, and so on, are all also psychic phenomena. Brentano classifies all such phenomena into three categories: (1) what he calls, using the difficult term, *Vorstellung*, 'merely thinking of something';[3] (2) believing and judging; and (3) volitional, valuational, and emotive activities. Further, the relationship among these is such that the last two are *based on* the first, and this is *essential:*

> Nothing is ever desired without being thought of [*vorgestellt*]; but the desiring is nevertheless a second quite new way of receiving it into consciousness. No more is anything judged . . . which is not thought of too. But we must insist that, so soon

as the object of a thought becomes the object of an assenting or rejecting judgment, our consciousness steps into an entirely new relation towards it. It is then twice present in consciousness, as thought of, and as held for real or denied; just as when desire awakens for it, it is both thought and simultaneously desired.[4]

Thus, for him, believing in something, denying it, as well as liking, wanting, or hating it, are not possible unless that 'something' is first of all merely thought by, or present to, consciousness. Simply thinking of or seeing the house is not itself a believing (affirming or denying) it as existent; that is a *higher level* act based on the mere visual seeing of the house. Hence, *all psychic phenomena are stratified and complex,* with 'mere thinking of' functioning as the foundation for all the others. Psychic phenomena are either, then, mere thinkings-of-something[5] or are based on them. These activities are always apprehended in what he calls 'inner perception,' for it alone presents psychic phenomena with immediate and evident certainty.[6]

By physical phenomena Brentano means only *sensory qualities,* such as colors, sounds, odors, and so on, apprehended by means of 'outer perception.' But, he argues,[7] since these phenomena are *sensations and not physical things,* reaching the latter from the former (the task of physical science) involves inferences and hence the always present possibility of falling into error.[8] Only inner perception has immediate, hence *certain,* access to its objects, and thus it alone is perception in the proper sense.[9]

The essential character of all psychic phenomena is, Brentano holds, that of their relation or directedness to their objects. What is essential is

the intentional (or sometimes the mental) inexistence of an object, and what we should like to call, although not quite unambiguously, the relation to a content, the directedness toward an object (which in this context is not to be understood as something real) or the immanent object-quality. Each contains something as its object, though not each in the same manner. In mere thinking something is merely thought of, in judging something is admitted or denied, in loving something is loved. . . . And thus we can define psychic phenomena by saying that they are such phenomena as contain objects in themselves by way of intention.[10]

Tracing this notion back through the Scholastics to Aristotle's *De Anima* (the sensed is in the sensing), Brentano lays stress on the *relation*, the activity of 'pointing' rather than that to which the activity points as object. It is clear, then, that Brentano holds: (1) the psychical is essentially different from the physical, and (2) must thereby be studied in a different manner. This way (3) is found in the nature of psychic life itself—namely, inner perception (itself a psychic activity), which can alone have the psychic as object and give it with certainty. Finally, (4) psychic phenomena are not 'things' extended in space, but processes, activities, and as such they have their own essential features: they are complex, stratified, inwardly cohesive and, principally, are 'intentionally directed' toward objects as 'intentionally inexistent.'

But Brentano holds a fatally ambiguous thesis. Turning to my own psychic life, I find its essential feature to be intentiveness—a *directedness-to-objects* and *objects-as-objects-of-psychic-activities*. Beyond such objects, however, he holds that there is yet *another* 'object,' namely the physical phenomenon—which is itself but a sensation functioning as a "sign"[11] of *still another* 'object,' the real physical thing (which, however, is *inexperiencable in principle*). In one experience, there are at least *two*, and probably, inferentially, *three objects*—seeing an apple is to have three objects: the 'intentionally inexistent' object, the physical sensation, and the real thing.

Surely, when I reflect, as Brentano also invites me to do, I find a seeing of the apple and the apple as seen. What justifies the supposition of yet other objects? The hidden assumption, which alone makes such a thesis intelligible, is that the *reflecting psychologist leap outside this setting* of 'internal perception,' and posit yet other 'objects,' which is possible only by quitting the arena of explicit discussion and adopting another standpoint while remaining, seemingly, within the first. He operates, in short, with a *fallacious double-standard*, the consequence of which is the wholesale importation of objects about which his psychology can literally say nothing (and which he argues cannot be experienced anyway). Brentano operates with the Kantian 'thing-in-itself'; only now, unlike Kant, the 'thing-in-itself' has become what the physicist studies, even though no experience of it itself is possible. This does not withstand criticism: as a psychologist, it is *illegitimate to draw* such a distinction, much less to maintain the 'real existence' (as opposed to 'intentional inexistence' of psychic objects) of material things, while at the same time maintaining the impossibility of experiencing them. All he can legitimately find, in his own terms, are psychic phenomena and their respective objects. Whether or not it is ever legitimate to posit any other objects is, at best, a quite separate question and, at worst, sheer indulgence in dogmatic metaphysics.

Husserl's Critical Response.

It is still true and important that Brentano's psychology set the stage for Husserl's work in positive ways, even though Husserl clearly saw the deficiencies of Brentano's theory, and despite the fact that although Husserl took over the *term* 'intentionality' he gives it *a wholly new significance and grounding.* Agreeing with the insistence that a study of mental life itself is a positive necessity, and that it is evidently different from physical things both as to essential characters and methods of study, Husserl proposes that consciousness be descriptively examined down to its most fundamental strata.

Like Brentano, Husserl sees an essential difference between physical things and consciousness, but his principle of differentiation is different, being drawn strictly from the reflective analysis of these affairs without relying on any uncritically accepted assumptions about 'real' physical things. Briefly, he points out[12] that a physical thing *cannot* be experienced in any possible process of consciousness as a *really immanent component of consciousness.* Consciousness, a stream of ongoing processes *(Erlebnisse),* cannot by essential necessity have any things in it; its only 'things,' if you will, are processes of consciousness. To speak of mental activities as 'intentionally inexistent,' or as 'images,' 'copies,' etc., is either a fatal ambiguity or outright nonsense. Rather, the objects of consciousness are all *other than the activities having ('intending') them as objects.* Negatively, the objects are *nonimmanent;* positively, in Husserl's technical term, they are *'transcendent'* to the stream of mental activities—where 'transcendent' means only that these objects are not themselves immanent components of the stream of mental life itself. As we shall soon see, the sole exception to this eidetic law is found with the temporal phases of the stream of psychic processes themselves, disclosed in reflection to be immanent to consciousness. But even here, to reflect on the noetic phase of an experience is to have as one's object something (namely, the mental process) *other than* the act of reflecting. Thus, in the strictest sense of transcendence, even this is no exception.[13]

As contrasted with the transcendent ('other than') status of its objects, *every process of consciousness is given reflectively as immanent to some consciousness, as a really inherent component of that consciousness.* Being thus essentially different from the status possessed by objects of consciousness, Husserl will also insist (in agreement with Brentano) that their respective modes of givenness differ, but he will draw these distinctions with far greater precision, as we shall see. To speak only of what Brentano calls physical and psychic phenomena, however, Husserl shows that while the former are always experienced perspectivally, the latter are not; hence, the evidence for them will also differ.

At every point, Husserl emphasizes that the critical philosopher remain strictly faithful to what the phenomena reveal to reflection, and that he import nothing into the inquiry. In other words, it is imperative *to practice and sustain a rigorous disengagement and systematic neutrality,* to maintain the critical attitude as regards everything not actually and evidently found in consciousness.

Although emphasizing this essential difference, Husserl also stresses that the psychical can only exist as one component of a psycho-physical being, of an animate being. The notion of a disembodied consciousness is an essential absurdity. Hence, at some point, the connection between these must be established, just as that between the psycho-physical animate being and the world must also be displayed. An adequate account of the psychical, thus, would be only a

part of a more complete theory of man. Thus far, Husserl
is not very different from many other thinkers. But he draws
from this essential and fundamental difference between mental
life and physical things a crucial methodological consequence
for a 'pure' theory of consciousness. In order to ascertain
clearly and distinctly the differences between them (including
the somatic as well as the physical), it is essential first to
develop the theory of the psychical *on its own.* Pure psychology
must become a rigorous science of the psychical, disregarding
its real relations to the somatico-physical; 'pure' somatics
(neurology, physiology, anatomy, etc.) and 'pure' physics,
must be developed disregarding the real relations to the
psychical. The principle is just that it makes no sense to
attempt to study a relationship before the relata have been
thoroughly accounted for.

As matters stood when Husserl began his efforts, there
was already a rather thoroughly worked out 'pure' physics,
for natural science had been developed by systematically,
although rarely self-consciously, disregarding the real relations between mind and matter. The science of somatic behavior, to the extent that it disregarded the psychical (unhappily, this has not been consistently done), would be a
distinct advance. But as for the correlatively 'pure' theory
of consciousness, it was at the time practically nonexistent—
at best only partially and sporadically developed, and at
worst a morass of confusion and dogmatism.

As has already been suggested, one of the reasons for the
sorry state of the latter discipline was the widespread doubt
and even disbelief that such a study could be developed as
a genuine 'science,' justified by evidence and verifiable by
any competent observer. This issue calls for some additional
comment. It is clear, as we saw, that each of us in daily
life simply (uncritically) accepts himself and others as real
human beings living in the real world of everyday life with
all its real things. But what evidence is there for these ac-
ceptances? It would seem that I have better evidence for
my own being, superior to the evidence I have for the being
of others, for I can immediately apprehend my own psychic
life whereas I cannot have *this* kind of evidence of the other's

mental life. I do, of course, directly experience the other's somatic behavior and aspects; but I do not have the same direct access to his mental life *as he himself does,* nor he to mine. This is *not* to say that his existence is doubtful; it is only to indicate (1) the way in which I experience the other person differs from that in which I experience myself, and (2) that the best access to consciousness available to me is through my reflection on my own mental life.

Of course, if the project of the critical philosopher were merely to hang his private laundry on the public line, it would hardly be warranted to project the discipline as a genuine science. Still, the 'pure' science of consciousness which Husserl sees as urgently demanded by the very character of philosophy, not to say by the current crisis, *does not purport to be empirical or autobiographical, but eidetic.* What is at issue are those features by virtue of what any possible process of consciousness is what it is, or without which it would not be that which it is. It seeks to ascertain the *generic nature of any possible* mental process, and to delineate the generic types, interconnections, and foundations. In view of that, empirical evidence concerning *de facto* cases is neither relevant nor sought for. Hence, the skeptical doubt about the *possibility* of such a science itself presupposes precisely the kind of access to eidetic possibilities and impossibilities that the phenomenologist seeks in his critical work—how else could the skeptic claim the essential impossibility of the discipline?

This entire issue merely underscores two obvious but frequently overlooked points: first, every philosopher purporting to theorize about consciousness supposes (most often presupposes) that he indeed has access to it in order to be able to theorize; and second, there is *a systematic demand for co-subjective verifiability of all results.* Thus, the claims emerging from phenomenological reflection are at once *epistemic and communicative guides.* As for the first, although the claims are *a priori* (necessity and eideticity), they are at the same time *necessarily open to criticism.* As for the second, the claims are designed to assist the work of others in bringing the affairs talked about to self-givenness—i.e., are methodological.

Requirements for the Theory of Consciousness.

What is required in order to develop such a pure science of consciousness? First, *we must each do it ourselves,* carefully and rigorously refraining from prejudgments in both senses: from hasty ones, and from judgments issuing from uncritically accepted preconceptions and biases. That is the *ideal;* in practice, it is a matter of striving toward that ideal. Second, I (you) must attempt to consider psychic life *just as I (you) find it,* disengaging from and remaining neutral toward all theories, information, beliefs, attitudes, etc. pertaining to it and related matters, which I as this particular human being inevitably carry with me as part of my biographically and socially determined stock of knowledge. This implies that I must restrict myself to my own consciousness, since there I find that I have the best available evidence for establishing the generic character of psychic life itself.

Broadening the term 'presentation' to fit the descriptively evident state of affairs, Husserl speaks of this 'best possible access' as the 'originary evidence for' or as the 'originary *presentation* of' mental life. The *kind* of 'presentation' here, obviously, is not sensory, but *reflective.*[14] As opposed to being 'straightforwardly' cognizant of objects (sense perceptually, memorially, valuationally, etc.), I am now *reflectively* cognizant. Of what? In simplest terms, my reflective apprehension is a grasping of a *complex* affair, for what I grasp is a *process of consciousness* (or better, a *'consciousing'*)[15] *with its specific object.* The whole noetic-noematic complex is what is reflected on:

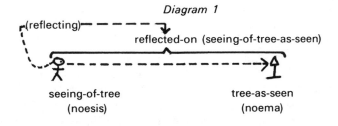

Diagram 1

(reflecting)

reflected-on (seeing-of-tree-as-seen)

seeing-of-tree
(noesis)

tree-as-seen
(noema)

My reflecting, then, is by no means a seeing of the tree, nor simply a grasping of the seeing alone. *It is rather an apprehension of the entire noetic-noematic complex.* Most striking about this complex is just this *correlation.* The most generic feature, we shall say, of any possible consciousing is that it is 'intentive' to objects, and these objects are 'intended by' the consciousing. My reflecting reveals that my mental processes are essentially intentive,[16] that they are intentive toward objects of various types, and that different processes can have the same object. Thus, I can see my dog, Irving, remember the house I once lived in, love my family, feel pride in my profession, and so on. I can also see my dog, remember him, love him, feel pride in his uniqueness, defend his peculiar traits before skeptics, and the like. I can also see the dog, see the grass where he lies sprawled, see the trees behind, and the like. Different consciousings can have the same or different objects, and the same type of consciousing can have the same or different objects.

Further reflection shows that my usual attitude is a straightforward concern with the various objects I encounter in my life. It is rarely a concern with my own mental life, much less with its intentive or eidetic character. I note, too, that there are moments when I do engage in a kind of reflection, as for instance when my eyes begin to hurt, or when I stop and wonder if what I saw really was what I thought I saw. But this kind is not what is called for now: I must be *critical,* I must focus my reflective attention on my own mental life as it is presented to me 'in person' *(leiblich),* engaging in an active attending to and reflective experiencing of my own consciousness and its objects, and on that basis to describe, explicate, and analyze it as it is itself evidently presented to me originarily.[17]

I can now also apprehend that my mental life is presented *as a reality,* a really existent affair standing in real relations with other affairs I in my naive life also experience and take to be realities (physical things, cultural artifacts, values, other persons, and so on). But my reflective project demands that

I disengage myself from all such taken-for-granted beliefs, hence from all things presented as realities and their real relations—not to deny or affirm them, but to study them *as* denied, affirmed, doubted, believed, loved, judged, and so on. *They obviously do not magically disappear;* I *note* their experienced status *as* realities, but now I remain neutral to that status in order more clearly to focus on mental life itself. They no more disappear than does the glass when I focus on its color; and judgments are just as much possible in the one as in the other case—only, what is judged changes, for I no longer pronounce on the existence of things, but only on their experienced status *as* existent.

More exactly, my disengagement and neutrality signifies, not ignoring, but refraining from accepting this reality-status (or any other experienced status various objects of consciousness may have), which in my daily life I simply take for granted as the unquestioned, but always open to question, basis of my living and acting. The same holds for the phenomenological inquiry into, science, religion, or any other human engagement. Thus, part of the fundamental *problem* for critical philosophy will be *to account for how it happens that my own mental life, body, and world in general are experienced by me* (indeed, by 'you,' 'us,' 'we,' 'they,' and 'them') *as real,* or as having any other status they may have (really past, fictive, valuative, emotive, and so on). The principal theme of critical philosophy turns out to be the explicative analysis of the intentionality-character of every possible process and activity of consciousness, for it is in virtue of this character that physical and cultural objects, animate beings, other humans, the life-world and myself come to have the various and complex *meanings* they are reflectively discovered to have. All objects, within the sustained attitude of disengagement and neutrality, are now considered strictly *as intended, as* meant, or *as* experienced in such and such intentive consciousings, which are themselves considered strictly as processes intentive to such and such objects, in these and those ways.

This systematically sustained critical attitude shows two sides: it is a refraining from 'living-in,' accepting and being busied straightforwardly with the objects of the various psychic processes *(neutrality);* second, it is a 'stepping-back-from' in order to be able to apprehend and explicate this straightforward positing and accepting of objects and the world as real *(disengagement).* Together, these constitute the epoche—a methodological move which has applications, we saw, and is, in fact, practiced with greater or lesser strictness as regards many different issues and concerns. But here, as elsewhere, *the meaning of the step is determined strictly by the themes and issues to be investigated.* Since we are to embark on an exploration of the foundations of consciousness, and from there the grounds of all human engagements, the sense of this specific epoche is that it is a *radical one,* one carried out with respect to every possible prejudgment, preconception, belief, bias, and so on.

This methodological move, moreover, has a consequence: it establishes or results in a *specific philosophical attitude or thematic concern* which, as we saw earlier, alone makes genuine criticism possible. This consequent attitude or systemic concern Husserl calls the 'reduction' and, again, has different levels, *each of which is strictly defined by the kinds of issues and strata that are made thematic.* What level of 'reduction' the critical philosopher must adopt strictly depends on which strata he wishes to 'thematize' or 'objectivate.' Since the term 're-duction' has such unfortunate connotations, however, especially conjuring up images of 'reductivism,' however irrelevant these may be, it is advisable to forego using it. I shall instead speak equivalently of the *critical attitude* at one or another level of thematic concern.

The procedure of 'imaginative variation' ('free variation') must be brought to bear here. What I as phenomenologist am seeking are those features of any possible consciousing, of a specific type, and more generally of consciousness as such, without which it would not be that which it is, or by virtue of which it is what it is. I seek the *eidetic* characters of a particular type of psychic process, by systematically varying examples in order to ascertain the *invariant* features. This method again, is not infallible: I may not vary widely enough, or be slipshod, or momentarily blinded, or foggy-headed (as Descartes knew so well), etc. But my eidetic descriptions can be verified and, for them to become part of the corpus of critical philosophical knowledge, *must* be verifiable. If such critical claims are shown to be illegitimate or in need of revision or modification, then what must be said is not that the eidetic claim was falsified, but that I mistakenly believed it to be eidetic (if it is shown to be 'false,' it is shown to have *always* been false, such being the inherent sense of eidetic claims).

Finally, it must be acknowledged that just as not every one can or even should be a carpenter, scientist, or artist, so not every one can or should be a philosopher, or critical phenomenologist. Not everyone is able to do the thing required, for many reasons, among them the fact that making accurate reflective observations and explications of one's own mental life is not an easy matter, nor one that just anybody can do. Just because we all have hands does not mean that we are therefore able carpenters; nor, because we all have minds and think, that we are thus critical philosophers. This circumstance no more vitiates the necessity or validity of critical conclusions than does one's blundering clumsiness with a hammer and saw mean that carpentry is either foolish or impossible.

The requirements for developing a pure critical theory of consciousness are, then, before us: I must reflect on my own consciousness, systematically disengage and remain neutral toward all my prior knowledge of whatever kind, adopt a critical attitude, and engage in careful imaginative variations. These we may call our 'methods,' if we want; but there are even more of them, as we will see, a whole battery of them, each with its specific focus and theme, and each having the double significance of being epistemic and methodological communicative guides.

The Most General Characters of Consciousness.

I (and you) reflect, then. What stands out through such reflective observation as the most general or universal characters of mental life? I have already discovered one: *intentiveness.* This feature and several others will suffice to illustrate the theory of consciousness and the way of proceeding which supports it. A second character involves a distinction found in every possible consciousing: whereas many of them are describably characterized by the presence of an 'I' living in them attentively busied with their respective objects, others do not have this dimension. The first may be called, with Husserl, *acts in the strict sense (Ich-Akte),* or processes in which the 'I' is actively engaged; the second may be called *operative* processes or consciousings (those in which the 'I' is either not now engaged, but could become so, and those in which the 'I' could not in principle be actively engaged, such as the phases of inner-time consciousness to be discussed in a moment.)[18] A third character of consciousness is that every process, whether active or operative, always is a specific *position-taking* (or has a specific positionality) and *modality-character.* By far the most fundamental is intentiveness; indeed, everything else said of consciousness is an explication of another dimension of intentiveness, and should always be understood as such.

The Noetic Stream of Intentiveness.

Suppose I focus my attention on only the present noetic phase of my own mental life, ignoring for the moment its noematic correlates (except tangentially). I reflectively perceive it as *a phase of an intrinsic temporal continuum,* metaphorically as a 'stream,' having other phases as well. To describe it as a 'stream' is to note that (1) the particular phases of the continuum are related to one another as earlier to later, and vice versa. One moment happens before, or after, another. (2) Each phase always has the same temporal relations to all the other phases: if a phase A occurs earlier than B, then it is always earlier, whether or not I may sometimes mistake the temporal successions and relations. (3) Again, each phase has continuously changing relations to the present phase: as I keep my attention focused on one phase, I note it changes from being present to being past, becoming continuously 'paster and paster' (clap your hands and 'watch' the phenomenon). Meanwhile, the later phases (to which I was not then attentive), which were in the future, have become successively present, and they in turn, become 'paster and paster'. This continuous changing of, and interrelations among, phases is the 'stream' of consciousness *(Erlebnisstrom)*. Although each phase has describable differences from other phases, all are alike in that they are intentive.

Thus, if I am listening to three notes on the scale (say, C, E, and G) *sounded* successively, the temporally sequential phases of this auditory consciousing are related as earlier to later (C sounded earlier than E, E earlier than G), and vice versa. Whatever else may occur, in whatever sequence, *these* relations in *that* experience retain their relative temporal positions, as well as their specific functional significances in the whole of which they are intrinsic components, as can be seen in reflection. As 'C' sounds (t_1), moreover, I can, so to speak, 'watch' it become progressively past, while 'E' is then sounded (t_2) and 'G' (t_3) is still to come. And, as each sounds, the same changing relations to the present stand out:

Diagram 2

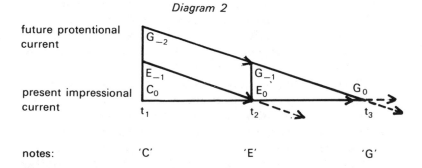

And, as for the movement into the past:

Diagram 3

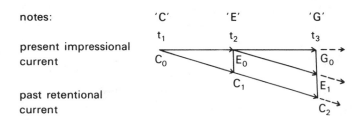

It is thus necessary to say of any actual or possible phase of consciousness that it is *essentially complex* as regards its intentive objects—that is, those affairs to which each phase is directed. There are two aspects to this complexity.

(1) Most fundamentally, *any temporal phase is intentive to other temporal phases of the same mental life* as 'earlier' or 'later' phases relative to itself. In different terms, each phase is always 'thick,' including within itself automatic or operative intendings to phases which are past relative to itself and future relative to itself. To take Diagrams 2 and 3 together, say at t_2, not only are there 'protendings' (operative anticipatings) of the phases just to come (and even further ones, of course), as is shown on diagram 2, but also operative retentions of phases just past (Diagram 3). At t_2, when note 'E' is just beginning to sound, there is the operative retention of note 'C' as having just sounded and the operative protention of note 'G' as just going to sound. Each phase of the temporal continuum is intrinsically *'intentively retentive'* to past phases, and *'intentively protentive'* to future phases, of the same mental life's continuum. At any one phase, then, there is a complex of intentive objects, each of which is an immanent component of the same mental life. It is important to stress that it is *not the notes* which are present or 'in' consciousness, but rather the *retention* of the past auditory hearing of the note, and the *protention* of the auditory hearing of the next note to come,

which are simultaneously present with the hearing of the note now sounding.

What the words describe can be readily apprehended if I carefully reflect. Earlier phases are retained, not 'in' the present, any more than are later phases protended 'in' the present. There is nothing in the present phase except the present itself as a complex series of consciousings. *There are no 'mental images' within the present phase of past or future phases or of their respective objects.* What is present, in more general terms, is the noetic intending, the processes of retaining and protending affairs that are not present but, precisely, past or future relative to that present complex consciousing. Each phase is *complexly intentive;* it retains earlier and protends later phases of itself *as* earlier and later, and *as* themselves being similarly intrinsically retentive and protentive to other phases. Among those protended by the earlier phase, which was protended then as a phase that will be retentive of the past phases of itself and all their specific contents, is the present one. Thus: phase t_3 in Diagram 3 is one which retains phase t_2 *as a phase which was itself similarly complex,* as one which protended t_3 (among others) as a phase which will retain t_2 (and others as well)—and all their specific contents. When the note 'G' sounds, note 'E' is retained as having happened earlier and as having been auditorily apprehended by a phase of the same mental life which protended (among others) the sounding of note 'G.' Moreover, t_3 retains t_1 as well, as a similarly complex phase protending t_2 (which retains t_1, and protends t_3) and t_3 (which retains both t_1 and t_2 as similarly protentive and retentive), as well as each of these phases being intentive consciousings of their own specific musical notes (noemata). Even more, t_3 retains t_1 both directly and indirectly, through retained t_2, which retained t_1:

Diagram 4

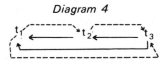

(Note: the solid lines represent retentions, and the broken lines protentions.)

In more general terms, it is descriptively evident, for instance, that I now expect to remember tomorrow (and other days, too) what I wrote today; when tomorrow comes, and I do remember what I wrote today, I remember today as a day in which I then expected to remember tomorrow. . . . Furthermore, I wrote yesterday, and expected (among other things) to remember today and tomorrow; and I now remember that yesterday I expected to remember today. When tomorrow happens, I will remember both today's remembering of yesterday, and yesterday itself. Tomorrow, for instance, I might have to correct my present recollection of yesterday. More simply, I can always 'pick up where I left off ', and when I do leave off some task, I know very well that I will be able to pick it up again (reading a book, digging a ditch, resuming a trip, and so on)—all of which necessarily presupposes as its foundation the temporal structure briefly delineated above.

Thus, the extraordinarily complex structure of intentiveness is easily grasped, but devilishly difficult to express in words: each phase, whether past, present, or future, is *essentially* retentively and protentively intended *with all its own specific complexity of content and temporal interconnections and relations.* What was said of retention holds for protention as well, with some obvious exceptions. Future phases of mental life, as phases that will be similarly complex, are protended as 'going to follow' the typical course of mental life's past phases. Despite the linguistic acrobatics one must perform in order to do justice to these complexities, it is clear that most former conceptions of time were utterly naive: the temporal continuum is neither a mere succession of 'nows' strung together like beads on an imaginary string, nor a movement of temporally discrete clutches of moments, nor a snowball of pure and simple duration.

(2) The second aspect of the complexity of every phase of mental life can now be indicated. Not only does each intend other phases of the same temporal continuum as objects

(in this case, 'immanent' objects, of course), but each also intends objects as not really intrinsic components or really immanent to the stream of consciousness. That is, there is always an awareness (a consciousing) *of something experienced* (intended) *as other than or transcendent to* the stream. These objects (the notes in our previous examples) are experienced (intended) as many different kinds: physical things, numbers, theoretical affairs, musical notes, values, judgments, relations, things past and future, and so on. To each kind of object there is correlated a specific set or type of noetic consciousing; and more importantly, for each 'transcendent' object there is *a most originary mode* (optimum conditions) of experiencing (intending) it. Or, to each type of noematic correlate belongs essentially a *specific type* of originary noetic process. Thus, to the class of physical things is correlated the set of intentive consciousings called sense perception. To the class of colors, that of visual sense perceiving is correlated, and among these, a set of originary seeings: as opposed to seeing a red ball at night, under candlelight, in fog, with blue glasses, the 'best' (relatively, obviously) way of visually experiencing the red is to see it itself under as optimal conditions as possible.[19]

The point can be made in another way, in which such distinctions are perhaps clearer. Suppose I want to discover the originary presentation of either a lighter or of mental life. What I would *not* do, forthwith, can be instructive. I would hardly proceed to mow my lawn, get a haircut, build a boat, *in order to* obtain an originary encounter with that cultural-practical instrument, 'lighter'. Nor would I simply sit and 'look' at it, or just touch it, etc. I would *use* it, for just this mode of its being presented to (experienced by) me *as tool* is the originary mode for that noematic character. If I were interested in its color, however, no amount of use would *as such* be relevant; only looking at it under as optimal conditions as possible would do. Similarly for mental life: to have it directly presented in the best possible way, I must not go swimming, drink tea, fly kites, and so on, but turn to the 'thing itself' in the way through which it is it-self presented, and experienced directly—reflection.

And so, *universally,* for all possible objects other than (transcendent to) consciousness: to each belongs a best pos-sible way of encountering it—even where, perhaps, obtaining that access may not be *de facto* possible, or perhaps impossible in principle (one cannot have a total view of a material thing, since that is a necessarily infinite process, as we saw). But the basic point is made anyway: part of the complexity of the phases of the stream of consciousings is that each will have its own specific 'transcendent' objects, which 'having' is not always the most originary having possible, but always includes inner-horizonal protentions to other 'havings,' among which is the most originary one (whether or not this can ever be actualized in fact or in principle). Indeed, part of the task of criticism is to establish these distinctions among the eidetically possible, impossible, actualizable, and so on.

Intentive Syntheses and Inner-Time Consciousness.

There thus emerges another feature of consciousness: *in-tentive synthesis.*[20] Each phase of mental life, being intentive (retentively and protentively) to other phases of the same mental life, is also intentive to their respective transcendent objects. Hence, an *additional complexity* appears as I focus more attentively. Namely, each phase has *its own* transcendent objects, but also retains and protends the transcendent ob-jects *of every other phase*—and these retentions and protentions go on quite operatively, without 'my' having to explicitly pay attention to any of this.

To illustrate, using an example from the level of explicit activity, I now remember seeing Jones, but I also remember Jones himself as I then saw him, where Jones is the *primary* object of that past seeing and the *secondary* object of my present remembering (I remember Jones *as then seen*)—but it is the *same* Jones in both. Similarly, I now see Jones, as I had expected yesterday to see him, today, where the primary object is Jones as I now see him and the secondary object is Jones as I now remember having expected to see him. These are very simplified examples, for at any moment there is not just one, but a multiplicity of primary and therefore also of secondary transcendent objects. The secondary objects, of course, were the primary objects of other phases: I now expect to see Jones tomorrow; that is, Jones-as-expected is the primary object, and Jones-as-I-expect-to-see-him-tomorrow is the secondary object of the present phase, but will be the primary object of tomorrow's seeing (if, of course, it actually happens).

Because of this further complexity, I now reflectively grasp, *no phase intends its own objects as exclusively its own, but each intends its objects as also the objects of other actual and possible phases of the same mental life* (not to mention intending them as the actual and possible objects of the other's experiences). Hence, in every phase of mental life there occurs what Husserl calls an "intentive synthesis," the most fundamental kind being a *continuous identifying synthesis,* which is simultaneously a differentiating synthesis:

Diagram 5

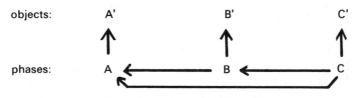

objects: A'   B'   C'

phases: A ←———— B ←———— C

(lower arrows indicate retentions)

Suppose I am hearing a single tone (A' through C') being sounded and enduring for a short span of time (A through C). The tone is synthetically identified, operatively, as the same tone throughout the phases of its endurance, and is identified at C as the same tone as what sounded in the retained phases B and A; at the same time, phase C retains A as 'when the tone began to sound,' and retains it both directly and indirectly (through retained phase B). With these retentions, there is retained as well the respective phases (B, for instance, is retained by C as that specific phase with its specific noema, **B'**). There is an operative, continuous identifying synthesis among the temporal phases, with their respective noematic objects, of the tone as *the same throughout* the multiple noetic phases of its being heard. At the same, there is a differentiation of the tone as heard in the first phase, the second, and the third ('beginning,' 'continuing,' and 'continuing, then ending').

Suppose another case: A is a cat-perceiving, **A'** the cat-as-perceived; B is a retaining of a cat-perceiving and an explicit remembering of the cat, thus **B'** is the cat-as-remembered; C, then, is a retentive consciousness of the cat as perceived in A and remembered in B, but C is another perceiving of the cat, thus **C'** is again the cat-as-perceived. Noetically, *the phase A is the same A as directly retained by C and as retained by retained B*. Similarly, the cat as seen in A (**A'**) is experienced as the same cat as remembered in B (**B'**), and when C occurs, the cat now seen (**C'**) is identified operatively as the same cat seen in directly- and indirectly-retained A, and as in retained B, itself a remembering of the cat seen in A. As Diagram 5 shows, then, each later phase retains earlier phases along with their own respective objects, and inherently running through this 'stream' of temporal phases are these continuous identifying syntheses.

But there are also *discontinuous identifying* syntheses, where objects of different phases are operatively identified and differentiated, but the different phases occur discontinuously. An example would be reading a book at night, going to sleep, getting up and going through one's day, then picking up the book again the next night: the book is operatively identified as 'the same' book as that put down last night.

Sacrificing some exactness, the Jones I saw last week and now remember, and remember as having been seen by me then, is experienced as 'the same' Jones in both phases. And should I see him tomorrow, he will be then experienced as the same Jones I saw last week and remembered today. Even if it should happen that I am mistaken, the fact of the mistake itself makes sense only if identifying syntheses are already operatively at work: to mistake is to mis-take what was taken as 'the same,' and to experience instead 'something different' —which is itself synthetically taken as 'the same' throughout the phases of its being experienced. I do indeed, I see on reflection, experience things of all sorts as identically the same throughout a multiplicity of different experiences of them (the thing I see and then touch, for instance). The ground for this ongoing noetic and noematic identification is in these syntheses.

A further point is worth mentioning, if only briefly. As I can grasp reflectively, it is essentially absurd to characterize the experience of recollection in terms of the well known 'trace' or 'image' theory: that whenever something is experienced, it leaves a trace or image in the mind—which trace is always present. Memory, in this view is a matter of apprehending that trace, which somehow of itself is supposed to refer to the past—that past time when it first occurred. Both the remembering and what is remembered (the trace) are *present;* the past event to which the trace somehow points is never itself apprehended by memory. Quite to the contrary, reflection on memory shows that the things remembered are *themselves now experienced as past:* the experienc*ing* (recollecting) is present (and shows all the temporal structures of retention and protention already disclosed—the recollecting itself has phases to it!), but what is experienc*ed* (the past event) is manifestly past. This can be seen in another way: not only can I recall visually seen things (and when I do, I recall them as having been seen from a particular point of view, within a particular context, environs, and so on), I can also remember another activity, such as remembering; I can also recall smells, odors, imaginative objects, values once held—as well as the *noetic* intendings correlated with these, all of which are themselves recalled as past. In short, the 'image' theory is false; at best, it is naive and hardly adequate to the descriptively evident character of memory. I can, obviously, also recall having seen pictures, just as I can now see a picture, say, of my wife. But to confuse the past seen picture with something present is as absurd as confusing the present seen picture with my wife.

The decisive role these syntheses play in the life of consciousness can only be indicated here. Think, for instance, of a judging: 'The pen is black.' While saying 'pen . . .,' then '. . . is . . .,' and finally '. . . black,' not only must the subject term 'pen' remain and be intentively experienced (identified synthetically) as the same (as 'subject'), but the pen itself as seen, must also remain the same throughout the remaining phases of the judging process. Otherwise, it would be plainly impossible ever to say anything at all, for if, while saying '. . . is black,' the pen were not synthetically experienced as identically the same pen and as the same subject of the judgment, the '. . . is black' could not at all function as applying to the subject. One could not predicate anything of the subject for there would not be any 'the same subject' throughout the judging. This kind of *"syntactical synthesis"* holds universally for all judgments and their noetic judgings, just as the underlying syntheses of identification and differentiation hold universally for all experiences.

Other syntheses can be seen, having significance for other problems. Thus, what Schutz calls the 'reciprocity of perspectives' in daily life (we assume [idealize] that we can 'change places' thus experiencing more or less what the other experienced),[20a] involves not only the syntheses already indicated, but another type. Husserl variously calls it the 'associative transfer of sense,' 'association synthesis,' or appresentational pairing.'[21] Most simply, it can be illustrated as follows:

Diagram 6

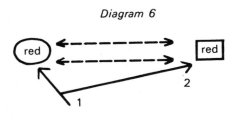

Imagine that my (your) visual field is homogeneously grey, and there then appears a circular red spot in it, after which there appears a square-like red spot. The first spot attracts my visual attention and I advert to it, seeing it as a 'red-round-spot' (it has that 'sense' for me). When the second spot appears, it also solicits my advertance, and obviously appears *after* the first has already appeared and has been visually perceived with its specific sense. That is, while now attending to the 'red-square-spot,' the 'red-round-spot' is retained *as such* (as already perceived with its specific sense), and there then occurs a kind of 'overlay' of senses—the tendency of all consciousness (as Hume, too, had noted) is to transfer its past to its future. Remembering now our discovery of protentions, and the tendency of consciousness to protend operatively its own further continuance as typically like what its past has been, we can note that the happening of phase two at once *fulfills and fails to fulfill* what phase one protended. Two fulfills one, for it is a visual perceiving (as was one) of a 'red' (as was one) which is also a 'spot in a homogeneous grey field' (as was one): in Husserl's terms, the *sense* 'red-spot-on-grey-field' is *operatively transferred and confirmed* (fulfilled). But phase two fails to fulfill (disconfirms) phase one's protention—partially, as well, for it is a seeing of a 'square' while phase one was a seeing of a 'round': in Husserl's terms, there is a conflict of senses and, hence, the tendency to expect uniform continuance breaks down, or the sense 'round' fails to transfer.

But that very failure has a vital import: as the dotted lines in Diagram 6 indicate, because of the disconfirmation of the transferred sense 'round,' *both acquire an additional sense* for consciousness: namely, the second is now experienced intentively as 'square *and not round,*' and conversely the first spot now acquires the sense 'round *and not square.*' By virtue of this synthesis of associative sense transfer, several decisive features of consciousness generally now stand out.

(1) The partially successful transfer of the sense 'red,' for instance, coupled with the partially unsuccessful transfer of 'round,' signifies that there is *'a common,'* which now stands

out and may thus be apprehended and explored—namely, 'red' itself stands out as *exemplified* in the one and in the other of the two spots, and that itself may be noticed and grasped. If so, then consciousness has before it the *rudiments of a material universal, and has exhibited the elementary form of idealization* —that is, *conceptualization:* the explicit grasping of 'the common' in a multiplicity of instances, or the explicit grasping of individuals as *exemplifications.*

(2) The same occurs in a different way, connected with the partially unsuccessful sense transfer of 'round' and conversely with 'square.' For not only are there now the two new senses, 'not-round' and 'not-square,' but there has also appeared *another 'common':* namely, *'two* spots' have synthetically emerged, and that itself may be adverted to and grasped. If so, there emerges the sense 'twoness' or 'pair' (hence Husserl's term 'associative pairing'), and the apprehension of that is one of the crucially important features of all cognition—the, in this case, rudimentary *apprehension of formal universals.* The further explication of these phenomena would eventually yield a phenomenology of cognition or thinking.

Still other syntheses are found at the roots of consciousness, but what has been pointed to thus far should suffice to suggest the kind of complexities that must concern the critical phenomenologist. In general, in order to be aware of anything at all, from geometrical affairs to beads on a necklace, this awareness (intentive consciousing) must go on for a certain span of time. That being so, intentive syntheses are necessarily at work in an operative manner, that is, these syntheses are *not* explicit connections made by a wide-awake self, but go on quite without any such explicit attentiveness. They are not 'my activities,' but operative consciousings. Without them, I could not be aware of any object at all as 'the same' object of which I was aware a moment ago, last week, and so on. Furthermore, in order to have 'concepts' of any kind, there must be the sort of operative sense transfers and confirmations and disconfirmations already mentioned, along with the rudimentary advertances called 'idealizations.'[22]

Each phase protends (operatively anticipates) or pre-delineates future possible intendings, among which are future possible intendings of something as the same as what is now intended (and among these are protended both the same and different *kinds* of intendings of the thing as 'the same'). The subsequent course of mental life may or may not actualize a certain predelineated process. But if this occurs, there happens an identifying synthesis ('That's the same guy I met in New York last year'), which may not be a perfect one, of course ('But he has certainly changed'). It is worth stressing again that *every phase* of mental life is re-tended or protended *as having its own complexity, relations to other phases, and its own complex inner horizons.* This predelineated inner horizon is always *at least* a protention of a certain *typical style* following at the least the typical style and objects of the past phases of the same mental life. Normally, such protentions are rather fully mapped out or filled in; for instance, few of us expect or plan literally nothing during the usual day; and what we do expect and plan for typically occurs with some modifications and alterations—this is especially plain if we think of the minute-by-minute course of the day.

But since it is evidently true that each phase has a protentional inner horizon, it is also true that *not every* protention could possibly become actualized. What occurs is that protentions come in sets, contexts, more or less organized, and if one set is actualized, others are made impossible (having already gone to Houston, I cannot at the same time stay in Austin), while still others are made more or less likely or unlikely (being now in Houston, say, it is more likely that I can see my friend there, but less likely that I can still get back to Austin tonight).

Furthermore, some future intendings are protended not only as possible identifying syntheses, but, in addition, as *fulfilling* syntheses of some present intentive experience. Such fulfillment, I reflectively grasp, is a 'more or less,' ranging from more or less disappointment to more or less confirmation of what was protended. Thus, not only are there syn-

theses of fulfillment (the blind date Jones arranged turns
out to be as pretty as he said she would be), but also *syntheses of annulment* or negative fulfillment (the blind date,
though pretty, is dull, unlike what Jones promised). But,
short of a *literally total collapse* of all protentive intendings
(for instance, my death), no actualization of a protention is
ever a complete annulment or fulfillment, but always a 'not
so but otherwise' experience.

The future phases of mental life are not descriptively protended as unambiguous; but neither are they protended
emptily. Rather, the future is protended operatively (and to
some extent anticipated actively) as a multiplicity of mutually exclusive sets of possibles, the general style of which is
protended as 'having the same type' as what has already
occurred, having the same typical ways and kind of objects,
processes, the same typical sorts of events, and so on. The
general style of the past casts its shadow over the future (in
Husserl's phrase). In short, there is always a certain weight
given to those processes of the same type that occurred in
the past as going to continue in the future. This feature has
been noted numerous times by others; what Husserl insists,
and I (you) can reflectively verify, is that it is founded in
the *complex synthetic structures of inner-time consciousness and is
an eidetic necessity of every actual and possible process of consciousness.*

My reflection also shows that by virtue of this eidetic
structure, the past itself, as the retentional current (as experienced within inner-time consciousness, for example), has
its own style of change and possibilities. After having touched
red things for a while, a child (by virtue of the syntheses of
identification-differentiation, and sense transference) expects
to be able to touch any red thing presented to him, until
he touches the red heating element of an electric heater and
gets burned. The experience rebounds to other things both
past and future, which acquire the sense 'be careful,' even if
experienced before. Slowly there develops, through what
Husserl calls 'sedimentation,' a building up of *senses, of types
and differentiations into subtypes,* resulting, finally, in the stock of

knowledge at hand that each of us has and brings to bear at every moment of his life. Finally, in the same way the past has its own style of change, it also has its own style of possibilities: after having actualized some but not other protendings, those which were not still have the sense of 'had X or Y been done, then thus and so would have occurred,' or, 'if I had only done Z, then. . . .'

Intentional explication is largely a matter of making explicit (thematic) in imaginative reflections these sorts of intentional horizons that are only implicit or operative. In other words, any possible type of experience can, and must for critical purposes, be made thematic. What is focused on in reflection are the ways in which objects of whatever sort could be brought to self-givenness: if certain potentialities were actualized, then certain chair-perceivings, value-intendings, number-intendings, and so on, would be actualized.

As regards any possible noematic correlate of the now protentionally predelineated phases of consciousness, there are protended many different possible ways of experiencing an object. Seeing a tree now outside my study, there are already implicitly delineated other ways of seeing it (in fog, at night, as grown, as cut down, etc.), and other ways of experiencing it, too (making judgments, remembering, valuing, sitting under it, etc.). The noema of any noesis is horizonally predelineated as *able to be experienced* in many different ways, settings, and under different circumstances. I now see the lighter before me and there is implicit in the seeing of it the possibility of touching it, using it, and the like. Hearing the doorbell is already to set in motion certain typically habituated potentialities, such as getting up, walking, reaching out, turning, pulling, saying, and so on. Every noematic correlate of any possible noesis is encountered, not as insulated and unconnected with anything else (one of Hume's prime mistakes is here; or, to have failed to inquire into the nature of 'belief' itself), but as surrounded by a penumbra of aspects and determinations, which are not now presented but horizonally predelineated.

And, as there is this inner horizon of potentialities, so there is an *outer horizon* of the noema. Simply expressed, everything is encountered as *being-in-a-context*, a field, of other things.[23] I see the tree as outside my window, next to the swings, behind the porch, in front of the hill—in short, as *set off from a background of coperceived things* (among them, my own body), and so on. More generally, I apprehend myself as located within a kind of zero-point, 'Here' and 'Now,' my own living body, around which are concentric zones of 'far' and 'near.' This is not only spatial and temporal, but also social, historical, economic, political, and so on. There are zones within my actual reach, within my restorable reach, and within my potential reach.[24] Each thing I experience has these surrounding zones, outer horizons of other things, is set off from them, and, as Natanson shows, only by virtue of this kind of outer horizonal structure is the phenomenon of self-placement as "here and now" (in all senses) even possible.[25]

All of these highly complex temporal strata and interrelations can be diagrammed, using Cairns' extension and reinterpretation of Husserl's presentation in his *Phenomenology of Internal Time-Consciousness.*[26]

Diagram 7

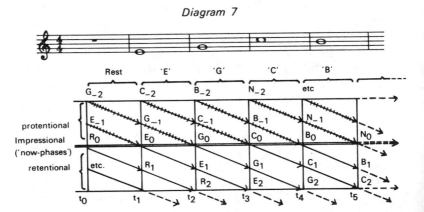

We have already seen the meaning of protention and retention; 'impressional consciousness' signifies here the ongoing continuum of 'now-phases' of the auditory consciousing of the notes of the scale. Thus, the line R_0 through N_0 is the ongoing succession of hearings of the notes. The vertical lines (t_1, t_2, etc.) are artificially distinguished cross sections of the internal time continuum, each having a temporal 'spread' and 'depth,' such that at any one time (t_2) there is an impressional ('now') auditory awareness of the beginning of the note 'G' and its duration, retentions of just past phases (E_1 and R_2), and protentions of phases to come (C_{-1} and B_{-2}). Thus, at t_2 there is impressional consciousing of 'G' and its duration, retentions of past note 'E' and the just-just past rest ('R'), and protentions of the notes to come ('C,' then 'B'). But this is, obviously, just a short cross section: at t_2, not only 'C' and 'B,' but also 'N' future notes and their correlated phases (C, B, N . . .), are protended; and phases earlier than R are also retained. Everything else already noted can also be seen here, and a good deal else as well, although there is not enough space in this study to explicate it sufficiently. Hence, I leave the matter and move on to another crucial feature of intentionality.

Evidence.

I am able, focusing merely on a single temporal phase of the life of consciousness, to make explicit a considerable amount of its remarkable complexity: its intentiveness, noetic-noematic structure and complexity of objects both immanent and transcendent, a variety of syntheses, and something at least of the temporal complexity and interconnections of the phases of mental life. With these thematized features, it is easy to see how it happens, for example, that the 'present' is concretely experienced not only as *'present'* but *as one phase in a continuum of phases:* it is precisely by virtue of these 'transversal intentionalities'[27] (retentive and protentive) that the 'present' is experienced and constituted synthetically as present, as are the 'past' and the 'future.'

Beyond these, there emerges a further and quite important

disclosure. Any phase of consciousness is either an experiencing of something as itself presented in person, either now or as past (in memory), or it is an experiencing of the something as not itself presented, but 'merely intended,' in one of two basic ways. There is a general distinction between something *really itself presented,* something *represented* (depicted in some mode), and something not presented nor represented but *'non-presented.'* I can, in other words, evidently distinguish among: really seeing Jones himself here and now in person or clearly remembering Jones as I saw him yesterday, where in both cases it is Jones himself whom I experience (though in different ways); seeing, not Jones, but a depiction (photograph, painting, sculpture, etc.) of him; or trying to 'call to mind' the man's name, which I cannot quite recall, and thereby to call him to mind. In the second case, Jones is represented (well or poorly); in the third, he is neither presented nor represented, but non-presented—a category that includes the phenomenon of symbolization generally (specifically designated 'appresentation' by Husserl).[28] Thus, a case of appresentation would be the use of the mark ' + ' which can call to mind something else neither represented or presented: the arithmetical operation of addition, or the religious Christ, or even a footnote, and the like. Finally, another mode of non-presentation can be seen: I may think of the man but be unable to recall his name, where his name is 'emptily intended,' until that moment when it finally 'dawns' on me.

I can thus distinguish among *presentational, representational and non-presentational (in particular, appresentational) modes of consciousness of one and the same thing.* To confuse these is to invite utter confusion, especially the anomalies, contradictions, and mistakes of much traditional 'theory of ideas.' In any case, if I now focus my attention more specifically on these phenomena, I can note that every possible *intended* object, regardless of its specific kind, *has its own type of presentedness.* For every intended object, there is correlated a most originary type of consciousness of it (whether actualizable or not).[29]

An earlier point[30] can now be picked up and given further grounding. It was mentioned in passing that there is better evidence for a judgment about something (e.g., 'the Statue of Liberty is colored green') when that state of affairs is itself actually presented, than there is when one only recalls having seen it, has only a picture of it, has heard someone else talk about it, or simply goes on hearsay. Clearly, there are differentiations of evidence in each case. Having a clear, as distinguished from a rather confused, recollection of the color of the statue as I once saw it, does provide some evidence for the judgment about its color. Similarly, if I can in some way be assured about a color photograph (where critical considerations about these 'assurances' must be given), seeing a picture might be taken as giving some degree of evidence. And, supposing I have good reasons for trusting someone, then again his 'word' gives some reason (evidence) for the judgment. But none of these provides as good evidence as actually standing there and, while viewing it under optimum conditions with adequate sensory apparatus, judging step-by-step 'The Statue of Liberty is green.'

To make such a judgment is to make a claim (supposal) *about* the state of affairs itself in respect of what is able *to be given visually*—experienced in the way appropriate to the specific affairs judged about. Similarly, if I judge 'Every process of consciousness is essentially characterized as intentive,' the judgment itself appeals to evidence of some order—to something, in other words, which is itself susceptible of being 'checked' in order to determine whether there is such an affair and whether it is as claimed. In order to 'check' it out, one must go to the 'thing-about-which' the claim is made and determine the evidence. *One must 'check' the evidence for the claim by consulting, in the appropriate ways, the 'thing-about-which.'*

To 'check' the evidence is to turn to the affairs judged about in the specific way or ways appropriate to them. As Husserl expresses it, "Evidence is, in an *extremely broad sense*, an *'experiencing'* of something that is, and is thus. . . ."[31] As was already stressed, moreover, the particular evidence appealed to in a specific case may be more or less adequate, more or less perfect, for the affairs in question. Not everything about which we make claims is of the same kind, or can be experienced in the same way. I can and do judge about numbers, values, the past, assess the validity of an argument, etc.—and with each of these, and all other things-about-which judgments can be made, to verify them is to check the evidence for them, and this necessitates *turning to the things themselves* in respect of the specific features, qualities, or aspects judged about. But each of these affairs is *accessible in different ways:* I can no more auditorily perceive the validity of an argument than I can cognitively apprehend musical tones. Hence, if evidence is a matter of turning to the affairs in question as regards a specific claim, of 'experiencing' them (in the "extremely broad sense" [*Erfahrung*, not *Erlebnis*] Husserl notes), then *evidence will differ with each particular kind of affair.*

Not only does evidence show differentiations as to the kinds of claims and underlying experiences pertaining to each, but also shows *various degrees.* For instance, I know now that the Pythagorean theorem is true *a priori,* but I remind myself that this means *a priori* true in the context of Euclidean geometry and its system of definitions, axioms, rules, etc. In that context, it is unquestionably true, and I know it; but my knowledge now is merely a 'knowledge-that,' not a 'knowledge-why' (or -how). I remember having once seen it proved, and even of having done it myself; but I can no longer call to mind the steps of this proof, and even some of the axioms, etc. are no longer 'with' me. My present judgment, '$a^2 + b^2 = c^2$' does have some evidence for it, but not at all as strong (adequate and perfect) as it would be if I were now able to articulate clearly and distinctly each component of the judgment, understanding what each signifies, cognizing the sense of the expression, relations and operations, and then grasping the whole formula itself *as a whole.*

Each of us can think of similar instances. One believes 'patriotism' is the 'proper value' for 'all true Americans,' and supposedly has evidence for this claim. The best evidence would obviously require the clear and distinct understanding of each expression, the interrelationships, as well as apprehending that value in the way proper to it—actually practicing it in living, with clear-headed understanding and consistent actional embodiment of it. Another believes that 'biological engenderers of progeny are responsible for the welfare of same'—and, again, the same kind of considerations must enter in.

There are, thus, different *kinds* of evidence relative to different *kinds* of affairs judged about, and different *degrees* of perfection and adequation relative to any one kind of affair. Reflection shows also that I can generalize: *a consciousing of something as itself presented in person in respect of the feature judged about* (the 'relevant feature') *is originary evidence for it.* On the other hand, a *clear recollecting* of the thing as it itself but now 'past presented' is *non-originary evidence,* but evidence nonetheless. Evidence, both originary and non-originary—the first is more perfect and adequate than the second—is a process of consciousness, an experiencing, each phase of which is a consciousness of the affair in question and a retentional consciousness of past phases. The latter, in turn, are themselves originary consciousings. Non-originary evidence is, then, a *modification* of originary evidence, and reveals precisely the same complexity of structure. There are phases of the process of recollecting, including retentive and protentive phases, no less than with any other process—but this structure does *not* make the *thing* remembered something present; that would be tantamount to importing things (past things) into the temporal stream of consciousings, and a blatant reification.

As opposed to these kinds, degrees, and modes of evidence, neither representational nor nonpresentational (or appresentational) consciousings provide evidence for the things represented, appresented, or 'emptily meant,' [32] in the *strict sense* of an experiencing of the things judged about themselves (either now or as past experienced). On the other hand, our imaginative variations do provide evidence—not, as Gurwitsch stresses,[33] for the *actuality* of the things in question, but only of their *essential possibility.*[34] Thus, by systematically varying (in fictive or imaginative reflectings) consciousings of a certain type, I am able to determine those invariant features of any possible examples of the type in question. A study of representations gives me no evidence for judgments about the thing or things depicted—not in the strict sense of evidence. But I must also note that I may reflect on the type, 'representational consciousness,' and thereby ascertain the eidetic features of that mode of consciousness. This reflection shows that, among other things, evidence *in the strict sense* is an impossibility for this mode. I cannot have evidence for what is depicted thereby; to get that, I must move from a representational to a presentational consciousness of the depicted affairs.

All of this would have to be further clarified and explicated. Already, however, I note that a synthesis of identification in which *either* (a) the object of a nonpresentive consciousness and the object of a subsequent presentive consciousness are identified as experiences of the same thing, as 'it itself' presented 'in person'; *or* (b) the object of an imperfectly presentive consciousness and the object of a later more perfectly presentive one are synthetically identified as of the same thing itself—can both be called the *verification* of the object in question in respect of those features it is intended as having. Imaginative variation yields only *eidetic clarification,* never verification, and provides *evidence only of essential possibility and impossibility,* never of actuality, just as verification (harmonious fulfillment of protentions) yields evidence for *actuality.*[35]

Actional and Operative Strata.

It has been necessary to wade through all these details, as opposed to providing a mere summary and capsule definitions of concepts, because that is what is demanded not only of criticism, but also of any serious understanding of Husserl's work. Even so, as should also be clear, I have dwelled merely on the outer fringes both of Husserl's theory and of the dimensions of consciousness, and shall continue to do so.

In addition to being intentive, with all the complexities

this involves, I note as well that some of my mental processes have a sort of I-presence, while others either have it only more or less marginally, or not at all. Among the latter, I notice that some *could* have such an in-living I-presence, while others simply do not admit this even as a possibility. Without in the least posing, much less trying to resolve, the difficult issue of selfhood, I can descriptively find such a presence, but only as regards some mental processes. An illustration will help clarify this.

Suppose this time I take a more complicated experience, again focusing mainly on several of its single phases, but presupposing now everything said thus far. A photographer comes to my home to take pictures of my wife; after doing so, he then sends me copies of a number of them (consider only two of these). I look at one, then at the other, and so on. Now, while the act (in the strict sense) goes on, I know (I who reflectively consider this act) that during its course what I (the perceiver of the pictures) attend to can vary. Reflecting on it, there is descriptively a consciousing of the thing depicted (my wife), of the picture itself (the physical thing as a depicting), and of the physical stuff (the paper, forms, blocks of color, lines, etc.). I can busy myself with (focally attend to) the depicted, and say, for instance, 'This is my wife standing by the fireplace.' Or, I can attend to the picture itself, saying 'This is not really a good likeness.' But I can also focus on the physical stuff (as an amateur photographer, say), noting its grain, the kind of developer, and the like. Regardless of how this I-advertance varies, the experience is a continuous consciousing of a physical thing (presentationally given) as a picture (representationally depicting my wife) of my wife.

A similar complex act reveals the same variational I-advertance, while the consciousing remains the same. For instance, while drinking a glass of beer and disliking its flavor, I can advert to the taste itself, saying 'This beer tastes "green."' Or, I can advert to the disliking, saying, 'I don't like "green" beer.' I find, on reflection, that in some of my mental processes I am livingly busied with and attentive to their respective objects, that this attentiveness can vary and furthermore that whether I advert to one or another object or aspect depends upon a complex set of considerations. What 'motivates' one or another focalizing depends upon my own biographical situation generally, and on my specific project at hand in particular (whether I am a professional photographer, an interested amateur, or just concerned to have a 'good' picture). Ultimately, as Schutz points out.[36] what I attend to now and then, here or there, will depend upon my plan of life, and more particularly on the complicated texture of choices, decisions, and projects I make every day in light of that plan, and even more immediate ones.

Thus, reflection discloses not only mental processes of many different kinds, but also different degrees of I-advertance ranging from full, 'wide-awake' attentiveness, through more or less marginal attentiveness, to a lack of any such advertance at all. The latter, as indicated, falls into three classes. (1) There are consciousings with whose objects I once was busied (volitionally, memorially, perceptually, etc.), but am no longer, though I might 'reawaken' them for one or another reason (thus, I was listening to the radio, then turned to my writing, and during its course the radio's noises slowly crept into my awareness forcing me to advert to it, say, angrily). (2) A second class are those processes with whose objects I have as yet not been attentive to, but may now become so (for instance, I might never before have been explicitly attentive to the slightly fuzzy aspect of distantly seen things, and now that I am, I go to the optometrist for tests and possibly to be fitted with glasses). Finally (3), there are consciousings to whose objects I cannot be actively attentive, and in whose noetic stream I cannot 'live' or be engaged. The most obvious of the latter are the impressional, retentive, and protentive phases of inner-time consciousness in their subtle moment-by-moment flux. Nevertheless, it is equally obvious that I who reflect can and clearly have already reflectively apprehended all these cases—which is, in a sense, but another instance of the necessity for keeping *reflecting* rigorously distinct from what is *reflected-on.*[37] I am able to reflect on inner-time consciousness, to explicate its features, and so on, but this in no way means that I, the reflective philosopher, 'live in' that noetic stream or am actively busied with their noematic objects.

The Self.

Continuing briefly, I also begin to observe that *the 'I' on which I reflect is itself experienced by me;* that it has and continues to develop typical ways of doing, thinking, and being; that it has and develops habitualities, has its own specific history; and, finally, that it appears, through the multiplicity of mental processes by which it is cognizant of objects, as self-identical and continuing. I note, however, that *this is strictly a matter of experience:* that is, these critical reflective observations are *not metaphysical interpretations,* so long as I sustain my disengagement and neutrality. Thus, whether the 'ego,' 'self,' or 'subject' *really is* a self-identical, self-subsistent substance is not at all within the range of my present concerns as critical philosopher. Rather, my interest here is *solely in making thematic the operative dimensions of 'self' in so far as and only in so far as it experiences itself,* in the various ways in which this occurs. This is in no way to deny that there are metaphysical or ontological issues here, as elsewhere; it is only to stress that such concerns are not those immediately relevant to the task of criticism.

Continuing my reflection, I (you) find that this 'I' is livingly present as described, has typicalities and habitualities, interests, concerns, values, goals, and some form, however vague, of a plan of life, or experiences itself as in some way purposive and in the process of growth. In a sense, the self has a unique tripartite status for itself.[38] First, this 'I' is aware of the world, others, and objects (including its own body), by means of its own consciousings, and in various ways: in actional modes of valuing, wishing, emoting, striving, worshiping, and also in modes of knowing, etc. It develops not only a stock of knowledge in the sense mentioned, but also various 'moods,' 'attitudes,' 'styles of thinking,' and the like. Second, the self (which is always *my* self) is disclosed, as it were, as 'living in' the consiousings mentioned, directed intentively to their respective noemata. It seems as if it 'inhabits' its own mental life not unlike mental life 'enacts' and 'is embodied by' its own animate organism. At the same time, 'inhabiting' its own mental life, it also is subject to the peculiar traits and processes of that specific consciousness, as can be made explicit when I consider that there are moments when I become quite upset at the 'way my mind works' (or, does not 'work') as regards some problem, or the way I can be quite delighted that my mind functions so well sometimes—as if I were but a witness to its operations (as is sometimes reported by creative artists, or even scientists, for example). In short, it is reflectively evident that *I am not identical with my mental life;* I in a sense 'have' it, but am simultaneously (even, dialectically) 'had' by it.

A third character of self also stands out: not only are there the kinds of 'cross-transversal syntheses' mentioned concerning inner-time consciousness, by virtue of which one can legitimately speak of consciousness as *self-consciousness,* but also *'I' am aware of myself* in many other ways. I can remind myself to do something, be angry with myself, feel embarrassed over my actions, love or hate myself, disappoint myself, be in wonder over myself, and even (most intriguing), become awakened to myself or discover me to myself in that remarkable experience Spiegelberg calls the "I-am-me experience."[39] Indeed, there is much that is attractive in the suggestion that this *I-who-reflects* on this *I-who-lives* in consiousings, is precisely this third stratum of self.

It is clear that this I-presence in consiousings, by virtue of which Husserl calls such processes 'acts' in the strict sense, is a highly stratified, subtle, and fugitive affair indeed. It seems clear, too, that at least the features indicated do characterize this elusive and problematic phenomenon.[40] But more of this in the next chapter.

Positionality and Objective Sense.

There are other operative and thematic strata that should be noted, if only briefly. The way in which 'I' can alter my attention as regards an object shows a correlative noematic distinction. In any act, the self is busied with some object, X, having such and such determinations; the object thus attended to has a certain *'objective sense'* for the self. But, in as much as the self's attentiveness can shift from the object, X, to one of its determinations (from the wine to its color), while all along intending the object, X, it is necessary to say that the *'objective sense' of the specific attentional focus* is not exactly the same as the *'objective sense' of the total intention.* Thus, while attentively focused on 'The victor at the battle of Jena,' or 'The vanquished at Waterloo,' the *explicit objective sense* of the attentional focus may vary while the intended object as a whole (the sense of the total intention) remains the same. The former varies, but all along it is 'Napoleon' who is intended as the object, X, having those explicitly focused senses. In James' terms, the 'object' (Napoleon) can remain the same while the 'topic' (victor at Jena) can vary. Which specific objective sense (topic) is explicit at any time, finally, depends on the self—its concerns, interests, plans, or, more generally, what is *relevant* at the time.

The noematic correlate, then, has a *specific relativity* to the noetic intending. As the noesis varies, the explicit objective sense also varies, even when the total object (or the coherent systematic unity of noemata, as Gurwitsch puts it) remains the same. In terms used earlier, the self, by varying its attentional focus, *objectivates* different noematic senses. Hence, I cannot speak simply of a consciousness of . . .' (wine, Napoleon, etc.), but must distinguish between various modes in which the noematic object is intended (Napoleon intended *as* 'husband of Josephine,' or *as* 'victor at Jena'). In still different terms, I must *distinguish between the object-which is intended* (the object, X) *and the object-as it is intended* (the explicitly focused object-determination).

But when I objectivate this or that specific determination or quality of an object—for instance, when I turn to Napoleon *as* victor at Jena—my objectivating is also, I grasp reflectively, a *thematizing* of that determination. I objectivate the *object-as,* as opposed to the *object-which* (which I may also objectivate, of course). Or, through attentional focusing, I make this specific objective sense *explicit,* and this thematizing can and is done in a variety of modes. Thus, I can advert to (thematize) it cognitively (e.g., being concerned with historical research pure and simple), valuationally (I might think it a fine or an evil circumstance), or emotively (I like, dislike, am unhappy, or perhaps delighted), and so on. My attentional focusing can vary in its specific mode, and correlatively what is thereby focused or thematized also varies— while all along the total noema, the object-which, remains the same.

In different terms, while James' distinction between object and topic seems correct so far as it goes, it does not allow for making the much more exact distinctions reflection shows must be made. Beyond this, I find an evident difference between simply believing in the affair in respect of this or that quality, positively believing it on the basis of sound evidence, disbelieving or even doubting it; and, on the other hand, liking, or disliking it, positively or negatively valuing it, wanting it, and so on.

There are two general distinctions that can thus be made, both noetically and noematically, which serve to clarify this situation: (1) my advertance to a noematic correlate in one or another mode of belief (ranging from simple taken-for-granted and unquestioned acceptance, to positive disbelief); (2) my advertance to it in one or another mode of valuation, volition, or emotion (positive, negative, or relative neutrality—such as when I say 'I don't care one way or the other'). These two modes of intending are, it is clear, ways of 'taking a position' toward the noematic correlate, or, in Husserl's terms, of *positionality.* The first mode can be called, with Hume, 'belief,' or in Husserl's more general term, *'doxic'* (from the Greek, *doxa*). The second mode may be called 'feeling' (valuative, emotive, or volitional); but since that term is so ambiguous and vague, it might better be termed, with Husserl, *'non-doxic,'*[41] or (to avoid the negative, which can be misleading), *sentic.*

Both doxic and sentic modalities are *noetic* positionalities, ways of 'taking-positions-toward' the intended object. If the self, say, positively believes that Napoleon was the victor at Jena, then it is reflectively evident that the self posits the *object-as* intended ('victor at Jena') as *positively existent,* and posits the *object-which* is intended ('Napoleon') as also existent *as intended* explicitly (as existent, at least, as the victor at Jena).

I may also, obviously, like or dislike this fact at the same time as I positively believe it. Suppose that I like it; then, in addition to the doxic positionality (with its specific modality, 'positive belief,' and its noematic correlate, 'positive existence as intended'), there is also the *sentic positionality* of liking the fact, and it, too, has its specific modality (i.e., 'liking' with its correlate 'really good *as* intended sentically'). If the *noetic side* is either doxic or sentic (or, as is usual, both), the *noematic side* may be termed the *specific thetic quality* (posited *as* existent, *as* doubtful, *as* probable, etc.; posited *as* good, *as* beautiful or ugly, *as* desirable, etc.). Hence, *the two simultaneous intendings, sentic and doxic* (an insight Brentano also had), *have the same intended object, but differ in respect of their specific positionalities and correlative thetic qualities.* The obvious lesson of this is, simply, 'experiencing an object' is plainly a gross characterization. Moreover, wherever one finds it evidently possible imaginatively to vary one component without altering the other, as we did many times already, then one is confronted with evident eidetic differences.

Another, more simple example will help here. Something can be experienced sentically or doxically (or both) in a variety of ways: I can visually perceive the apple, taste it, smell it, touch it; I can remember it (as seen, tasted, smelled, etc.), expect it, or imagine it (again, in a variety of ways). Other affairs cannot be sense perceptually given, but only given or presented in reflection (for instance, my own mental life); or only in a specific kind of cognition (for instance, numbers); or by using them (for instance, hammers *as* tools for hammering nails); and so on. In other words, the various, practically infinite number of objects with which I deal or can deal in the course of my life are given (presented, encountered, experienced, or intended) in many different ways. Designating this feature the 'mode of givenness' *(Gegebenheitsweise)* of the particular affair or determination of it, Husserl points out that this mode is *strictly correlative to the self's objectivations:* seeing the ashtray visually, I can then turn to a touching of it to determine if it has a chip on it, or whether what seems a chip is due only to the way the light shines on it. When I do thus objectivate, everything thus far said about intentiveness holds, but the mode in which the ashtray is experienced or given varies.

Thus, through my reflective explicating, I note that the thetic quality, the objective sense, and the mode of givenness are evidently distinguishable but inseparable components of the noema, and can be objectivated. This objectivation, explication, description, and analysis is not normally done by me. But what reflection reveals as different components can be attended to even in my usual affairs to some extent: a sketch artist will explicitly focalize the mode of givenness; someone interested in art will sometimes objectivate the thetic quality of a painting correlated to his sentic positing ('I like it because of . . .'). Just so, I will momentarily focus the specific objective sense of an intended object when, say, something in my environs conflicts with what I thought I really saw ('That was not a man, but only a tree limb which looked like a man'). But these objectivatings are not critical in the sense required of critical philosophy. Only critical phenomenological reflection takes as part of its unique task the systematic, sustained thematizing of these operative dimensions of *this or any possible act or process of consciousness,* seeking what is *eidetic* as regards the essential *type* of process and correlated noema.

Further details could and should be drawn out, but what has been done thus far seems adequate here. Not being mere curators of mental life, though, it is necessary to assess the significance of our findings and draw some general conclusions.

Review: Stratification and Foundedness.

What stands out above all is that even the simplest psychic process in its individual temporal phases is a fundamental *set of complexities,* which have different dimensions. Every single phase of every possible consciousing whatever is (1) a noetic-noematic correlation, shows (2) a reciprocal interlacing of temporal phases constituting the noesis as a phase in a unitary stream of other systematically interconnected phases, has (3) a complexity of intended objects, both immanent (other phases of the same mental life) and transcendent (things 'other than' the stream of phases), has (4) a multiplicity of primary and secondary transcendent objects. The noetic correlate is also complex in that it shows (5) a diversity of strata—doxic and sentic positionalities, active (attentional focusings) and operative (implicit) dimensions, and a complexity of temporal and meaning syntheses. Furthermore, (6) the noematic correlate shows the complex structures of inner and outer horizons, thetic qualities, modes of givenness, and objective senses (object-which is intended and object-as intended). In general, these and other dimensions not mentioned here, are *all included in the generative concept of intentionality.*

Beyond these prominences on this roughly drawn map, we were also obliged to make numerous methodological markings—guides, as it were, for reading the map. Principal among these are rigorously adopted disengagement and neutrality; the effort, reflectively, to explicate (thematize or objectivate) the implicit or operative strata of human life generally and its many engagements, and mental life in particular; and finally the imaginative variation practiced to enable each of us to 'see for himself' the lay of the land— the eidetic possibilities and impossibilities pertaining to consciousings as such. At every point, the prominences found, and the markings both leading to and disclosing those prominences, are two sides of the same coin: criticism or phenomenological exploration of foundations.

One significant aspect of this compounded complexity was only hinted at, however, and to fill out even the barest of outlines, it is essential to bring this to explicit attention. Several times it was pointed out that every consciousing is *stratified;* to say that is to insist that reflection discloses not only *different levels* of consciousings but that there are important relations among them, which can and must be specified if we are to understand critical philosophy in its proper sense.

I (and you) reflectively grasped an evident distinction between acts in the strict sense and merely operative consciousings. The former stand out from a background comprised of the latter. Thus, when I am visually busied with seeing the house, the whole series of complexities mentioned are not at the focus of my attention. I see the house, and the rest is only operative; the house I see stands out from a background of implicit features. I could, if either I chose or my circumstances obliged me, advert to one or another of these operative features: to the color, the value, the wish to sell; or, as the case may be, to my headache; or something else. That there are such operatively ongoing components of the experience can be readily grasped, say in the case of a headache: while writing, for instance, my attention is directed to the ideas to be expressed, the words best suited to say them, and so on; but slowly, my aching head begins to creep into my attention, increasingly demanding my advertance and that I do something about it (such as take an aspirin). Now, suppose I do turn to it, dislikingly. When I do, reflection shows that the headache did not just begin when I adverted to it, but rather that it was going on all along, only I did not pay attention to it. My advertance to it is such that the headache has the sense for me of 'having already been going on, even though I did not pay attention to it' (or, perhaps, attended to only marginally, and then more focally).

Or, *quite in general, all such active advertances emerge from, refer to, and are, in Husserl's term, 'founded on' the already ongoing operative processes of consciousness.* I could not possibly advert to a headache unless *some* kind of 'awareness' (operative consciousing) of it were already ongoing, and when I do so advert, it has the sense of having already been there. Active attentional focusing does not create its objects, but, as it were, receives them ready-made from the lower, 'founding,' stratum of the process in question; and phenomenological analysis is this process of 'unfolding' these 'layers' of consciousings. The various strata of consciousness are related to one another in the relation of "foundedness" *(Fundierung),* and with certain strata there is a relation of 'mutual foundedness' (for example, the color and extension of a material thing; or, as might be argued, the relation of consciousness and body, where one 'embodies' and the other 'enacts').

Or, consider another case in point—say, a photograph in the newspaper of the president kissing a baby. There is a presentive sensory consciousing of the picture and a representive consciousing of the president kissing a baby, where the representive consciousing is necessarily founded on the presentive consciousing. That is, there is clearly a *sui generis* relationship (noted already by Brentano) of foundedness here: *a priori,* there can be a representive consciousness only on the basis (foundation) of the presentive consciousness of the picture as a depiction. And the latter is itself founded on an even lower or founding stratum: that is, a sensory perceiving of the physical stuff (paper, ink, specific configurations, etc.)—such that none of the above is at all possible except on the basis of the latter.

A further and quite important instance of the founding-founded relation must be mentioned. Suppose I consider a specific sentic positionality: say, liking the house (or, loving my wife, disliking totalitarianism, desiring to live in a different part of the country, striving to climb a mountain, etc.). *Universally, such sentic positionalities are essentially higher-level or founded strata: they are necessarily founded on doxic positionalities, ultimately, in the sense that there cannot possibly be sentic acts without doxic ones, whereas the latter do not, in the fundamental strata, require the former.* (I may judge, a doxic positionality, on the basis of a liking; but that liking itself is founded on a more fundamental doxic positionality.) In general, I cannot like something that I do not, *in some modality, believe* in (if only in what Husserl calls the 'proto-doxic' modality, that is, simply accepting something as what it presents itself to be without question, but also without positively affirming it). To desire, love, hate, and the like (anything at all), is *already* to posit or accept (or doubt, deny) it as existent, in some modality. The same holds, it seems reflectively evident, throughout the entire range of consciousness and its objects.

Hence, *the fundamental principle defining the stratification of every noetic-noematic correlation is that of foundedness.* If this is so, *there is a strictly connected methodological demand on critical thinking.* If the thing to be investigated displays a specific structure, then one is obliged to remain rigorously faithful to that structure itself and impose nothing on it in his inquiry. More particularly, if a specific experience shows, on descriptive explication, the structure of founding-founded strata, *then one must always inquire into the founding stratum first* before any sense can be made of that stratum founded on it. The methodological principle, thus, has two formulations.

First, in general, one's method must always conform to the actual structures of the phenomenon being investigated, reading nothing else into it; thus the method of studying consciousness must conform to the character, stratification, and eidetic features of consciousness itself as disclosed in reflective explication. Second, *descriptive explication* is the first method to be used, and is that method which detects the lay of the land (like Hume's 'mental geography'), its various components, levels (like Kant's 'dissection'), functions, prominences, and so on. But that 'laying-out' (descriptive explication) is only the *first* stage of critical inquiry, and must be completed by another. Specifically, as now appears plain from the foregoing, *what has been explicated must be analyzed,* where 'analysis' means *strictly the inquiry into the founding-founded relations among the explicated strata of whatever is in question.* To analyze, in the critical-phenomenological sense, is to objectivate the lower (founding) strata *to the roots,* all the while making explicit how the various strata specifically interlace and interconnect (a method Husserl sometimes calls the 'zig-zag').

This discussion brings up a final point, first made quite early in this study. How does it happen, it was asked, that objects of any particular type have the sense they have been described as having? For instance, some objects have the sense, 'other human beings,' while others do not have that sense, but rather that of 'physical thing,' 'animate being,' 'number,' 'art object,' and so on. Since these objects descriptively disclose such meanings (and these meanings or senses are far more complex than this), *for or through consciousness,* there is a significant methodological demand here, too. By explicating the context of meanings a particular type of object has for and through consciousness, the critical philosopher has before him a crucial set of *'clues' (Leitfaden),*[42] which 'point back' *(zuwenden)* to the various typical sets or modes of consciousings having that specific type of object as their noematic correlates. *The intended object functions as a clue to the synthetic processes which intend it, and tracing out the kinds of syntheses we have mentioned* (and others besides) *is what is strictly meant by phenomenological 'constitution.'* When we earlier discussed sense perception, we took as our 'clue' the house itself as seen from the front, and from there, after unraveling some of the complexity of the set of noematic correlates, moved back to the specific types of noeses that had as their specific intended object that house as 'the same.'

It thus happens that several methods are to be added to the battery of critical methods we have already been using: that of 'analysis,' and of 'clues.' Still further methods are found to be necessary, but it is not possible to mention them here. Enough has been indicated, however, to show *a basic order of inquiry* generally, one which is not imposed from without, but is, rather, *derived from and grounded in* the materials themselves to be studied. If we take any intended object whatever, we find that it leads back to a great variety of actual and possible intendings of it.

From this, we can say that, first, *we should investigate all possible intendings of the object as 'the same,' those that are the most originary consciousings of it.* The possible modes of originary consciousings and their noematic correlates must be explicated and analyzed prior to the modes of non-originary, representive, and non-presentive consciousings, along with their respective noematic correlates. Second, *the founding strata must be analyzed before the founded ones,* since the latter presuppose the former. Third, since acts (attentional focusings by self) are possible only by their standing out from the milieu of *operative consciousings,* the latter *need to be investigated before acts in the strict sense.*

The order of inquiry is, then, a kind of *regressive* one (which might well have been the sense of Husserl's use of the term 'reduction'), where *'regressive' is defined by the phenomenon of foundedness.* Precisely this regressive explication and analysis is what is meant by 'constitutive analysis,' and that, in turn, is the meaning of what Husserl calls *"genetic phenomenology."* It must be emphasized again that such analysis moves through all the various strata, dimensions, aspects, features, and so on, we ourselves (and others as well) have discovered thus far. It must also be stressed unambiguously, because the point has so frequently been distorted and generally confused, *that 'constitution' in critical philosophy in no sense whatever means 'creation'*—as if consciousness literally gave birth to its objects. There is a perfectly proper place for the concept of creation, and that is precisely where it is actually found— in such activities as art, religion, speculative philosophy, statesmanship, literature, and other such affairs.

We thus can reach some understanding of what it means to demand, with Descartes, Hume, Kant, Husserl, and others, a rigorously grounded science of foundations—criticism in its deepest meaning. The demand on thinking is nothing short of 'going to the roots'; but the demand carries with it an equally radical responsibility—to the 'phenomena themselves' first of all, but also to one's own philosophical, socio-historical, and life-worldly milieux as well. In the final chapter of this study, therefore, we must weigh carefully the sense of philosophy itself, not alone in its critical dimensions, but in its critical locus in the life of man generally.

4

The Exigency for Transcendental Philosophy

"But there must be an end to this:
a sharp end and clean silence: a
steep and most serious withdrawal:
a new and more succinct beginning
. . . Nor may this be lightly undertaken: not lightly, nor easily by any
means: nor by any hope 'successfully.' "

James Agee,
Let Us Now Praise Famous Men

"All life," Husserl wrote, "is taking a position, and all
taking a position is subject to a must."[1] That "must" is
nothing short of the demand—inherent to life and especially
to the life of thought from which no human being is exempt
—to open one's "positions" to critical study, whether by
oneself or by another. Being human inextricably engages
one in 'taking a stand,' making up one's mind, choosing
among alternatives. Thus criticism is demanded. And criticism is, in essence, the serious effort to describe, explicate,
analyze and assess, in the light of all available and the
best possible evidence, the texture of every actual and pos-

sible position-taking. This undertaking is not something to be taken lightly, nor is it an easy calling. But the stakes are high in any life, for as Ortega y Gasset emphatically reminds us,

> Life is fired at us point-blank. I have said it before: where and when we are born, or happen to find ourselves after we are born, there and then, like it or not, we must sink or swim . . . there is no escape: we have something to do or have to be doing something *always;* for this life that is given to us is not given us ready-made, but instead everyone of us has to make it for himself, each his own: the strangest and most confounding thing about this circumstance or world in which we have to live is the fact that within its inexorable circle or horizon it always presents us with a variety of possibilities for action, a variety in the face of which we are obliged to choose and hence to exercise our freedom.[2]

This having to choose and take a stand is not accidental, but essential to human life. We, of necessity, take positions, and therefore are enmeshed in the responsibility inherent to these positions and their consequences. All human life demands criticism, so that critical phenomenology is imperative.

To assist in developing this necessary critical attitude, I have tried to bring out as clearly as possible and with a minimum of overly technical jargon,[3] at least some of the necessary tools of criticism, and to show something of their actual use as regards the life-world, sensory perception, and consciousness. My hope has been to have provided a sensible and intelligible way into that undertaking, the many 'ways' which can lead to it, some of its historical background and the contemporary urgency for its careful working out, and a glimpse at some of the prominent terrain the phenomenological explorer must traverse in order to fulfill his mission as a genuinely critical philosopher. The issues of methodology were deliberately interlaced with these concrete issues and soundings, for the two can be only artificially divorced, and then only at the considerable risk of completely misunderstanding the central meaning and tasks of phenomenology.

The Problem of Transcendental Phenomenology: Preliminary Considerations.

Many of the leading notions of phenomenology have been treated here, to greater or lesser degrees. But one really important theme has been prominent by its almost complete absence. It is one which has proved to be most thorny, dividing philosophers into sometimes warring camps, having the antagonism usually found only among the mythic forces of primeval dieties. This theme concerns Husserl's distinction among different *levels* of phenomenological problematics—principally between 'psychological phenomenology' (or, sometimes, just 'phenomenology') and 'transcendental phenomenology.' He additionally wrote of an 'eidetic' level of phenomenology, which was conceived as applicable both to the psychological and the transcendental levels.

Husserl continually struggled to develop a correspondingly stratified system of epoches and reductions, but was never satisfied with his results and, indeed, was not always consistent in his usage of these notions. Nor have many of them been used with the same meanings by subsequent phenomenologists. The controversies continue, both as to methodology (some claiming as many as six or more different 'reductions,' others that the entire notion of 'method' has been grossly exaggerated), and as to the very sense of speaking of a transcendental level of problems (indeed, few have been willing to follow Husserl to the transcendental). I have tried to make it plain what sense it makes to speak of 'epoche' and 'reduction,' using terms that strike me as more intelligible in English and as carrying the most consistent meaning I find in the literature. The question of the 'transcendental' range of phenomenology has been especially complicated, however, by Husserl's repeated assertion that it is a transcendental 'idealism,' [4] but not like Kant's.

Just because of these controversies over the latter, which are serious to the *very sense and range of criticism*, I cannot hope to do more than make a few suggestions; I hope these will provide some guidelines for further thinking; I do not pretend to have laid the issues to rest. I must stress again, however, that what is at stake is no mere family squabble clamouring for public recognition; the stake is focused on the nature of philosophical criticism, wherever and whenever it may be found. I am reminded of one of Agee's wonderful aphorisms: "The tigers of wrath are wiser than the horses of instruction." [5] One learns little or nothing if he avoids the central tigers of his discipline or craft, even though remaining with the gentle, domesticated horses may seem safer. It is necessary, then, to enter the fray; not for me to pretend to instruct, which is for horses, but rather to take up the issues directly, inviting you to think through with me the sense of criticism and its demands on thinking.

Think back to the place where we mentioned the striking feature of human being;[6] that man experiences himself as being at once an object in the world among other objects and a worldly subject for whom these objects are at all objects. Two features of this dual status are compelling. First, I am a *subject who experiences myself as subject and as object;* whatever may or may not be said in other contexts, my experience is that way (and so, I claim, is yours). Thus, my own *status as object* is itself as much a matter of my experience (by which we now must understand intentiveness) as is my *status as subject.*

Second, the essential condition for the very possibility of experiencing and apprehending myself as *worldly* object and *worldly* subject is that this *experiencing and apprehending is necessarily at another level than* these worldly statuses. Now, call that 'other level' what you will, it is experienced as necessary and essential and, more, is already implicit in that dual status.

Descartes already had a glimpse of the eidetic necessity of another status, but he made two decisive errors in assessing the significance of this insight. If we look at these, we can advance our own understanding. (1) In analyzing the discovery of the *cogito, ergo sum,* he consistently viewed the 'ego' as *he-himself, that particular worldly man as worldly,* but considered it in abstraction, in respect only of his cognitive faculties primarily—i.e., thinking *(res cogitans)*. Hence, for Descartes, the ego is conceived as *one* of the two metaphysical *substances*. But the rub of this interpretation was simply that the domain of the *res cogitans* was somehow given the essentially absurd role of establishing the authenticity of the other, *equally mundane* piece of reality, the *res extensa*—thus, among other things, seriously compromising its status as a genuinely metaphysical substance. One *part* of a whole (Reality) was made to account for the whole, and that just will not stand up. As Husserl expresses it, Descartes' mistake was to have thought it possible to

> rescue a little *tag-end of the world*, as the sole unquestionable part of it for the philosophizing Ego, and that now the problem is to infer the rest of the world by rightly conducted arguments, according to principles innate in the ego. [7]

(2) The insoluable problem this presents seems to have been seen by Descartes, but his effort to get out of the impasse led to a second crucial error. The impasse, inherent to much traditional philosophy, can be put quite simply. Here I am, this particular man, living and thinking within the world I find before me at every moment. I know, when I stop and think, that all my knowing, perceiving, willing, and so on, goes on within me; all the distinguishing between genuine and deceptive experiences also goes on in me as part of what I call my thinking. Every truth, every object, every event, is something I myself experience in myself. The great problem is: How can I ever get outside myself? How can I ever, with evidence and certainty, legitimately believe that what I thus experience, know, believe, has *objectivity?* I am an object in the world, a status that Descartes believes can be doubted. But if so, what can possibly assure me that there is anything beyond this pure, encapsuled immanence?

Clearly seeing the impasse, Descartes tries to find a way out by appealing to *divine veracity;* but that effort just as clearly reinforces the sheer immanence and intensifies the encapsulation and impasse. To make that appeal, he is obliged to appeal to *his own immanent and innate ideas of* a perfect being (where the 'of' in no way suggests a conception of intentionality, however), and then, without the least criticism, to adopt the Scholastic distinction between formal and objective reality as the sole way of salvaging himself from the *aporia*. In the end, Descartes failed to recognize what is implicit in his apprehension of himself as both object and subject in the world. His effort to conceive the worldly *ego cogito* as a purely apodictic *axiom* from which to deduce the *res extensa*, not only obfuscated the ever present mundaneity of the ego, but also forced the equally and necessarily obscure move to God as that by whose divine benevolence alone could any guarantee of the ontological status of the *res extensa* be secured. By failing to see the eidetic necessity of a status other than worldly or mundane, and inherent in the very experienced duality of subject and object, Descartes failed to make the transcendental turn.

He thus remains in the absurd position of maintaining an ontology on the grounds of an essentially *psychological* basis, even though the mental steps of deduction and intuition that this ego performs have other than psychological meaning and status. By so conflating ontology and psychology, Descartes also seriously confused the sense of a genuine psychology. As Gurwitsch has shown in detail, most psychology after Descartes is worked out on an essentially Cartesian dualism. Despite his genuine and undeniable insights, therefore, two serious confusions ensue from his efforts, leading to deep misunderstandings of the sense of genuine criticism and psychology.

Psychology, Phenomenology, and Transcendental Phenomenology.

We are already familiar with two points. First, I (you) noticed that in the course of my normal living I am rarely attentive simply to one item, and then only for a few moments (or longer, depending on one's skill). In any case, the corresponding phenomenon is the *shift of attention, of focal interest*. Sometimes, my attention is solicited by my environs; other times, I voluntarily shift it, bringing into focus all manner of items.

But one such attentional shift is peculiar: instead of being immersed in and directed toward the objects of my experiences, I can and sometimes do *shift to myself.* This can occur in normal life in various ways, as we saw: I can 'think back' over something I once saw, over the feelings I had at the time, over other aspects of the now recollected circumstances, objects, and situation at the time. My 'thinking-back' is not synonymous with the recollecting but occurs, as it were, within it. Thus I might, while remembering my hometown nostalgically, stop and think back at my very nostalgia, wondering why I should feel that way about that town; or, I might, while remembering a feeling of dread once felt whenever I walked by a certain house, not only remember the dread and the house, but also think back ('think over') that dread itself, wondering whether, for instance, what I then felt was really dread or perhaps something like a child's anticipatory curiosity. This type of thinking-back is not the same thing as remembering, although it can certainly go within memory. Similarly, I can do the same as regards presently ongoing experiences: while viewing a painting, I might wonder what it is that makes me like or dislike it, where the 'thinking-back' is not the same thing as the present perceiving, although it can be simultaneous with it. Again, the same can go on as regards expected events or experiences: anticipating with joy that I shall soon see my friend, I stop and 'think over' my own feelings, or why I think I shall at that future time be 'joyful,' and so on. [8]

Such pauses to 'think back over' are not unfamiliar. They typically are focusings on myself in my individuality; and, although I know that with practice I can become better at this, it still involves all the difficulties of any self-observation and self-assessment generally. Such *pauses to 'think back over' are autobiographical,* referring to me, 'this man,' with all my own biographical situation, stock of knowledge at hand, particular habits, style, beliefs, and so on. In a way, there is nothing surprising about their occurrence, even though what I may thereby discover may well be surprising.

There is a second point with which we are also familiar—namely, what have been called the disengagement, neutrality, and the critical attitude. It seems obvious enough that these can go on at different levels, just as can the shifts of attention —and both seem correlated, in that they both vary as the themes or problems vary. The juror on a panel is asked to dissociate himself from, remain indifferent to, and have an open attitude toward everything except what directly is relevant to the issue at hand (as this is defined by the court). The medic in treating a disease is called on to dissociate himself from the concerns of his own 'normal' life as husband, father, citizen, etc., while doing his job. The physicist, legislator, teacher, and others, are similarly supposed to practice this kind of dissociation for the prevailing purposes at hand. Whether, or how well or poorly, this is done is quite another issue. Here, again, there is nothing surprising about such demands; they are a normal part of our usual taken-for-granted style of life in the social world.

But we also learned something else—namely, that these demands can be brought to bear on still different concerns, practiced with greater care and in a more sustained manner, for the purposes of the problems at hand. For instance, I could become interested in studying psychic life itself; in order to do so, I must again practice a kind of dissociation, a kind of indifference,[9] and an openness to whatever presents itself to me, for the special purposes I would then have (where such notions are strictly *methodological, not moral, ones*). Or, in order to differentiate the kind of thing involved in this, as opposed to the usual practice in the life-world generally, I shall speak here of a *systematic disregarding, refraining, and objectivity* as prerequisites for the study.

If I want to study psychical life, I may take my 'subject matter' from many places: myself, what I can learn from others in a variety of settings (clinical and otherwise), and groups (children, adults, students, etc.). In any case, I am called on in such an empirical endeavor to practice the kind of methodological demands mentioned. If, on the other hand, I want to study the "psychic" purely in itself, regardless of its real relations with other things around, then the demands are more stringent, and I must make a very specific shift of attentional focus: I must disregard those relations, for the present at least; I must refrain from allowing my own biographical situation to enter into the framework of the problematic (except as it is relevant, and established as such); and I must strive for observations that can be repeated by an indefinite number of other equally careful persons (objectivity).

Since I am in that case concerned with the psychic itself, and am therefore concerned to obtain the best available samples of it, then I must take my own mental life first of all. But, to distinguish this kind of thinking from that of everyday life, and from empirical observation of other persons generally, when I focus on my own actual psychic life itself (we may call this *introspection),* my concern is not with my own idiosyncratic situation (autobiography), nor with finding out about 'people' generally, but with what mental life, in fact, is.

If I thus become concerned, I can then notice, among other features, that my own mental life is presented to me as a reality, one among others, and that it has many complex real relations with other things presented to me as also real: my own body, physical things, cultural artifacts, values, and so on. In order to concentrate my introspective attention on just one problem at a time, I find I must do more than dissociate myself from, be indifferent to, and remain objective as regards what is specifically autobiographical. For I am not interested merely in the autobiography of myself, but in mental life as it actually is in the context of the actual surrounding world. My attention might then become focused on the normal functionings and structures of actual mental life, or it might be to focus on the deviations, abnormalities and the like.[10]

To carry out such a project properly, I must practice a rigorous methodology. Whatever I find, moreover, is a matter not only of gathering as much actual experiencing of mental lives as possible but also of introspecting as regards my own actual psychic life. More particularly, I must become an acute observer of my own actual mental life, whether my interest be in the 'normal' or the 'abnormal' course and structures of mental life.

If I am successful at doing this, I will have begun to develop a *phenomenological psychology,* and if I focus more especially on mental life itself, without regarding its connections with other realities, I will be on the way to developing a *'pure' internal* phenomenological psychology. My 'science,' then, will be a science of actualities, the most fundamental meaning of 'empirical.' My attentional shift was *from* the objects in the environs and my usual autobiographical thinkings-over, *to* mental life for its own sake, as observed wherever I can find it (normal or not); and *from* that *to* mental life regardless of its actual relations with other things, being concerned only with its various developmental functions, structures, faculties, or what have you.

Having made such shifts of attention, with their corresponding methodological demands, something else begins to appear as increasingly pressing. In my psychological inquiries, especially in the 'pure internal' sense (such as done by William James, for instance), I begin to notice certain constancies, for what I have been considering thus far has been taken simply as this or that specific mental life (and most immediately my own), whose actual and possible relations with other types of actualities have been systematically disregarded for the purposes of my psychology. But I notice the fact that *these specifics are also instances or examples of actual mental life as such.* Apprehending this is already to make an important advance beyond psychology, pure and simple. What I, in effect, apprehend is that my inquiry thus far is *essentially incomplete:* what, after all, is it in virtue of which a mental life is what it is? Of what is it an 'instance'? I realize that my initial project *stands in need* of further probing. Grasping this incompleteness is tantamount to grasping that every empirical science of actuality involves epistemic claims and presuppositions, that *these judgments and presuppositions themselves stand in need of being grounded*—which demand, I begin to see, is inherent to their very meaning. Still more fundamental considerations are called for, before I can fully understand what mental life is, much less how it relates to other affairs.

I thus find it necessary and natural to move a step further in my attentional shiftings of focus, concentrating now on these specifics themselves *as examples of a generic type,* 'actual mental life.' To bring my attention to bear on this, however, I now realize that other methods and systemic requirements are in order. For, if I have been taking certain matters for granted, and have apprehended the incompleteness of my efforts, which presupposed those matters, then it must be a positive requirement that I *no longer take them for granted.* I must focally attend to the best possible instance of mental life, the one to which I have the clearest and most direct access—and, as I have already seen as a psychologist, this is my own.

Remembering that I am no longer concerned with autobiography or psychology (empirical or 'pure'), I must rigorously refrain from simply accepting my own mental life as it presents itself, but must now take it as merely *one instance* of actual mental life as such. In order to make possible what I now recognize is a necessary further inquiry, I must not only disregard and dissociate, but *positively disengage myself from* my rootedness in, my engagement with, the entire framework of suppositions, beliefs, and theses taking 'the world' as 'really there.' While not denying or affirming this rudimentary thesis and rooted engagement in the world, I must 'step back from' it in order to view it and descriptively explicate it. Furthermore, it is no longer sufficient merely to refrain, but I must *rigorously neutralize* all such usual lifeworldly and empirically scientific concerns and presuppositions. And, most importantly, I must pursue scientific objectivity to its fullest extent; that is, I must adopt *a strictly critical attitude*—concentrating now on explication, analysis, and assessment of actual mental life as such.

In short, my concerns must become *philosophical,* focused on the foundational presuppositions of any actual mental life and worldly experience generally. To make these requirements and demands possible, I now find it imperative to *make another shift of attention,* now becoming *reflective in the strict sense*—that is, to focus on mental life and its processes as instances of generic types, in order to explicate what is *eidetically* necessary to the generic types themselves. That reflection must become *a strict imaginative variation,* and my concern must now be to do what has been outlined in the last two chapters, and more besides. By now, that is, I will have apprehended the eidetically necessary intentiveness, positionality, and the like, already noted.

I will, in different terms, have apprehended and explicated, if successful in my inquiry, the sense of myself as both object and subject in the world in which objects are at all objects. I will have developed not only an 'internal psychology' of mental life, but now a *strict philosophically critical phenomenology.* Having completed the inquiry into consciousness, I could then go on to pose other phenomenological problems: concerning the eidetic ways in which consciousness relates to its own animate organism, how the latter acquires the sense of being 'mine' (and hence is a genuine *Leib* and not just a *Körper);* how it happens that certain objects in my field of experience acquire the sense of being 'other human beings'; and even further problems. I would also be in a position to develop at least the beginnings of a theory of science, showing the ways in which the various scientific disciplines interact, interrelate, and so on, and articulate the sense of 'science' itself. In brief, I will have begun to develop a systematic conception of the totality of actual human life and the modes in which it is engaged, studied, thought about creatively and epistemically, and there develop a general philosophical anthropology.

But, as I now pause again and look over the results of such efforts, I find that *something is still not complete.* And, this incompleteness, though difficult to specifically locate as yet, seems genuinely *urgent.* For, if I have, after all, set out to give a *rigorous account,* then inherent in both terms is the *essential idea of ultimately grounded knowledge.* I notice that everything I have done thus far can be seen as a process of making explicit what is implicit, or that my reflections are a regressive uncovering of layer after layer of operative strata sedimented in the typicalities, habitualities, and stock of knowledge at hand at any moment of my life—and that this sort of 'archeological' uncovering is found as regards any actual mental life. My consciousings, furthermore, are all *positional* (doxically and sentically). My explications can then be seen as presuppositional thinking in the specific sense of the uncovering of the stratifications of positionalities inherent to every consciousing and its horizons. But I realize, too, that the project, as initially conceived, was one of developing a 'presuppositionless' philosophical criticism—the effort to explicate and examine every presupposition whatever, as the ideal towards which critical philosophy strives, according to its integral meaning.

This pause to look back over what has been accomplished, then, shows a striking incompleteness, not as regards the acknowledged sketchiness of the presentation, but that a still further layer of sense or presupposition, of thematic concern, has yet to be uncovered. This further level can be expressed in several ways.

The 'Disengagement' as Radical.

It is unquestionable that I can dissociate myself in the ways indicated. Just as medics, lawyers, jurors, clothing buyers, psychologists, so can I myself. Furthermore, just as this dissociation, as a methodological demand, can and does apply to a vast range of matters, depending upon the particular circumstances, so it can be practiced upon me myself. In the latter, even though there is really nothing surprising, since we do it a good deal already, there is yet something quite unusual. To dissociate is at once to ignore certain affairs and to focus attention on others, those which are specifically relevant to the task at hand. Similarly, as regards the psychological disregarding, some matters are ignored for the sake of focusing on others.

But in the case where *I reflect on myself* (in the philosophical sense), this specific *disengagement* is most unusual, for the disengaging is a 'stepping-back-from,' in order to focus on *myself.* But, (1) this stepping-back is a stepping-back *from myself,* my own mental life; (2) it is also *an action I myself engage in, something which I experience* and, by experiencing, experience something else—namely, myself. Hence, (3) I disengage from myself in order to engage myself in myself critically, and this constitutes a complex mode of experiencing and self-experiencing.

Without pretending to be able to unravel this apparent paradox, I can at least note the following. First, the *fact* is that this activity occurs, even in the cases of introspection and autobiography in everyday life. Second, the issue is not so much *how* such an action is possible as *what* can descriptively be found about this self-disengagement focusing on my self that would permit me to understand it, and thereby to account for it. To put the issue as one of finding the conditions for the possibility of disengagement would invariably lead to argumentation (in order for x, y must be posited, etc., regardless of whether there can ever be any object, 'y,' which is experienced or not, or found as an inherent component in every experience), but that argumentation itself would still have to be grounded in more than the formal validity of inference. Ultimately, all arguments must consist of *claims about* some state of affairs, and it is to the latter that I must turn if I would hope to account for this peculiar disengagement. Or, the question of 'conditions for the possibility of' can be answered only by, first of all, investigating the deeper layers of the affairs themselves—in the present instance, 'disengagement' of self in order to permit the self to view itself critically. What will make our results, if any, 'transcendental' is *not the argument* that only if x then y, but rather the disclosure of a deeper status of self and its consciousings, 'deeper' in the specific sense that everything else is founded on it while it is the founding stratum for everything else. The 'founding-founded' relation is a matter of the inherent sense or meaning of the affairs themselves; and sense or meaning is a matter of experience, of the self's experience. If there is not this kind of experiential ground, then one cannot speak of 'transcendental' anything except in the most empty of formalistic senses.

Husserl sometimes speaks of this phenomenon of disengagement as involving a "splitting of the Ego [*Ich*]: the phenomenological Ego establishes itself as *'disinterested onlooker,'* above the naively interested Ego." [11] When I disengage or become 'disinterested,' I in effect 'split' myself up into the types of Ego mentioned. This seems to me a most unfortunate way of putting it, for it invites all manner of irrelevant interpretations: from the view that there must be two, three, or four egos (as if phenomenological criticism necessitated the psychosis of multiple personality), to the view that the self (Ego) is a kind of schizophrenic (one being 'usual' and the other 'philosophical.')

Still, it is always necessary to see beneath the sometimes unhappy formulations of philosophers to the point at which they are driving. And what Husserl here expresses, though in a way easy to misunderstand, is something correct and fundamental, I think, judging from my own reflections. Allow me to put the same point in quite another way. I say something to my friend, and he says that that is not at all like me. I stop and think, and then say, 'I guess you're right, I didn't mean what you thought, but rather. . . .' Now, clearly, my saying the latter came after my stopping and thinking over; I dissociated myself from what I first said (I 'stepped back from' it in order to 'see' it), and then went on to say what I 'really' meant to say. 'I' did not suddenly become *two* selves, one who said the first and the other who thought and then said the second. Rather, *I am the same self all along,* but was able to 'step back' or dissociate—or better, *to 'distance' myself from what 'I' had said in order then to go on to say what 'I' (the same 'I' as before) 'really' meant to say.* Other examples could be given, but the point remains the same: although it is *as if* I 'split myself up,' *in truth* I do not. I merely do what is utterly unsurprising about all human conduct (until one stops to think about this itself!): I 'distance' myself from myself, and *this is the phenomenon upon which I must fasten.*

What, then, does happen? I am, quite frankly, not altogether sure (which should not surprise anyone), but I do have several suggestions, which take me to the second path.

Reflexivity: Self as Transcendental.

When I 'think over,' introspect, or reflect, it is the same, self-identical 'I' who do these—a judgment I (the same 'I') make on the basis of my own reflection on the matter of 'distancing' or 'disengagement.' It is not something I conclude on the basis of argument, but something I reflectively apprehend (experience) with evidence, in the specific sense developed in the last chapter. I 'distance' myself: that is, I 'step back from' and 'view' something—myself—with one or another specific thematic concern, as we saw (autobiographical, psychological, phenomenological). *This distancing or stepping-back is itself something that goes on; it is itself a reflective experiencing of something: myself.* What is this 'something' that 'reflective stepping-back' shows? I ask, not how is reflection possible, but *what is this reflection itself, at whatever level it is practiced?* One need not focus just on phenomenological reflection proper: *any possible type of 'distancing'* must show, as an exemplification of a generic type, the eidetic features for which I seek.

Having clarified the issue somewhat, I now offer what may well be a rather unsatisfactory suggestion (one piece at a time for the tigers to gnaw upon). I cannot simply be an object in the world; that is already to assume for myself the status of a subject for whom any object (including myself) is object: for something to 'stand over against' *(Gegen-stand; ob-jectum)* is for it to stand over against a something or other (call it 'self' or 'subject,' or whatever) *for whom* it 'stands there.' I experience myself as both object and subject for whom objects are at all objects. This we saw. But that is an *essentially incomplete* descriptive explication. For, *I am aware* (I experience, I am intentively cognizant) *of myself as both object and subject.* This feature is unique: it exhibits a *reflexivity status of self* that has not been hitherto explicit. To note that I am aware of

myself as having that dual status is implicitly itself a phenomenon that can be thematized and explicated. To focus
on it is to have before me something at another level than
either what I get by introspection or reflection: namely, that
reflexivity itself, that *very being-able-to-distance-myself-from-myself*
—and this is a *genuine phenomenon for study* on its own. But to
focus on this, as opposed to reflective consciousings, *is to
have made explicit another status of the same unitary being called
'I' or 'self.' That reflexive status, since it is apprehended as that by
virtue of which any possible reflection, introspection, or autobiographical
thinking-over is at all possible cannot, by eidetic necessity, be at the
same level or have the same status as the latter.*

If the self who 'thinks over,' introspects, or phenomenologically reflects is 'worldly,' then this other status of the same
self may be called 'transcendental.' The transcendental status
of self is that pertaining to the philosophically reflecting self;
the reflexivity of selfhood grounds that philosophical activity itself—
not to mention introspection and autobiography. To say that
the possibility of philosophical criticism is eidetic is not by
any means to suggest that it is necessarily actualized as regards every being properly called a 'self.' But it is an eidetic
possibility, and as such grounds every actualizing of philosophical reflection. The evidential apprehension of that ground is
a 'transcendental' apprehension or experience; its systematic
exploration is the thematic concern of transcendental phenomenology.

Allow me to try one further way of getting to this phenomenon. Again, much is at stake here. To be a subject
over against an object is for that object to be related to that
subject and vice versa. But in this relation, the subject is
related both to the object and to the relation itself; and the
same is true of the object. Thus, I see the tree, and this seeing of the tree is a noetic positionality related to the tree as
the noematic objective sense of the noetic seeing. One can
no more speak of the tree as not in principle seeable (or,
in this case, seen) than one can say wishes are horses. Seeings
are of objects as seen by the seeings. To speak of *consciousness as intentive to objects* (of whatever type) *is to characterize*

consciousness; it is an eidetic feature of consciousings universally. But this intentiveness is two-sided: it has its noetic and its noematic correlates, with all the complexities noted. To be sure, then, while this descriptively evident feature of consciousings can in no sense be characterized as a relation in any usual sense, it, nevertheless, can be called *a relation of its own kind.* It is not a 'relation,' in other words, which, like the 'theory of ideas,' surreptitiously smuggles in a kind of ontological realism—a position that some have tried to see in this unique relation. *Intentiveness is a sui generis type of relatedness,* a thesis in critical philosophy, including within itself its noematic correlate, the 'tree-as-seen,' and its noetic correlate, the 'seeing-of-the-tree.' But I must be extremely careful *not to reify* anything here—and consciousness *(Bewusstsein)* most of all. Consciousness is but a convenient substantival term referring to a concatenated system of consciousings, by and through which what we call 'I' or 'self' achieves cognizance of its environs, in many different ways, modes, positionalities, and so on. It is a 'something,' of course, this consciousness: namely, a temporally ongoing series of sedimented habitualities and typicalities of experiencings through which is built up a correlatively sedimented system of coherent, harmonious noemata. Hence, the substantival term, 'consciousness,' is not altogether improper so long as one is not misled into reifying it into a 'stuff.'

But none of this, not even the mentioned transversal intendings (retentive and protentive) of inner-time consciousings, *says one word about reflexivity,* about the self who thus philosophically apprehends and experiences himself and his multiple consciousings of world and himself. 'I' (you) reflectively observe that complex of intendings called inner-time consciousness; 'I' (you) view the concatenated system of intentive consciousings of objects and world, and the latter as intended. *Who is this 'I' who thus reflects, explicates, analyzes, and, in these specific modes, experiences himself?* What is this reflexivity by virtue of which that reflection is itself even possible, at whatever level and with respect to whichever thematic objects it may be brought to bear? Kierkegaard, I think, came as close as anyone to suggesting what is at stake here:

> . . . what is the self? The self is a relation which relates itself to its own self, or it is that in the relation that the relation relates itself to its own self; the self is not the relation but that the relation relates itself to its own self. . . . If . . . the relation relates itself to its own self, the relation is then the positive third term, and this is the self.[12]

Precisely that unique and uncanny phenomenon, I am suggesting, is itself something for critical philosophy to explore. To distinguish its task from both internal psychology and phenomenology, I interpret it as transcendental phenomenology, and thus find myself in full agreement with Husserl's repeated insistence that "a system of *phenomenological* disciplines" necessarily unfolds, "which treat correlative themes and are ultimately grounded, not on an axiom, *ego cogito,* but on an *all-embracing self-investigation.*"[13] What distinguishes these levels of investigation, to repeat, is strictly and only *the specific thematic concerns* prevailing at the time. This consequentially developed self-explication, carried out to its fullest extent and completion, is precisely transcendental phenomenology, having the form

> of a systematic egological science, an explication of my ego as subject of every possible cognition, and indeed with respect to every sense of what exists, wherewith the latter might be able to *have* a sense for me, the ego. This idealism is not a product of sportive argumentation, a prize to be won in the dialectical contest with 'realisms.' It is *sense-explication* achieved by *actual work,* an explication carried out as regards every type of existent ever conceivable by me, the ego, and specifically as regards the transcendency actually given to me beforehand through experience: Nature, culture, the world as a whole. But that signifies: systematic uncovering of the constituting intentionality itself. *The proof of this idealism is therefore phenomenology itself.*[14]

It must be added that this 'self-explication' refers ultimately to that *reflexivity* essential to selfhood. Hence, the 'idealism' to which Husserl refers is not at all a metaphysical stance. It is rather a descriptive methodological concept indicating that the completion of criticism is found in the subtle reaches of the 'I,' the self in its deepest levels as a 'relation which relates itself to its own self.' It should also be clear that to refer to 'self' by means of the substantival term is *not* equivalent to an explicit or covert reification: 'self' is no *thing*, no stuff or substance, but that reflexivity Kierkegaard refers to with a noun clause—'*that* the relation relates itself to its own self.'

If this suggestion about the thematics of transcendental phenomenology is at all sensible, several consequences follow, which I shall merely mention here. First, the conception of that critical discipline *must receive its sense,* as do all other philosophical (and other) disciplines, *from its specific 'subject matter,' its specific thematic concerns.* This means that transcendental phenomenology cannot be conceived merely as a critique of knowledge, but rather, and more broadly and deeply, as *a criticism of the total range of human experience with self-criticism as its foundational base.* Hence, absolutely everything found in human experience will also of necessity be found as essential themes in transcendental phenomenology. Similarly, whatever is problematic in human social life, empirical psychology, internal psychology, and phenomenology, will also be found at the transcendental level. *It is not a question of a metaphysical stance, but only of the completion of the sense, requirements, and tasks of criticism as regards the manifestly different levels of thematics.*

Second, there cannot be criticism without self-criticism; indeed, *criticism is necessarily self-criticism,* and in both senses: as a criticism of self, and as a criticism of transcendental phenomenology itself. Criticism essentially, as Husserl emphasizes,

leads back to criticism of transcendental-phenomenological knowledge (in the first place, criticism of transcendental experience[15]); and, owing to the essential reflexive relation of phenomenology to itself, this criticism also demands a criticism. In this connexion, however, there exist no endless regresses that are infected with difficulties of any kind (to say nothing of absurdities), despite the evident possibility of reiterable transcendental reflections and criticisms.[16]

There is no *regressus ad infinitum,* precisely because the essential feature of 'self' is its reflexivity. The criticism of 'reflection,' though reiterable (that is, the fact that *any* evident insight must be essentially repeatable, both by oneself and by others), and thus perchance circular, is by no means a vicious circle. Methodologically, reflection upon reflection does not lead to a still further reflection. The phenomenon of reflexivity is disclosed the very first time as that which is eidetic and foundational to any possible reflection.

The Exigence of Philosophy: Why Philosophize?

In his perceptive critique of modern culture, Marcel addresses himself directly to this question:

> What we have to do with, really, is a decisive option: the choice between being and not being. Today, however, we must recognize that it is possible for non-being to be preferred, possible also for it to wear the mask of being, and it is just such masquerades which the philosopher is in duty bound to denounce.[17]

In slightly different terms, the decisive option is between reason and unreason (criticism in its fullest sense and nihilism), and it is possible for men to choose unreason or to mask their unreason with the face of reason. It is quite possible for philosophy to be damned and nonphilosophy preferred, and yet for the latter to masquerade under the guise of the former. Marcel continues with two further remarks, which strike me as relevant to our present question. It is incontestable, he feels, that

> We are living in a world which seems to be founded on the refusal to reflect. It is the place of the philosopher, and perhaps his place only to attack this contemporary confusion, not in a presumptuous way certainly, not with any illusions about what the effect of his attack is likely to be, but with the feeling that here lies a duty from which he cannot withdraw himself without betraying his true mission.[18]

Obviously, Marcel's conception of the place and vocation of philosophy in the world is bound to get a philosopher into deep and troubled waters. But the risks need to be carefully understood, where understanding itself requires the courage and stamina to withstand the dangers and to keep faith with that vocation:

> It follows from all this that the situation of the philosopher as he confronts our contemporary world is almost the most risky and exposed situation one can imagine. I do not merely mean that the philosopher may expect to pay for his rashness in the depths of some . . . prison. The danger is also, and perhaps above all, an inner one. It is very hard for the philosopher today to resist the temptation to flee, I will not say into the realm of science—for science, where it is truthfully pursued, retains even today all its value, all its dignity—but into the realm of some pretended science . . . [or] into mysticism. . . .[19]

For Marcel, as for Husserl,[20] the fate of philosophy and that of civilization are intimately bound together. Indeed, Husserl forcefully points out that the very ideas of the fulfilled human being, culture, and civilization in western history are deeply tied to the idea of philosophy.

Max Scheler once remarked that "in no other period of human knowledge has man ever become more problematic to himself than in our own days." And, Husserl insists in *Krisis,* if it is true that the very existence of man appears critical and problematic, this can only be because man has become unfaithful to that fundamental set of ideas of himself, his culture, history, and *polis,* which are intimately bound up with his fulfillment in genuine philosophical activity. *Philosophy in this sense is nothing short of radical criticism—* that is, transcendental phenomenology. Only by critically explicating and analyzing the founded-founding strata of the natural, the social, the human, consciousness—and, ultimately, self—can there be any hope of rescue from the obliterating confusions and agonizing torments of the current crises blasting out from every corner of the world.

Again, it is that masterful philosopher, Ortega, who expresses the exigency of philosophy with artful and impressive insight. Speaking, in his last work, of the way in which Roman culture became increasingly gross with luxuries and pleasures— literally stupified and hence stupid—he wrote:

> The capacity to take a stand within the self, to withdraw serenely into one's incorruptible depths,[21] was lost—as it

threatens to be lost in Europe if something is not done to prevent it. Nothing is talked about but action. The demagogues, impresarios of *alteración*,[22] who have already caused the death of several civilizations, harass men so that they shall not reflect, see to it that they are kept herded together in crowds[23] so that they cannot reconstruct their individuality in the one place where it can be reconstructed, which is in solitude. They cry down service to truth, and in its stead offer us: *myths.* And by all these means they succeed in throwing men into a passion, in putting them, between ardors and terrors, *beside,* that is, *outside of, themselves.* And clearly, since man is the animal that has succeeded in putting himself *inside himself* [*ensimismamiento*], when man is *beside himself* [*alteración*] his aspiration is to descend and he falls back into animality. Such is the spectacle—always the same—of every period in which pure action is defied.[24]

Most of these remarks speak for themselves: the crisis facing modern civilization is widespread and deeply rooted, both historically and structurally, in the tissue and fabric of our culture.

The Necessity for Radical Philosophical Thinking.

What is perhaps not so apparent, however, is the tie between these soundings and the sometimes thick thematics of this study. Perhaps the point can be made most directly by way of a contrast. It is unquestionable that critical philosophy as conceived here—transcendental phenomenology—is not the most common conception of philosophy or of criticism, at least in the Anglo-American community. More generally, of course, philosophy, however conceived, has yet to become an activity which is normally understood and accepted as a prerequisite for any educated man, as well as for the one whose profession is in the academic disciplines. However that may be, for better or worse the conception of philosophy as a rigorous science is not as yet at home today.

Typically, philosophy is conceived quite differently in Anglo-American philosophy. It can be said, without too much distortion, that A. J. Ayer's characterization captures the tenor and direction of this typical conception when he distinguishes between the pontiffs and the journeymen of philosophy.[25] The former are the princes of metaphysics, those who believe that it is possible to develop a total system of knowledge that encompasses the totality of 'what is' (Being, Reality, or what have you). The 'archpontiff' of the nineteenth century is Hegel; that of the twentieth is Heidegger, the 'high priest' of that strange and curious crew of anguished souls, the existentialists. In the end, for Ayer and other journeymen, the pontiffs are ultimately mystics, imaginative indulgers in literature, poetry, and other forms of philosophic vices. The journeyman has to remind himself that the history of philosophy is largely a parade of pontiffs anyway.

The journeymen have none of the pretensions of the pontiffs, and are far more modest in their understanding of their role. Essentially, says Ayer, the journeymen are really nothing but 'technicians,'

> Believing, as they do, that the only way to discover what the world is like is to form hypotheses and test them by observation, which is in fact the method of science, they are content to leave the scientist in full possession of the field of speculative knowledge. . . . The task of the philosopher . . . is rather to deal piecemeal with a special set of problems . . . [which are] in a broad sense semantic . . . [but more exactly] I think it better to resume their philosophical activities under the general heading of logical analysis.[26]

Their historical tradition is, as everyone knows, that of the British empiricists, principally Locke, Berkeley, Hume, Mill, and later, of Russell and Wittgenstein.

The journeyman is very fond of referring to Locke's "Epistle to the Reader" in his *An Essay Concerning Human Understanding:*

> but everyone must not hope to be a Boyle or a Sydenham: and in an age that produces such masters as the great Huygenius, and the incomparable Mr. Newton, with some others of that strain, it is ambition enough to be employed as an underlabourer in clearing the ground a little, and removing some of the rubbish that lies in the way of knowledge. . . .[27]

Finding this underlaborer role congenial to themselves, the journeymen set out to clear away that rubbish standing in the way of true knowledge—which is to say, science (if it is knowledge of 'the world') or logic (if it is 'language').

This rubbish, for latter-day laborers, consists largely of forms of misuse and abuse of language: confusions of things with words, vagueness, ambiguities, and a general abuse of the common tongue. Metaphysical pontiffs, specializing in such linguistic vageries, must then be exorcized, and logic is the prime instrument for this solemn task. Philosophy, then, is but "the piecemeal solution of logical or linguistic puzzles." [28] Hence, the philosopher is a kind of janitor in the hall of science.

Such a view and its variations (not everyone is as blunt as Ayer) have received severe criticisms,[29] just as the pontiffs have come in for their share of animated rebuttal. It is not my desire to enter this battlefield and engage, as Husserl remarked, in sportive argumentation. After all, every philosopher worth his salt knows full well the dangers of linguistic idols, just as he knows the corrolary trap of a cavalier and uncritical definition of his activities as 'myth' or 'nonsense.'

The basic problem with the common way of conceiving philosophy in the Anglo-American philosophical community is that it simply does not understand that such alternatives and oppositions are unwarrantably narrow, and that such sport does not get to the vital point: what is it, to think philosophically, whether as pontiff or as journeyman? And, as a necessary continuation of that, what is it that is demanded of *radical* philosophical thinking? We have already seen a good deal of what must be done in answering these questions. But a final comment is clearly in order to drive home the signal point with precision. To do this, it will be helpful to consider Locke himself, taking him at his own words, disregarding what he claims to have found, and concentrating solely on how he conceives his task and problems as a philosopher. His praise of Newton, Boyle, and the others, it turns out, while obviously as genuine as was his distrust of the abuses of some other philosophers, is hardly to the point.

Reading his "Epistle" and "Introduction" is as instructive as was our reading of Hume's "Preface." Whatever else may be said of Locke's *Essay,* he is unambiguously clear on several things. He conceives his task in such a way that the critical viewing by others of "like minds" is a positive demand. But these others, to be at all helpful in the undertaking, cannot take the *Essay* "upon trust from others," but must "make use of their own thoughts in reading" it (p. ix). Thus, Locke insists,

> For, though it be certain that there is nothing in this treatise of the truth whereof I am not fully persuaded, yet I consider myself as liable to mistakes as I can think thee; and know that this book must stand or fall with them; not by any opinion I have of it, but thy own. (p. x).

The first point, then, is identically the same as what was stressed as regards Descartes, Hume, and Kant: (1) one's philosophical thoughts stand in positive need of critical examination by others, who must patiently 'think along with' the philosopher; and (2) there is a decisive difference between (a) the *epistemic claims* made, and (b) the *confidence* with which the philosopher asserts them (and most, like Locke, are not shy on confidence).

Of course, it is quite true that neither Locke, Kant, nor Hume saw in this point much of methodological or epistemic significance. And, while Descartes did seem to see more to it, still it did not, in the end, come to have the importance that phenomenological criticism insists it must have. Namely, this invitation to others, and the distinction between the epistemic claim and one's confidence in his own insight leading to the claim, is *a fundamental principle of criticism:* every claim is at once epistemic (with all the strata we have delineated) and methodological (serves as a communicative guide for others). This means that the appeal to others is of *systemic significance,* and is an inherent component of every philosophical (every epistemic) activity whatsoever.

Locke goes on in his "Epistle" to state unambiguously what his project purports. Puzzled over some aspects of "a subject very remote from this," he and "five or six friends" could arrive at no satisfactory solution, and he notes that

it came into my thoughts, that we took a wrong course; and
that, before we set ourselves on inquiries of that nature, it was
necessary to examine our own abilities, and see what objects
our understanding were or were not fitted to deal with (p. x).

After railing, doubtless with good cause, against those who
abuse language and mistake vague terms for science (pp.
xii–xiii), Locke points out "that the taking away false foundations is not to the prejudice, but advantage of truth. . . ."
(p. xiii). Thus, one would naturally suppose that when Locke
goes on to say that it is "truth alone I seek" (p. xiv), he
means that *he, too, seeks the true foundations.* Clearing away the
brambles of false foundations can only mean that he seeks
to uncover the true ones. He goes on in the "Introduction"
to Chapter I of Book I to set out his project.

It is the "understanding that sets man above the rest of
sensible beings" (p. 1), and thus it forms a proper and
legitimate subject for inquiry. Besides, those who claim
knowledge do so on the basis of the functioning of the
"understanding"; hence, clearing away confusions and the
like positively requires a careful examination of this affair.
But,

The understanding, like the eye, whilst it makes us see and
perceive all other things, takes no notice of itself; and it requires
art and pains to set it at a distance, and make it its own
object (p. 1).

Only by getting clear about it, about the "origin, certainty,
and extent of human knowledge, together with the grounds
and degrees of belief, opinion, and assent" (p. 1), can knowledge of anything else be at all hoped for. Locke goes on to
specify this project, its methods, and his own hopes for it;
but what is vital for us has already been stated. Whatever
one may think of his results, there are three points of considerable importance for grasping the demands of critical
philosophy. (1) Locke's insight into the *necessary order for inquiry*
is one such demand: before one sets out to inquire into
anything else, it is necessary first of all "to examine our
own abilities," that is to turn to the "understanding" itself.
In our terms, the *fundamental task of philosophical thinking is
critical explication and analysis of consciousness.* (2) Locke insists

that while the understanding is actually at work it is like the eye: it "takes no notice of itself." But, unlike the eye, which cannot make its own seeing an object, *one can and must* make the understanding "its own object." To do this, it is necessary to "set it at a distance," a step that takes "art and pains," but can and must be done. In other words, to accomplish the critical task, *it is essential to disengage, neutralize, and sustain the critical attitude.* (3) The general aim of the *Essay* is to determine what the understanding is properly fitted to deal with. Ultimately, the project must conclude with a critical explication, analysis, and assessment of the mind itself, as Kant later saw.

Now, although Locke did not seem to appreciate the sense of his own emphatic points, the last shows clearly that *the self* which engages in critical explication and analysis *must have a status other than its status as geared toward the world.* Its mundaneity does not give the possibility for doing what Locke sets out to do; only by virtue of its *transcendental status* is such a project anything more than fanciful nonsense. To 'set at a distance' is an *experience,* whether Locke saw it or not—an action performed by the thinking self—and this 'distancing' is ultimately transcendental disengagement, neutrality, and criticism.

Concluding Remarks.

If Descartes, Locke, Hume, Kant, Brentano, James, and others are at all correct in their commonly shared, but rarely understood, insights regarding the fundamental task of philosophy and its methodological demands, then Husserl's claim that phenomenology brings this signal feature of western philosophy to its fruition must certainly command the respect of every philosopher. For, as I have tried to show, phenomenology *is* critical philosophy, now with established systemic and methodological foundations, and carried out with rigorous, intersubjectively verifiable insight. Inasmuch as phenomenology insists upon a rigorous examination of experience—no longer conceived narrowly—it is perfectly proper and necessary to characterize it *not only as 'transcendental idealism' but as a new empiricism,* so long as one knows whereof one speaks when using such labels. It is 'transcendental' because it is *foundational,* seeking to uncover and explicatively analyze the necessary presuppositions of every actual and possible object and process of consciousness, leading ultimately to the grounds for philosophical reflection itself (reflexivity). It is, therefore, also 'idealism' because, *as criticism,* it is obliged to turn to consciousness, to consciousings themselves as those acts and processes by and through which alone are objects of any and all types whatever at all presented, experienced, or in some manner made known. It is, finally, an 'empiricism' precisely because it insists that positing anything beyond all possible experience of any kind is sheer nonsense, and that it is to the 'things' of experience that one must ultimately appeal for all evidence and knowledge. But it is a 'new' empiricism, because 'experience' has been critically disclosed as manifestly richer and enormously more stratified and differentiated than any traditional empiricism understood it to be. And, I might add, it is properly and necessarily designated as *critical philosophy,* inasmuch as its fundamental concern lies in the explication, analysis, and assessment of every actual and possible experience, opinion, belief, value, attitude, activity—every mode of consciousing and every current and modulation of life whatever. And it does this with an explicitly developed and rigorously formulated and executed *battery of methods,* which are themselves systemic components of the very task of criticism itself.

Much, as I have often stated, has been left out of this study. Perhaps the most glaring lacunae are the almost complete absence of the themes of intersubjectivity and embodiment. My excuse for this is quite simply that they are so complex and difficult as to have required an unpardonably lengthy study. They figure so prominently in the literature, however, that one can easily find out their problematics for himself with little difficulty. Beyond this, it seemed to me that the themes of the life-world and perception are equally, if not more, important, and that the seminal works of Alfred Schutz and Aron Gurwitsch on these issues deserve to be better known than they are. As for the thematics of consciousness, I felt it essential to give at least some clues to the immense lay of this land as studied by Husserl (and made wonderfully clear by Dorion Cairns), for the theory of consciousness, especially in respect of its transcendental status, is fundamental to everything else.

My hope is to have done enough to permit and encourage the further study of the continent which the discipline of criticism focuses upon.

Epilogue

"We shall not cease from exploration
And the end of all our exploring
Will be to arrive where we started
And know the place for the first time."
T. S. Eliot,
Little Gidding *(Four Quartets)*

In one way or another, practically every work Husserl himself published was conceived by him as an 'introduction' to phenomenology. Continually plagued by the inordinate difficulties of bringing others into this rigorous, critical dimension of philosophy, he was also continually disappointed with his own efforts to introduce it. At one point he remarked, with some disenchantment, that, though phenomenology seeks to get beyond all the quarrelsome parries and thrusts infecting philosophy today, and to achieve objectively valid results in collaboration with an essentially indefinite number of other laborers,

> how could actual study and actual collaboration be possible, where there are so many philosophers and almost equally many philosophies? To be sure, we still have philosophical congresses. The philosophers meet, but, unfortunately, not the philosophies. The philosophies lack the unity of a mental space in which they might exist for and act on one another.[1]

In the light of the crisis in philosophy today, I can here offer but a small plea for that *solitude* of which Ortega so perceptively speaks in the passage quoted in the last chapter, and without which the disclosure of reflexivity simply becomes impossible. It is this solitude alone which can "break this enchanted circle of *alteración*, which hurries us from one folly to another."[2]

Philosophy is the quest for the truth that can alone free us *from* the bondage of the cave and *for* that self fulfillment which is potential for every human, each in his own way and according to the dictates of his own essential solitude. But if it cannot combat such follies, and philosophers cannot mutually engage in that dialogic criticism which is essential to the very sense and mission of the discipline, then I very much fear that Ortega's biting words will quickly become actually and terribly real: "in the world today a great thing is dying: it is truth. Without a certain margin of tranquility, truth succumbs."[3]

That solitude I have tried, in a perhaps cumbersome way, to present here is what alone permits the systematic regressive or reflexive withdrawal into one's own self and mental life. And that withdrawal, it seems to me, is what alone can make sense out of human life generally. For human life is nothing if it is not first and foremost selfhood—that strange and uncanny reflexive solitude that relates itself to its own self, and in so relating reflexively, inwardly relates to the other selves about him. This vision, alive at least since Herakleitos, is the primal source and theme of critical philosophy.

Philosophy in its critical discipline cannot tolerate what is hidden, unexamined, ulterior, and taken for granted. Its principle task is the explication of these, wherever they may be found. In this sense, critical philosophy is the *rationale* of every human engagement, seeking to make intelligible, explicit, and analytically clear, every dimension of human life, thought, and action, including itself—so far, obviously, as this ideal can be accomplished. As Natanson says, philosophy

is the critique of man's experience through a persistent effort to explore its foundational presuppositions, its claims to truth, its dreams of justice, and its moments of transcendence.[4]

But critical philosophy not only criticizes all claims and dimensions of human life, it also *seeks* foundations. Hence, it is essential that philosophers be *responsible* in their craft and discipline: *responsive* to the criticisms of others and themselves, and thus exhibiting *critical openness*—to their own folly as well as to the possibility of truth. Critical philosophy is the rigorous science of presuppositions: of beginnings, origins, or foundations. It is this reflexive character of critical dialogue, grounded both in the things being examined and in the dialogic responsibility to others mutually engaged in the quest, which uniquely characterizes the discipline of criticism. To the extent that reflexivity is the essential, transcendental epiphany of human being, critical philosophy is a fundamental fulfillment of that being.

As Husserl says, concluding his *Cartesian Meditations,*

The Delphic motto, "Know thyself!" has gained a new signification. Positive science is a science lost in the world. I must lose the world by epoche, in order to regain it by a universal self-examination. "Noli foras ire," says Augustine, "in te redi, in interiore homine habitat veritas."[5]

Notes and Bibliography

Prologue

1. The reference is to Principle I of Descartes' *Principles of Philosophy,* in: *The Philosophical Works of Descartes,* Haldane and Ross edition (New York: Dover Publications, Inc., 1955; by arrangement with Cambridge University Press, 1931), Vol. I, p. 219: *"That in order to examine into the truth, it is necessary once in one's life to doubt of all things, so far as this is possible."*

2. Edmund Husserl, *Cartesian Meditations,* tr. Dorion Cairns (The Hague: Martinus Nijhoff, 1960), p. 2. Hereafter referred to as *CM.*

3. See Maurice Merleau-Ponty, *Phenomenology of Perception,* tr. Colin Smith (New York: The Humanities Press, 1962), p. xiv.

4. See his *Man Against Humanity,* tr. G. S. Fraser (London: The Harvill Press Ltd., 1952), p. 48.

5. See his *Creative Fidelity,* tr. & intro. Robert Rosthal (New York: The Noonday Press, 1964), Ch. 2.

6. *The Philosophical Works of Descartes, op. cit.,* Vol. I, p. 139. The "Objections and Replies" are found in Vol. II.

7. *An Essay on Philosophical Method* (London: Oxford University Press, 1933), pp. 1–2.

8. Martin Heidegger, *Being and Time,* tr. John Macquarrie & Edward Robinson (New York: Harper & Row, 1962), pp. 211–14.

9. Herbert Spiegelberg, *The Phenomenological Movement: An Historical Introduction,* Phaenomenologica 5 & 6 (The Hague: Martinus Nijhoff, 1960), pp. 1–23.

10. Edmund Husserl, *Erfahrung und Urteil: Untersuchungen zur Genealogie der Logik,* Redigiert und herausgegeben von Ludwig Landgrebe (Prague, 1939; republished by Claassen Verlag, Hamburg, 3rd unaltered edition, 1964). Hereafter referred to as *EU.*

11. Husserl's training in mathematics, logic, and natural science (he received his doctorate in mathematics and had been one of Weierstrass' best students) naturally disposed him to explore the foundations of these, as well as questions of epistemology and methodology. While he did devote some efforts to questions of

ethics, the social world, history, and other topics, he did very little as regards aesthetics, religion, and other areas.

12. Thus, in *CM,* pp. 153–56, he insists that phenomenology must be rigorously scientific, in the most fundamental sense, and a *communal effort* grounded on "the intrinsically first being . . . [i.e.] transcendental intersubjectivity. . . ." (p. 156) This aim, we shall see, is of paramount importance for understanding the nature of criticism.

13. This has been contended, for instance, as regards Hegel, Peirce, and Brentano. See Spiegelberg's assessments, *op. cit.,* Vol. I, pp. 12–15, 17–19, and 27–49 respectively (also my Ch. 3, Some Historical Considerations: Franz Brentano); also pp. 98–101 (Meinong), 111–17 (James), 138–39 (Santayana), and 144–46 (Royce).

14. Dorion Cairns, "An Approach to Phenomenology," in *Essays in Memory of Edmund Husserl,* ed. Marvin Farber (Cambridge: Harvard University Press, 1940), p. 4. Unfortunately, this important book has been out of print for a long while.

15. Dorion Cairns, *op. cit.,* pp. 6–7.

Chapter 1: Ways to Phenomenology

1. Theodore Spencer, "The Enlistment," in *An Act of Life* (Cambridge: Harvard University Press, 1944), pp. 42–43.

2. Wallace Stevens, "The Man With the Blue Guitar," in *Poems By Wallace Stevens,* sel. & intro. Samuel French Morse (New York: Vintage Books, Random House, 1947, 1954), pp. 73, 79.

3. See Alfred Schutz, "On Multiple Realities," in his *Collected Papers, Vol. I: The Problem of Social Reality,* ed. & int. Maurice Natanson, with pref. by H. L. van Breda, Phaenomenologica 11 (The Hague: Martinus Nijhoff, 1962), esp. p. 229. Hereafter cited as *Collected Papers (I, II,* or *III,* as the case may be).

4. Edmund Husserl, *Ideas: General Introduction to Pure Phenomenology,* tr. W. R. Boyce Gibson (New York: Collier Books, 1962; by arrangement with The Macmillan Company, 1931), sec. 30. (Although this translation is very poor in most respects, until the new translation by Dorion Cairns is available, I thought it best to keep as many references to the English editions of Husserl. It is advisable always to check this translation against the German, however.) Hereafter referred to as *Ideas.*

5. Maurice Natanson, "Existential Categories in Contemporary Literature," in *Literature, Philosophy and the Social Sciences* by Maurice Natanson (The Hague: Martinus Nijhoff, 1962), p. 120.

6. See above, footnote 3.

7. See Hume, *Enquiries Concerning the Human Understanding,* ed. L. A. Selby-Bigge (London: Oxford University Press, second edition, 1902), pp. 25–27.

8. Alfred Schutz, "Concept and Theory Formation in the Social Sciences," *Collected Papers I, op. cit.,* p. 52.

9. See Husserl, "Philosophy as Rigorous Science," included in *Phenomenology and The Crisis of Philosophy,* tr., notes, & int. Quentin Lauer (New York: Harper Torchbooks, Harper & Row, 1965), p. 80. Hereafter referred to as *PCP.*

10. *PCP,* p. 79. Laurer points out in a footnote that this passage contains the basic intuition of the irreducibility of the psychic to the physical, which "set Husserl on the path to transcendental phenomenology." This is precisely the point of this section, although it must be shown. See also *Ideas,* secs. 33, 34, 39, 42, and 50.

11. *Cf., Ideas,* sec. 52, and *PCP,* p. 80.

12. *PCP,* p. 79.

13. See Hume, *A Treatise of Human Nature, Book I: Of the Understanding,* ed. L. A. Selby-Bigge (London: Oxford University Press, 1888), pp. 13, 67, 77, 84 & 187–218.

14. This criticism is an extension of Marcel's. See his *Metaphysical Journal,* tr. Bernard Wall (Chicago: Henry Regnery & Co., 1952), pp. 327–29; and *Creative Fidelity, op. cit.,* pp. 37–38.

15. Alfred Schutz, *Collected Papers I, op. cit.,* pp. 53–54.

16. *PCP,* p. 87.

17. *Ibid.,* pp. 89–90.

18. Edmund Husserl, *Die Krisis der europäischen Wissenschaften und die transzendentale Phänomenologie,* Hrsg. von Walter Biemel, Husserliana, Band VI (Den Haag: Martinus Nijhoff, 2. Auflage, 1962). Hereafter cited as *Krisis.* The first two parts of this study, given as lectures at the University of Prague (1935) and published in the Belgrade review *Philosophia* (1936), were all that Husserl regarded as complete before his death. With additional material, notes, appendixes, and Part III, they were published first in 1954 in Husserliana. Parts I and II are published together with "Philosophy as a Rigorous Science" in *PCP,* cited in footnote 9. Aron Gurwitsch has given a detailed summary of *Krisis* in *Studies in Phenomenology and Psychology* (Evanston: Northwestern University Press, 1966), pp. 397–447. An English translation of *Krisis,* by David Carr, has been published by Northwestern University Press early in 1970.

19. *Krisis,* secs. 9 & 10; *PCP,* pp. 182–83. That geometry is thus taken without appreciating systematically its origination in specific acts of consciousness, becomes a principal theme in Husserl's works. See the masterful study of these issues, among others, by Aron Gurwitsch, *Field of Consciousness* (Pittsburgh: Duquesne University Press, 1964); also see *EU.*

20. Whether it be Descartes' *res cogitans,* Locke's *tabula rasa,* Leibniz' *monad,* Hume's mosaic of impressions and ideas, or Kant's system of forms and categories.

21. Descartes: a *"figuram"*; Locke: a "copy"; Berkeley: an "idea"; Hume: an "impression"; Kant: a "material content"; for much contemporary psychology and philosophy: a "sense-data" or "stimulus." (A. Gurwitsch, *Field of Consciousness*, op. cit.)

22. Berkeley, an exception to this point, is nevertheless forced into serious ambiguities by his insistence that, though *esse est percipi*, yet all "ideas" are *"in* the mind."

23. Merleau-Ponty, *Phenomenology of Perception, op. cit.*, p. 5. Smith translates "le préjugé du monde" sometimes as "widely held prejudice," which unfortunately does not capture the central critical point against objectivism. See also Jean-Paul Sartre, *Being and Nothingness*, tr. Hazel Barnes (New York: Philosophical Library, 1956), pp. 310–15; and Gabriel Marcel, *Metaphysical Journal, op. cit.*, pp. 326–28.

24. Sartre, *Being and Nothingness*, p. 315.

25. Merleau-Ponty, *Phenomenology of Perception*, p. 5.

26. William James, *The Principles of Psychology*, 2 vols. (New York: Henry Holt & Co., 1890), Vol. I., p. 196.

27. See above, p. 14. It should be emphasized here that the reference to Descartes is neither a covert endorsement nor a denial of his views, nor is it the only reference that would be made. As we shall see in Ch. 4, Locke could just as easily have been used for this purpose. Descartes' statement of this essential point of critical philosophy is particularly clear.

28. *CM*, p. 6.

29. *Ibid.*, p. 10. *Cf.* also his *Formal and Transcendental Logic*, tr. Dorion Cairns (The Hague: Martinus Nijhoff, 1969), Pt. II, Chs. 4 & 7. Hereafter referred to as *FTL*.

30. *Ideas.* On p. 53, he explicitly says that it is merely an "instance" of a "procedure"—that, namely, of "disengaging" oneself from a "thesis" (the general thesis of the natural attitude) in order to focus on it critically in the sense developed here.

31. *Ibid.*, p. 54.

Chapter 2: The Sense of Phenomenology

1. James Agee, with photographs by Walker Evans, *Let Us Now Praise Famous Men* (Boston: Houghton-Mifflin Co., 1960), p. 11 (from the place used as the motto for my entire study).

2. See his *Discourse on Method, Philosophical Works of Descartes, op. cit.*, pp. 79–130, esp. pp. 84–89. All quotations from Descartes' works are from this edition, cited textually by essay and page number.

3. In his *Principles,* Part I, no. XXX, p. 231, Descartes makes this connection quite plain.

4. *Rules,* pp. 28–29, makes it clear that sense perception is only an analogy used to aid understanding in this case.

5. See, e.g., Gurwitsch's brilliant essay, "Husserl's Theory of the Intentionality of Consciousness in Historical Perspective," in *Phenomenology and Existentialism*, ed. by Edward N. Lee & Maurice Mandelbaum (Baltimore: The Johns Hopkins Press, 1967), pp. 25–57.

6. See Husserl's *Logische Untersuchungen*, Zweiter Band, I. Teil (Halle a.d.S.: Max Niemeyer, 4te Aufl., 1928), pp. 184–215.

7. *PCP*, pp. 113–15; and Quentin Lauer's "Introduction" to *PCP*, p. 20.

8. *Ibid.*, pp. 113–14.

9. Hume, *A Treatise of Human Nature, op. cit.;* hereafter cited textually.

10. As Hume states: "I can only observe what is commonly done: which is, that this difficulty is seldom or never thought of; and even where it has once been present to the mind, is quickly forgot, and leaves but a small impression behind it" (p. 268). Just this "what is commonly done" proves to be what Hume, with magnificent oversight, failed to probe, *precisely as it relates to his skepticism.*

11. *Krisis*, p. 100.

12. *FTL*, p. 256. See also Suzanne Bachelard's excellent *A Study of Husserl's Formal and Transcendental Logic*, tr. Lester E. Embree (Evanston: Northwestern University Press, 1968), pp. 197–204.

13. Aron Gurwitsch, "The Kantian and Husserlian Conceptions of Consciousness," *Studies*, p. 148.

14. *Ibid.*, p. 173.

15. Hume, *Enquiry Concerning the Human Understanding, op. cit.*, p. 13.

16. For a veiw which sees a closer connection than what I here suggest, see Paul Ricoeur, *Husserl: An Analysis of His Phenomenology*, tr. Edward G. Ballard & Lester E. Embree (Evanston: Northwestern University Press, 1967), pp. 175–201.

17. "Introduction" to *PCP*, p. 21.

18. *Ideas*, p. 166.

19. *FTL*, p. 258.

20. Bachelard, *A Study of Husserl's Formal and Transcendental Logic, op. cit.*, p. 202.

21. *Ibid.*, p. 203.

22. *Krisis*, p. 117; also p. 116.

23. Kant, *Critique of Pure Reason*, tr. Norman Kemp Smith (New York: Macmillan & Co., 1929), p. 272. Hereafter cited textually.

24. *Krisis*, p. 116.

25. As Gurwitsch says, "If one seeks a motto for the whole of Husserl's work, one could not do better than to refer to the few phrases Kant places at the head of his *Analytic of Concepts . . .*" which we just quoted. See Gurwitsch, "The Kantian and Husserlian

Conceptions of Consciousness," *Studies*, p. 148.

26. See, e.g., pp. 45, 66, 94, 95, 100, 106, 111, 161, 171, 176, 186, 206, 208, 228, 234, 263 n.a, 305, *passim.*

27. "Essence" may be understood as meaning "that by virtue of which a thing is what it is," or, negatively, "that without which a thing would not be what is." In these terms, Kant's efforts are clearly what Husserl calls *eidetic*—i.e. directed towards essences.

28. *Ideas*, pp. 165–66. Husserl notes here that "Phenomenology is then the natural ground for the so-called specific philosophical sciences." See also *Ideas*, sec. 26.

29. *Ibid.*, p. 166.

30. *PCP*, p. 141.

31. *Ibid.*, pp. 141–42.

32. In this connection, Julián Marías' discussion of the sense of *"problema"* and its relevance to our current situation is most important. See his *Reason and Life: The Introduction to Philosophy*, tr. Kenneth S. Reid & Edward Sarmiento (New Haven: Yale University Press, 1956), pp. 1–7 & Chs. I, II, VI & VII.

33. See above, pp. 73–78.

34. See *CM*, pp. 46 & 83–88.

35. Eugen Fink, "Les Concepts opératoires dans la phénoménologie de Husserl," in *Husserl* (Paris: Cahiers de Royaument, 1959), pp. 214–30.

36. *FTL*, p. 120–22.

37. See his *Principles of Psychology*, Vol. I, *op. cit.*, pp. 271-76.

38. See *CM*, pp. 39–49; and *Ideas*, Chs. 9 & 10.

39. Analyzed in depth by Gurwitsch, *Field of Consciousness*, *op. cit.*, esp. Part V.

40. *Ideas*, secs. 77 & 78; also *CM*, sec. 15.

41. Husserl also uses the term "thematic reflection," since what the philosopher who reflects does is to make thematic (explicit) what is operative (implicit): *FTL*, sec. 69. It should also be stressed for the sake of clarity that to thematize what is operative *does not transform the operative into the thematic:* simply because we make explicit the implicit features of epistemic claims, for instance, does not *alter* their character as operative. They are operative *for the claim*, but made thematic by the philosopher examining the claim's dimensions. So, too, for consciousness generally: to objectivate does not mean to objectify (reify).

42. *PCP*, pp. 88–91, 110–22, and 142–47.

43. The full meaning of "reflexivity," and the reason for its use, will not become clear until Ch. 4, "Psychology, Phenomenology, and Transcendental Phenomenology."

44. In these terms, Husserl's early insight is truly remarkable: "The spiritual need of our time has, in fact, become unbearable.

. . . Would that it were only theoretical lack of clarity regarding the sense of "reality" investigated in the natural and humanistic sciences that disturbed our peace. . . . . Far more than this, it is the most radical vital need that afflicts us, a need that leaves no point of our lives untouched. All life is taking a position and all taking of position is subject to a must—that of doing justice to validity and invalidity according to alleged norms of absolute validation. . . . In order to alleviate our need, we have no right to bequeath to our posterity need upon need as an eventually ineradicable evil. The need here has its source in science. But only science can definitively overcome the need that has its source in science . . . [Hence] there is only one remedy . . .: a scientific critique and in addition a radical science, rising from below, based on sure foundations, and progressing according to the most rigorous methods—the philosophical science for which we speak here." (*PCP*, pp. 140–42) The essay was written in 1910.

45. Descartes, *Meditations, Philosophical Works*, I, pp. 148–49.

46. One of the rudimentary assumptions of any quest for knowledge is that the direct presentedness of an affair provides better evidence for judgments made about it than would an indirect, or non-presentedness of it. For example, seeing a red wagon provides better evidence for the judgment 'The wagon is red' than does merely hearing about it, or even clearly remembering it. See below, Ch. 4, "The Most General Characters of Consciousness."

Chapter 3: The Theory of Consciousness

1. See the important essays by Alfred Schutz, "Multiple Realities," *Collected Papers I*, pp. 207–59; "William James' Concept of the Stream of Thought Phenomenologically Interpreted," *Collected Papers III*, pp. 1–14; Aron Gurwitsch, "William James' Theory of the 'Transitive Parts' of the Stream of Consciousness," *Studies*, pp. 301–31; *Field of Consciousness* pp. 21–29, 127–31, 184–88, 309–17; See also the excellent study by Bruce Wilshire, *William James and Phenomenology* (Bloomington, London: Indiana University Press, 1968).

2. Of Brentano's many works, the most important here is his untranslated *Psychologie vom empirischen Standpunkt I*, ed. & intro. Oskar Kraus (Hamburg: Felix Meiner, 1955; first published in 1874). See also the brilliant essay by Fred Kersten, "Franz Brentano and William James," *Journal of the History of Philosophy*, Vol. VII, No. 2 (April, 1969), pp. 177–91.

3. Usually translated as "representation," *Vorstellung* just does not have that sense here. The above translation is originally James', and is taken over by Kersten. It far more accurately expresses Brentano's meaning. See Kersten, *op. cit.*, p. 179; and William

James, *Principles of Psychology,* II, p. 286.

4. Quoted in Kersten, *op. cit.,* p. 178; originally, it is found in Brentano's *Psychologie,* II, ed. & intro. Oskar Kraus (Leipzig, 1925), p. 38. Again, Brentano's point is that something must already 'be present to' or 'be merely thought of' *(vorgestellt)* before it could possibly be judged, believed, desired, loved, and so on. This insight becomes crucial for Husserl, called 'doxic positionality.'

5. Kraus points out in his notes to Vol. I (p. 257, n. 10) that Brentano understands 'thinking' in the inclusive Cartesian sense of 'consciousness,' although this cannot be strictly true.

6. *Cf., Psychologie,* I, p. 137.

7. *Ibid.,* pp. 128–29.

8. *Cf., Ibid.,* pp. 28, 110, and 129. Since so-called 'outer perception' is essentially *mediate* (requires the mediation of sensations) and thus subject to error, it really ought not be called perception *(Wahr-nehmung:* literally, "truth-taking") at all, but *non-ception (Falsch-nehmung* rather than *Wahr-nehmung)!*

9. *Ibid.,* p. 137.

10 *Ibid.,* pp. 124-25.

11. *Ibid.,* p. 28.

12. *Ideas,* sec. 42.

13. It is critically important to keep this distinction between *the reflecting* and *what is reflected on* rigorously clear, for to confuse them is tantamount to committing the philosophical equivalent of the 'psychologist's fallacy'—the philosopher's fallacy, so to speak, which is to mix up his own experience as a reflecting philosopher with that experience on which he reflects.

14. Any mode of awareness (consciousing) of its objects as "they-themselves' presented 'in person,' Husserl calls an originary presentation or 'having,' whether it be sensory, recollective, reflective, imaginative, judgmental, volitional, valuational, cognitional, or whatever. He will also speak of these as "intuitions," and as "presentations originaliter."

15. This term, suggested to me by Prof. Sherman Stanage (Northern Illinois University), strikes me as a preferable shorthand way of speaking of consciousness, which is not a some*thing (res),* but a stream of processes *(Erlebnisse)* and activities *(Ich-Akte),* that is, consciousings with an 'I'-presence.

16. The English term, 'intend' has a narrow range, more so than the German *'Intentionalität,'* which expresses the essential directedness of every consciousing toward its specific object(s). Hence, I use 'intentive' rather than 'intentional' (which connotes a willfulness, i.e. only one particular kind of intentiveness in general).

17. Husserl will sometimes speak of this 'seeing of something as it-itself "in person" ' as an "intuition," and will use the notion

to characterize not only sense presentedness, recollective presentedness, etc., but also the presentedness peculiar to universals, numbers, and other ideational affairs. He speaks even of a peculiar kind of presentedness in intuition as regards essences *(Wesensanschauung)*—but this in no sense enters him in the contest between realists and nominalists.

18. *Ideas,* secs. 35, 37, and 80; *CM,* sec. 37–39; *FTL,* secs. 3–4. Husserl uses *"Passivität"* for these; Cairns has suggested "automaticity" as preferable to "passivity"—since the point of Husserl's analysis here is not at all that such *Erlebnisse* (consciousings) are passive in any usual sense, but neither are they "active" in the strict meaning of "having an 'I' presence." I find both terms unsatisfactory, for even though "automaticity" does avoid the wrong connotations of "passivity," it does make this stratum of consciousness sound far too mechanical. I, therefore, have decided to use both "implicit" and "operative" for this dimension of consciousings.

19. How one is to define 'optimal' may be debated, of course, but we have at hand already some rather good guidelines for this, and for other possible types of objects and their correlates. Thus, as Husserl remarks, more generally: "If one keeps no matter what object fixed in its form or category [type] and maintains continuous evidence of its identity throughout the change in modes of consciousness of it [i.e., throughout imaginative variations], one sees that, no matter how fluid these may be, and no matter how inapprehensible as having ultimate elements, still they are by no means variable without restriction. They are always restricted to a set of *structural types,* which is "invariable," inviolably the same: as long as the objectivity remains intended as *this* one and as of this kind, and as long as, throughout the change in modes of consciousness, evidence of objective identity can persist." *(CM,* p. 51.) The point here is just that this reflective procedure is not without limitations, some obvious and others not so obvious. In any event, in order to apprehend the essence of a specific kind of consciousing (or structural type), he must keep his imaginative variations within the limits of that type, in order to assure that his examples are all examples of the type in question.

20. See *CM,* secs. 17–20, 39 & 50–52; *Ideas,* secs. 113, 118, 122–23 & 140.

20a. *Cf.,* Schutz, *Collected Papers I,* pp. 11–14, 315–17.

21. See *CM,* esp. secs. 39 and 50–52.

22. See *FTL,* secs. 73–74; and *EU,* secs. 17–19, 24 & 51b.

23. *Cf.,* Gurwitsch, *Field of Consciousness,* Part V.

24. *Cf.,* Schutz, *Collected Papers I,* 222–26.

25. See Natanson's essay, "Being-In-Reality," in M. Natanson, *Literature, Philosophy and the Social Sciences, op. cit.,* pp. 55–61.

26. *Phenomenology of Internal Time-Consciousness,* pp. 49 & 21.

27. *Cf.,* Merleau-Ponty, *Phenomenology of Perception,* pp. 416–22.

28. *Cf.,* Schutz, *Collected Papers I,* pp. 287–356.

29. On this, see *CM,* secs. 5–7 & 23–28; *FTL,* secs. 58–61 & 84–87; and *Appendix* II; and *Ideas,* Ch. 12.

30. See above, Ch. 2 n. 46.

31. *CM,* p. 12.

32. A complication here is the evidence for other persons, whose mental processes are only *appresented,* never presented—and, indeed, never in principle presentable in Husserl's strict sense of "itself-presentedness in person." How one is to resolve this issue is quite difficult and the issue remains hotly debated. Merleau-Ponty *(Phenomenology of Perception,* pp. 346–65); Sartre *(Being and Nothingness,* pp. 221–430); Alfred Schutz *(Collected Papers I* [pp. 150–203, and 312–28] and III [pp. 51–90], *(Phenomenology of the Social World,* pp. 97–214); Edith Stein *(On the Problem of Empathy,* tr. Waltraut Stein, foreword Erwin W. Straus [The Hague: Martinus Nijhoff, 1964], pp. 4–84 esp.)—are all especially good samples of the problem. See also Husserl, *FTL,* sec. 96; *CM,* Meditation 5; and René Toulemont, *L'Essence de la société selon Husserl* (Paris: Presses Universitaires de France, 1962), esp. Ch. II, for a discussion of Husserl's views on intersubjectivity in relation to the general problematics of the social world.

33. See *FC,* pp. 213, and 288–90.

34. See *Ideas,* secs. 69–71; and *CM,* secs. 25–26.

35. In Husserl's terms, which should be easier to comprehend by now: "In the broadest sense, evidence denotes a universal primal phenomenon of intentional life, namely—as contrasted with other consciousness-of, which is capable *a priori* of being 'empty,' expectant, indirect, nonpresentive—the quite pre-eminent mode of consciousness that consists in the *self-appearance,* the *self-exhibiting,* the *self-giving,* of an affair, an affair-complex (or state of affairs), a universality, a value, or other objectivity, in the final mode: 'itself there,' 'immediately intuited,' 'given originaliter.' . . . All evidence, we may say, is *experience in a maximally broad, and yet essentially unitary, sense.* In the case of most objects, to be sure, evidence is only an occasional occurrence in conscious life, yet it is a possibility—and, more particularly, one that can be the aim of a striving and actualizing intention—in the case of anything meant already or meanable [intended or intendable]. Thus it points to an essential *fundamental trait of all intentional life.* Any consciousness, without exception, either is itself already characterized as evidence

. . . or else has an essential tendency toward conversion into givings of its object originaliter—accordingly, toward syntheses of verification. . . ." (*CM* pp. 57–58.)

36. *Cf.*, Schutz, *Collected Papers I*, pp. 67–96, 227–28, and his *Reflections on the Problem of Relevance*, ed., R. M. Zaner (New Haven: Yale University Press, 1970).

37. Which points to a highly significant issue that must be itself taken up in due time in any full critical study—namely, reflection on this reflecting, or a criticism of criticism itself. See Ch. 4, "Reflexivity: Self as Transcendental."

38. See my "Self-Awakening: Towards a Phenomenology of Self," in *Perspectives in Phenomenology*, ed. F. J. Smith (The Hague: Martinus Nijhoff, expected in 1970), for a study of several of these subtle and fugitive dimensions of self. Neither Gurwitsch *(Studies*, pp. 287–300), nor Sartre *(The Transcendence of the Ego*, tr., annot., & intro. Forrest Williams & Robert Kirkpatrick [New York: The Noonday Press, Inc., 1957]) would be in agreement with these suggestions, either about the 'self' or about the 'transcendental.'

39. Herbert Spiegelberg, "On the 'I-Am-Me' Experience in Childhood and Adolescence," *Review of Existential Psychology and Psychiatry*, Vol. V (1964), pp. 3–21.

40. There is considerable controversy over the status of self (see above, n. 38). See, in English, Gurwitsch, *Studies*, pp. 175–286 & 287–300; Maurice Natanson, *Literature, Philosophy and the Social Sciences, op. cit.*, pp. 44–60; Edith Stein, *On the Problem of Empathy, op. cit.*, esp. III & IV; Paul Ricoeur, *Husserl: An Analysis of His Phenomenology, op. cit.*, esp. Part IV; and Erwin Straus, *Phenomenological Psychology* (New York: Basic Books, 1966).

41. The difficulty of terms is particularly acute, since a single, unambiguous one is obviously desirable, but the fact is that English has no such term to cover the 'nondoxic modes.' Husserl's term, on the other hand, is unfortunate, since it is both negative ('non') and suggests a too sharp contrast with the doxic modes, or even that the 'nondoxic' is a mode of the doxic. I shall therefore use the neologism, 'sentic' (a contraction from 'sentiment'), even though I dislike neologisms, simply to indicate that the socalled non-doxic modes are quite positive and yet not doxic.

42. See *CM*, sec. 21.

Chapter 4: The Exigency for Transcendental Philosophy

1. *PCP*, p. 140.

2. José Ortega y Gasset, *Man and People*, tr. Willard R. Trask (New York: W. W. Norton & Co., Inc., 1957), pp. 42–43.

3. I agree with Marcel's judgment that "Philosophers ought not only to come back to the simplest words, but that they should give

these words a higher value by removing, as it were, the layers of grease with which they have become covered by impropriety in common speech." (*Man Against Humanity*, p. 85.)

4. See, e.g., *CM*, secs. 40–41.

5. James Agee, *Let Us Now Praise Famous Men, op. cit.*, p. 458.

6. See above, pp. 118–21.

7. *CM*, p. 24.

8. *Cf., Ideas*, secs. 77–78. It might be noted here that Schutz believes that reflection is a species of retrospection or recollection, a position with which I do not agree. See his *Phenomenology of the Social World, op. cit.*, pp. 45–53.

9. "Indifference" obviously does not signify that "I don't *care*"; the philosopher no less than the medic, I would argue, *must* care a great deal about what he is investigating. The 'indifference' is strictly a *methodological and not a moral concept.*

10. Several excellent examples of such psychologists: Jean Piaget, *The Origins of Intelligence in Children,* tr. M. Cook (New York: International Universities Press, 1952), and *The Construction of Reality in the Child* (New York: Basic Books, 1954); also, among the superb works of Erwin Straus, see *The Primary World of the Senses* (The Free Press, 1962), and *Phenomenological Psychology, op. cit.;* as well as William James' *Principles of Psychology.* Studies by Binswanger, van den Berg, Buytendijk, Sigmund Koch, Köhler, Koffka, and Kurt Goldstein also serve as excellent examples.

11. *CM*, p. 35.

12. *The Sickness Unto Death,* published with *Fear and Trembling,* tr., intro., & notes by Walter Lowrie (New York: Doubleday Anchor Books, by arrangement with Princeton University Press, 1941, 1945), p. 146.

13. *CM*, p. 156.

14. *CM*, p. 86.

15. I.e., a criticism of the reflective experiencing of consciousings, hence, a *criticism of reflection*—that is, reflexivity, must be critically studied as a genuine phenomenon on its own.

16. *CM*, p. 152.

17. Gabriel Marcel, *Man Against Humanity, op. cit.*, p. 95.

18. *Ibid.*, p. 98. The tone and content of this is certainly what Husserl deeply felt as early as 1910 *(PCP)* and at the end of his life *(Krisis).*

19. *Ibid.*, p. 97.

20. As is evident from *PCP* and *Krisis.*

21. The Spanish term is *ensimismamiento* (from *ensimismarse*), but is almost untranslatable. 'To contemplate,' 'to meditate,' or even 'to regain (restore) one's integral sense of himself,' seem to come closest. The notion of *reflexivity* I have used seems also very much

the same notion—though this would have to be established.

22. This is the counter-notion of *ensimismarse;* the closest English is 'being on the alert' for what lies outside, for what is 'other-than' *(alter),* that self-integrity achieved by *ensimismarse.*

23. See Ortega's brilliant study, *The Revolt of the Masses* (London: George Allen & Unwin, 1951; first published in Spanish in 1930, in English by W. W. Norton, 1932); and most of his other books, which in one way or another strike this theme.

24. *Man and People, op. cit.,* p. 33. Earlier, Ortega notes "the tremendous fact that, unlike all other entities in the universe, man is not and can never be sure that he is, in fact, man, as the tiger is sure of being a tiger, and the fish of being a fish . . . The condition of man, then, is essential uncertainty." (pp. 24–25.)

25. Of his many writings, the most relevant here is "The Claims of Philosophy," originally published in *Polemic,* No. 7 (March, 1947), pp. 11–33, and reprinted in *Reflections on Our Age: Lectures Delivered at the Opening Session of UNESCO at the Sorbonne University, Paris,* intro. David Hardman, foreword by Stephen Spencer (London: Allen Wingate, 1948), pp. 51–66; and also in *Philosophy of the Social Sciences: A Reader,* ed. Maurice Natanson, *op. cit.,* pp. 461–86. Also see Ayer's *The Problem of Knowledge, op. cit.,* esp. Ch. 1, and *The Foundations of Empirical Knowledge, op. cit.,* esp. Chs. 1, 3 & 5. The references to the pontiffs and journeymen are to the first essay above, as reprinted in the Natanson volume.

26. Natanson, *ibid.,* p. 471.

27. Locke's *Essay,* p. xii. References to this are to the edition in Sir John Lubbock's *Hundred Books* (London and New York: George Routledge & Sons, n.d.), which is an exact reproduction of Locke's "New Edition, Carefully Revised, and Compared with the Best Copies." (Further quotations from this *Essay* are made textually.)

28. Natanson, *op. cit.,* p. 475.

29. One of the more trenchant being by Peter Winch, *The Idea of a Social Science, and Its Relation to Philosophy* (London: Routledge & Kegan Paul, 1958), pp. 3–39.

Epilogue

1. *CM,* p. 5.

2. *Man and People, op. cit.,* p. 34.

3. *Ibid.,* p. 35.

4. "Philosophy and the Social Sciences," in *Literature, Philosophy and the Social Sciences,* by Maurice Natanson, *op. cit.,* pp. 165–66.

5. *CM,* p. 157. "Do not wish to go out; go back into yourself. Truth dwells in the inner man." *(De vera religione,* 39, n. 72.)

Index